The Financial Planner's Legal Guide

Eli P. Bernzweig, *J.D.*
Member of the New York Bar

A Reston Book
Prentice-Hall
Englewood Cliffs, New Jersey 07632

Library of Congress Cataloging-in-Publication Data

Bernzweig, Eli P.
    The financial planner's legal guide.

    Includes bibliographies and index.
    1. Investment advisers—Legal status, laws, etc.—
United States.   2. Brokers—Legal status, laws, etc.—
United States.   3. Investment advisers—Malpractice—
United States.   4. Brokers—Malpractice—United States.
I. Title.
KF1072.B47   1986   346.73′0926   85–14640
ISBN 0-8359-2032-1   347.306926

To Lorraine, Sara and Linda

Editorial production/supervision and
interior design by Norma Miller Karlin

The publishers gratefully acknowledge the review
of this text prior to publication by
Loyd Hall Black, Jr., Attorney at Law, Atlanta, Georgia.

© 1986 by Eli P. Bernzweig
A Reston Book
Published by Prentice-Hall
A Division of Simon & Schuster, Inc.
Englewood Cliffs, NJ 07632

10 9 8 7 6 5 4 3 2 1

Printed in the United States of America

Contents

chapter nine **MISCELLANEOUS LEGAL CONCERNS** **157**

Preface

As one who has chosen financial planning as a second career after spending years dealing with legal liability issues in other contexts, the author has had firsthand experience in trying to cope with the usual problems that beset every newcomer to this field. A good part of that process has involved just trying to keep abreast of all the legal requirements imposed on financial planners by statute, regulation, and securities industry pronouncements. Even as a lawyer I was amazed to learn how all-embracing was the regulatory environment I had entered. To say it was intimidating would be an understatement—threatening comes closer to the mark.

No sooner had I begun delving into the theory and mechanics of financial planning than I realized how little I knew about the many legal obligations and constraints that were to become an integral part of my professional life. Words and phrases with great legal significance were bandied about by colleagues who admittedly had only the vaguest idea what they meant or how they applied. I kept hearing words like due diligence, fiduciary, RIA, compliance, Reg D, OSJ, suitability rule, SROs, full disclosure, brochure rule, exempt offering, jurisdictional means, securities principal, private placements, public programs, selling away, off-book transactions, 10b-5 actions, and many others that I knew were significant, but did not fully understand. A quick search of the legal literature revealed that practically no information was available discussing the financial planner's common law liabilities to his or her clients, let alone any practical advice for coping with the customary legal issues faced by all planners.

This book was written to fill that perceived deficit. It reflects my realization that there must be many financial planners practicing today who have no legal background or training and who more than likely haven't the foggiest notion what their legal responsibilities really are or how to live up to them. It is my firm belief (1) that *authoritative legal information and the knowledge gained therefrom is a prerequisite to meaningful action,* and (2) that *the financial planner who knows and understands the legal consequences of his or her professional activities is more likely to act in a manner that will not only assure compliance with all statutory and regulatory requirements, but will greatly minimize the chances of being sued for malpractice.*

Although this book was written primarily for persons who are either practicing financial planners or students in the process of becoming financial planners, the principles and information it contains are equally relevant to other professionals in the financial services industry, including stockbrokers, lawyers, syndicators, accountants, money managers, insurance and real estate agents and brokers, investment analysts, and bank trust officers, among others. To better service their clients, many individuals in these categories have discovered the importance of acquiring more sophisticated financial planning knowledge and skills, and over the past several years growing numbers of them have been turning to financial planning as their principal professional activity. Thus, this book is intended to be a resource tool and practical guide for all who work in the financial services field, to help them meet their legal responsibilities to their clients, their employers, and to themselves. It is also designed to be a resource tool for those who teach financial planning.

I have tried to set forth in simple, understandable language an overview of the relevant legal problems and issues facing today's financial planner and to explain how to minimize the two primary legal hazards associated with financial planning practice: regulatory agency disciplinary proceedings and malpractice suits. I am aware of the fact that the law in general, and securities law in particular, is strange territory to many people. This book has been written to remove as much of the mystery and complexity as possible by taking you step by step through the maze of federal and state statutes and common law doctrines that vitally impinge on your daily practice as a financial planner. Each chapter appears in logical sequence so that the reader can obtain a good understanding of this fairly complex field with the least amount of difficulty.

The reader who follows this chapter sequence will learn in Chapter One about why it is important that all practicing financial planners, as well as those planning to enter this field, be familiar with the key legal issues that affect this area of professional activity. Chapter Two discusses the mechanics of obtaining your license to sell securities at both the federal and state levels. In Chapter Three you will learn about the extremely important issue of why and how to become a registered investment adviser. Experienced planners who have been contemplating becoming their own broker-dealers will learn in Chapter Four the pros and cons of so doing and the mechanics of the broker-dealer registration process.

Perhaps more important than anything else, this book will help you understand the legal mechanisms by which the Securities and Exchange Commission, the various state securities departments, and the industry self-regulatory organizations regulate your daily conduct—what they expect of you and how they go about enforcing their respective statutory responsibilities. In Chapter Five you will learn all about this, in addition to learning about the ethical standards applicable to your conduct as promulgated by the two principal professional organizations for financial planners, the International Association for Financial Planning (IAFP) and the Institute of Certified Financial Planners (ICFP).

Chapter Six addresses the topic of the financial planner's professional liability to his clients, giving illustrative examples of the type of conduct that is likely to make you most susceptible to a malpractice suit. In Chapter Seven you will learn about the judicial and nonjudicial processes available to someone who wishes to assert a claim against you as a planner and the legal and practical consequences of each. In Chapter Eight you will learn what you must do to develop a workable claims prevention strategy, and this chapter may well prove to be your most useful practical source of information on this very important subject. Chapter Nine contains essential information about the planner's potential criminal liability, why you should have malpractice insurance, and how to obtain further legal help on specific legal problems. The glossary and comprehensive index will make your task that much easier and, along with the detailed appendix materials, will make the book particularly useful as a desk-side reference source.

Discussing the law and legal matters is always fraught with problems because legal concepts tend to be encrusted with strange words, endless exceptions, and often-conflicting interpretations. With that in mind, I have attempted to write in a style that is easy for the layman to understand. Legal concepts and principles have been reduced to the simplest language possible, and the text has not been loaded down with footnotes (there aren't any) or with citations (only a few precedent-setting cases are cited). Throughout this book, the emphasis is not on legal theory but on practical suggestions that can keep you out of trouble with federal, state, and industry regulatory authorities, as well as help you to avoid becoming the target of malpractice suits brought by clients.

For those readers who wish to delve more deeply into specific topics, selected references have been included at the end of each chapter. In addition, to help reinforce all new material presented, I have appended a special section at the end of each chapter summarizing the key points to remember. Once you have read the entire book, you can review all the major legal issues covered simply by rereading the Key Points to Remember for each chapter.

A final comment about literary style—specifically, the use of masculine and feminine pronouns. This is a problem all authors face, especially when writing reference works such as this one where the principles being discussed necessarily apply to both sexes. It is awkward to have to write "he or she" in practically every sentence or, alternatively, to struggle to render sentences gender neutral. This only makes the sentence structure more contorted and the subject matter more difficult to follow. Parenthetically, it should be noted that judges and legal commentators traditionally have utilized the masculine gender in analyzing legal decisions and explaining legal doctrines and principles. Accordingly, although fully aware of the great sensitivity to this issue on the part of women generally, and fully aware of the vast number of women who are financial planners, for author's convenience and ease of reading I have chosen to follow the precedent established by most legal writers and have used the masculine pronoun throughout this work.

I would like to express my appreciation to a number of persons whose advice, information, and suggestions helped make this book possible. I am particularly indebted to Gilman Robinson, CFP, of Menlo Park, California, for reviewing the original draft of this manuscript and for his insightful and constructive comments and suggestions.

Grateful appreciation is due the following, who provided varying degrees of information and suggestions regarding technical issues covered in this work: Carol C. Schuder, Dick Williams, and Hewitt H. Covington of the International Association for Financial Planning; Mary Clark and Marvin Tuttle of the Institute of Certified Financial Planners; Bill Fishkind and Robert Butler of the Washington office of the National Association of Securities Dealers (NASD), the latter having since become an active participant in the securities industry, and Steve Algert, Edna Yee, and Chip Curtis of the NASD's San Francisco office; Mary Champagne and Jay Gould of the Washington office of the Securities and Exchange Commission; and Jonathan Boynton and Troy Stone of Private Ledger Financial Services.

I would also like to acknowledge attorneys William B. Shearer, Jr., Loyd Hall Black, Jr., Donald G. Davis, and Arthur H. Bill, whose excellent writings, seminar presentations, and audio tapes have stimulated me and helped me determine the proper focus and emphasis of this work. Similar thanks are due the various authors listed in the Selected References at the end of each chapter.

Finally, special thanks are due Susanne Dyer of the Santa Clara County (California) law library, for her gracious cooperation and assistance, whenever requested, during various phases of my legal research.

It is my hope that each person who takes the time to read the material contained in this book will become a better financial planner for having done so. At the very least, you should acquire a deeper appreciation of the many legal ramifications of your chosen profession and the way in which the law and the practice of the financial planning profession share a common objective in seeking to protect the rights of individuals—planners and clients alike—within the framework of our American system of jurisprudence.

ELI P. BERNZWEIG

chapter one

Introduction

THE NEED FOR FINANCIAL PLANNING AND FINANCIAL PLANNERS

The men and women who are entering the financial planning field at this time are part of an exciting new movement in American enterprise. Not that the field is really all that new; accountants, lawyers, estate planners, tax specialists, bank trust officers, professional money managers, sports and entertainment representatives, and even a few persons calling themselves "financial planners," have been providing specialized financial planning services to top corporate executives and the wealthy for many years. But a lot has happened in recent years to compel the need for personal financial planning services by hundreds of thousands of middle-income Americans, persons who have neither the time nor the inclination to keep track of their personal finances, even though they recognize the importance of so doing.

What are some of the factors that have brought this about? A major one, of course, is the ever-changing tax laws. Over the last 15 years alone a dozen major changes have been made in the tax laws, and a total revamping of the tax code is currently under consideration. Without question, still more changes are likely in the years ahead. Keeping on top of the tax laws has become a chore for even the most astute accountants and tax planners. How, then, is the layman whose attention is principally focused on succeeding in his own occupation supposed to keep abreast of the ever-changing tax laws and know how to take maximum advantage of those laws in order to save on taxes?

In addition to keeping up with the tax laws, the beleaguered middle-income employee and small businessman has had to contend with volatile interest rates, a wildly fluctuating stock market, and a seemingly endless array of new investment products constantly being issued by banks, brokerage firms, insurance companies, and proliferating financial super-markets, all of whom are competing for his investment dollars. Making wise investment choices in this type of environment is beyond the capabilities of many otherwise talented persons.

It would be a gross understatement to say that most of these individuals are confused by what is happening in the financial services industry, and more and more of them have come to recognize that the need for professional financial help is imperative. Little wonder that the field of financial planning should develop so rapidly to meet this increased demand for specialized financial help. A recent *Wall Street Journal* article estimated that as many as 200,000 persons currently may be holding themselves out to the public as financial planners, with new entrants joining the ranks every day. Presumably, the reader is, or plans to be, a part of that veritable army of new financial professionals who have begun providing the specialized financial planning services necessitated by the factors mentioned.

WHY TODAY'S PLANNER NEEDS LEGAL HELP

Beginning a new career in any field is a difficult process at best, and the financial planning field is certainly no exception. Everywhere one turns there is more to learn, not only about the planning process itself, but a wide range of related matters, including how to organize and run a business, how to prospect for new clients, how to manage the daily paper flow, how to maintain good client relations, and so on. As already noted, the tax laws affect everyone and seem to become more difficult to comprehend, let alone apply, with each passing year. Trust and estate law continues to play a vital role in the financial planning process, as does a working knowledge of corporation law, partnership law, real estate law, and insurance law.

Even the most astute professional cannot be an expert in every field and would be foolish to try. Imagine how much more difficult the task must seem for the inexperienced or beginning planner seeking the most basic information necessary just to manage his or her practice. Still, your survival as a financial professional is dependent in large part on your learning as much as you can as quickly as you can, and knowing the law that applies to your conduct is a vital part of that process.

There are a variety of reasons why today's financial planner needs a more thorough grounding in the legal aspects of practice, and especially a working knowledge of the applicable federal and state securities laws. For one thing, regardless of a planner's educational background or prior experience in tax planning, accounting, insurance, or real estate, his knowledge of law, and securities law in particular, is likely to be minimal. And yet he has entered what may well be the most highly regulated and legally circumscribed of all areas of professional activity, with ramifications that can be highly significant.

If you are a planner with a securities license, you need to understand that the moment you don your securities seller's hat you are subject to the most rigorous regulation by the federal and state authorities, as well as by the several self-regulatory organizations such as the stock exchanges and the National Association of Securities Dealers (NASD). In recent years, all of them have become considerably more vigorous in their enforcement activities, and this has important implications for you as a practicing financial planner, both professionally and financially.

A major concern of all financial planners is, and should be, knowing whether to register as an investment adviser. Because the potential for harm to investors is directly related to the number of persons giving investment advice, the federal government (acting through the SEC) and many state legislatures have begun taking a serious look at more effective ways to regulate the conduct of financial planners who give investment advice. California has taken the lead in this respect, having already held hearings on legislative proposals calling for the establishment of minimal educational and experience criteria for financial planners and fairly precise standards of conduct for their dealings with clients. Minnesota, Washington, Oregon, Hawaii, Maine, Massachusetts, Florida, Georgia, and other states are also exploring ways to improve the protection of investors by tightening their laws regulating investment advisers and sellers of securities.

Although most of the changes that are in the wind should ultimately prove beneficial to the financial planning profession, their immediate effect is to create an atmosphere of anxiety and confusion on the part of new as well as experienced financial planners, all of whom need to know with reasonable certainty that what they are doing in their professional practices does not conflict with the law. Securities attorney Donald G. Davis has stressed the importance of knowing the applicable laws thusly:

It is imperative to understand these licensing laws and how they relate to the way you conduct business. If you are conducting activity as a broker, you must be appropriately licensed as such. If you are conducting activity as an investment adviser, you must be licensed as such. There is no room for error in these areas. Proper licensing may constrain your activities, but failure to be properly licensed is courting total disaster . . . . You must know the laws, you must know how you may conduct business within those laws, and you must carefully comply. [D. Davis, "Know the Law," *Financial Planning*, vol. 12, no. 12, 68 (December, 1983). Quoted with permission.]

Perhaps an even more important reason for the financial planner to have access to legal information of the sort presented in this guide is the fact that financial planning is fast becoming a major risk profession in its potential for malpractice litigation. We live in an increasingly consumer-oriented society in which the prospect of being sued by a disgruntled client is no longer some remote possibility, but a constant threat. The legal risks of financial planning are real, and they can have serious financial and professional consequences for the planner who disdains them. True, the profession is still in its infancy and has not yet attracted the attention of the plaintiffs' bar to any substantial degree; but the honeymoon period will not last for long. It is a virtual certainty that malpractice claims against financial planners will begin to increase as the number of financial planners continues to grow and the full extent of their professional activities becomes more widely known.

For this reason alone, it is imperative for planners who value their reputations, to say nothing about protecting their personal assets, to become more familiar with the laws and regulations that affect their daily professional conduct. In the final analysis, the golden mean between fear and overconfidence is to know what the risks are and how to take reasonable precautions against them.

SCOPE OF SUBJECT MATTER COVERED

It should be made clear at the outset that this is not an encyclopedia nor a primer on the general subject of the federal and state securities laws. That subject is much too complex and voluminous to cover in a work of this sort, nor would it be of much help to the average financial planner. Nor does this book concern itself with the procedures relative to investigations or the rules of practice applicable to administrative proceedings before the SEC or the NASD, except in the most general way. Certainly, it will not help you decide whether or not financial planning is a proper career choice. By the time you begin reading this book, you should have made that decision. Nor is it designed to advise you on how to set up or manage your financial planning practice, how you should charge for your services, or anything else having to do with your mode of practice.

But sooner or later every financial planner finds the need for legal advice on some aspect of practice, and when that time comes, this book should help point you in the right direction. The three principal objectives of this book are (1) to give you an overview of the law applicable to the sale of securities and the giving of investment advice, (2) to serve as a guide to the basic legal requirements for engaging in practice as a financial planner, and (3) to alert you to the type of conduct that is likely to stimulate malpractice litigation and tell you what you can do to prevent this from happening.

When you have finished this book, you will have obtained answers to at least the following major questions: What licenses and registrations are necessary to practice financial planning, to sell securities, and to give investment advice? What agencies exercise regulatory control over your actions as a financial planner, how are disciplinary actions brought, and what sanctions may be applied to you? What are your legal responsibilities to your broker-dealer and what are the broker-dealer's special liabilities because of your conduct? Should you form your own broker-dealership, and, if so, how do you go about doing that? What specific types of professional conduct will give rise to your legal liability as a planner, and what are the legal consequences thereof? What positive actions can you take to avoid or reduce the likelihood of such liability? How are disputes against planners resolved, what forums are available, and what are the relative merits of each? What is your potential criminal liability as a planner? And, finally, why should you have malpractice insurance and what should your malpractice policy provide?

Throughout this book, various legal rules and doctrines will be mentioned or elaborated upon, but only to the extent absolutely essential for your understanding of the topic under discussion. The reader should bear in mind that securities law is in a constant state of flux. As times change, so does the law; new court decisions are being handed down every day, and the federal and state securities laws also undergo revision periodically. Although all legal decisions cited in this work are authoritative and current as of the time the book went to press, the possibility that some of them may be reversed or modified by later court rulings should be kept in mind.

Moreover, because the laws of each state differ so much (and are also undergoing change), it would be foolhardy to assume that every legal proposition or concept mentioned in this work can be applied in the same manner in every state. However, since the cases cited herein are used primarily to illustrate general legal principles or points of law rather than to serve as definitive guidelines for legal practitioners, the bulk of the material covered in this book should remain a reliable guide for most of the subjects covered for the foreseeable future.

Finally, a word of caution. *This book is not a substitute for specific legal advice.* It does not pay to be a do-it-yourselfer when it comes to legal matters involving the complexities of securities law. You will have to rely on experienced legal counsel to flesh out the material presented here and to apply the applicable law to your particular situation. Chapter Nine contains an extended discussion on how you should go about finding a lawyer and/or obtaining additional help in dealing with your particular legal problem(s).

WHO IS A FINANCIAL PLANNER?

One issue that must be resolved before we get started is establishing just who we will be talking about when we use the term *financial planner* in this book. Thus far, no federal or state governmental body has enacted legislation purporting to regulate persons practicing as financial planners or to delineate the legal scope of their activities. Because there are no formal legal requirements to become a financial planner, a multitude of persons with widely varying educational backgrounds and professional skills legally can, and currently do, hold themselves out to the public as financial planners, and this has caused considerable confusion.

In point of fact, many so-called financial planners are little more than financial hucksters—selling life insurance, stocks, bonds, mutual funds, annuities, and a multitude of tax-sheltered investments. Most persons in this category have little or no interest in preparing detailed financial plans or in advising their clients (more accurately, customers) on their long-range tax, retirement, estate planning, and investment strategies, and they are frank to admit it. Since they live on the sales commissions they earn, what financial reports or plans they do prepare merely serve as a backdrop for their sales activities.

Other individuals who occasionally refer to themselves as financial planners are primarily specialists in other fields (e.g., law, accounting, benefits and pension planning, real estate, or insurance) who provide various degrees of financial planning services as an adjunct to their primary areas of expertise. Although they may become deeply involved in financial planning for selected clients, this activity ordinarily is incidental to their customary professional orientation.

Finally, there are those individuals who have chosen to become financial planners in the most comprehensive sense of that term. They have made it their business to acquire the necessary education, training, and experience to enable them to determine where a client is financially and where he would like to be, and to recommend how to get from where he is to where he would like to be in the most efficient manner. Doing this requires preparation of a detailed financial plan for the client. Such a plan routinely will cover a variety of subjects, including cash flow control, tax planning, estate planning, retirement planning, risk management, and investment strategies, all aimed at helping the client achieve his particular personal financial objectives.

Unless the context otherwise indicates, the term financial planner as used in this book refers to men and women who fall within the last described category. This is the planner who (1) collects and assesses all relevant information about the client's financial situation, (2) identifies the client's financial goals and objectives, (3) identifies specific financial problems, (4) prepares a written financial plan containing recommendations and alternative solutions, (5) coordinates the implementation of recommendations, and (6) provides periodic review and update. These activities parallel the basic standards established by the International Association for Financial Planning (IAFP) for admission to its Registry of Financial Planning Practitioners and are similar to the criteria used by the College for Financial Planning in its Certified Financial Planner (CFP) program.

KEY POINTS TO REMEMBER

1. The ever-changing and increasingly complex tax laws, along with the revolution in financial services and products, have made it imperative for many middle-income taxpayers to obtain competent financial planning advice. This, in turn, has increased the demand for competent financial planners.

2. Most persons practicing financial planning today have had little or no legal background or training, yet their professional lives are intimately bound up with legal concerns and obligations.

3. Every financial planner needs a working knowledge of law, especially the securities laws and regulations that govern his or her daily conduct.

4. One of the most important reasons for a planner to become familiar with the law is the ever-present threat of being sued for malpractice. Knowing the legal risks

associated with the practice of financial planning and how to take precautions against them is the planner's best defensive strategy.

5. The three principal objectives of this book are (1) to give an overview of securities law as it applies to financial planners, (2) to set forth the basic legal requirements to engage in practice as a financial planner, and (3) to point out the type of conduct likely to stimulate malpractice claims against a planner and how to prevent this from occurring.

6. This book is not an encyclopedia, nor does it elaborate on the state securities laws. Moreover, it is not intended as a substitute for specific legal advice from experienced legal counsel.

7. The financial planner referred to in this book is one who performs the principal functions outlined in the IAFP's Registry of Financial Planning Practitioners.

SELECTED REFERENCES

Need for Financial Planning

"Financial Planners—How to Find the Right One," *Changing Times,* 28 (December 1983).

Dunton, L., (ed.), *Your Book of Financial Planning* (Reston Publishing Company, Reston, Va., 1983).

Legislation Affecting Financial Planners

Brown, J. T., "Taking the Lead," *Financial Planning,* vol. 14, no. 1, 38 (January 1985).

Wojtalewicz, P., "The Regulatory and Legislative Report," *California Planner,* vol. 2, no. 2, 17 (February 1985).

Who Is a Financial Planner?

Wunnicke, P., "A New Breed of Money Adviser," *California Planner,* vol. 2, no. 5, 13 (May 1985).

"What Is Financial Planning; Who Is a Financial Planner," paper published by the Institute of Certified Financial Planners (Denver, 1984).

"IAFP Announces Registry of Financial Planning Practitioners," *Financial Planner,* vol. 12, no. 5, 19 (May 1983).

Johnson, B., "Part-Time Planners," *Financial Planning,* vol. 13, no. 12, 124 (December 1984).

Why Financial Planners Need Legal Help

Davis, D. G., "Know the Law," *Financial Planner,* vol. 12, no. 12, 68 (December 1983).

Bernzweig, E. P., "Taking Care of Business," *Financial Planning,* vol. 13, no. 2, 119 (February 1984).

Bernzweig, E. P., "Common Legal Pitfalls," *Financial Planning,* vol. 13, no. 4, 143 (April 1984).

chapter two

Registration and Licensing Requirements for Selling Securities

For the individual who wishes to practice financial planning as a full-time professional, obtaining the necessary legal authorization to sell securities is clearly the first order of business. Assuming that the reader intends to conform to the financial planner profile described in Chapter 1, a number of preliminary factors must be taken into consideration before it can be determined which type of registration or license you must obtain in order to engage in practice. It is important to know, for example, if you intend to charge specific fees for preparing financial plans and for giving investment advice. Also, it is important to know whether you intend to sell stocks, bonds, mutual funds, insurance, annuities, tax shelters, or other investment products.

In addition, the state in which you intend to practice and whether your practice will include clients in other states are also important considerations, since all the states now have laws that govern the conduct of persons who sell securities or charge fees for giving investment advice. Thus, a number of important factors bear directly on the licensing and registration process. The principal focus of this chapter will be on the legal requirements for obtaining the necessary federal registration and state securities licenses, and the legal issues relevant thereto.

FEDERAL REGISTRATION TO SELL SECURITIES

Since a key element in financial planning is the implementation of appropriate investment strategies as outlined in the plan, and since nearly all investments qualify as "securities" under the federal and state securities laws, most financial planners will be obliged to obtain securities registration in order to engage in practice. There are exceptions, of course. The planner who prepares financial plans and gives investment advice for a fee, but does not sell any investment products, has no need to obtain securities registration. Nor does the planner who limits investment recommendations to the sale of life insurance or annuities. Generally speaking, however, if you intend to "effect transactions in securities" (meaning buy or sell them) for the account of others at any time in the future—a service most planners provide—then obtaining the appropriate securities registration is a legal necessity.

Background of Federal Securities Legislation

The sale of securities to unwary investors has been a matter of public concern in the United States since the early part of the century. Interestingly, the first attempts to regulate securities transactions began with the states, Kansas having enacted the first general securities law in 1911. The state securities laws were aimed at preventing the proliferation of fraudulent money-raising ventures of all kinds, many having to do with nonexistent oil and gas wells, gold and silver mines, and other illusory ventures.

The legislative thrust of these early acts was to discourage speculative schemes that, in the words of one court, had "no more basis than so many feet of blue sky." Today, blue-sky laws (laws aimed at preventing the fraudulent exploitation of investors) are on the books of every state, as well as the District of Columbia and Puerto Rico.

Federal regulation of securities, by contrast, did not begin until after the stock-market crash of 1929. At that time a large part of the public blamed speculation in the securities markets as the real cause of the crash and the disastrous depression it produced. The anger and frustration brought on by the depression prompted some to suggest abolition of all the stock exchanges; others believed tighter regulatory control would be a better solution.

Ultimately, President Franklin D. Roosevelt chose to adopt the approach suggested by his friend and adviser, Louis D. Brandeis, that is, the concept of full disclosure in all securities transactions. This philosophy, coupled with the then novel concept, "let the seller also beware," set the tone for the *Securities Act of 1933* (hereafter, the Securities Act) and for all subsequent federal securities legislation.

For the first year of its existence, the Securities Act was administered by the Federal Trade Commission. However, with the passage of the *Securities Exchange Act of 1934* (hereafter, the Exchange Act) the Securities Exchange Commission (hereafter, the SEC) was created and was given responsibility for administering both acts. To this day they remain the two most important federal statutes aimed at protecting the public in matters relating to the sale and distribution of securities.

Before enactment of the federal securities acts, investors faced practically insurmountable obstacles to the recovery of damages in state lawsuits alleging fraudulent or deceitful practices in securities transactions. The federal laws created new liabilities permitting an aggrieved party to recover damages in a civil action, while allowing the government to more effectively regulate the securities industry.

Scope of the Federal Securities Acts

The principal purpose of the Securities Act is to protect the public against being defrauded by unscrupulous issuers and dealers in securities. It does this by providing for full and fair disclosure of all relevant information regarding new offerings of securities intended to be sold in interstate commerce. In addition, it prohibits fraudulent acts and practices in the sale of securities, as well as statements, acts, and practices that misrepresent the facts about securities or tend to deceive investors.

With respect to the matter of disclosure, the Securities Act provides that, prior to the issuance of a security in interstate commerce, the issuer must first file with the SEC a registration statement containing prescribed information about the security, the issuer, and the underwriters. This information is required to be furnished to all potential investors by means of a prospectus. It should be noted that the SEC does not have legal authority to rule upon what securities may be sold to the public, nor does it exercise any judgment regarding the merits of proposed new issuances. Its responsibility under the act is merely to make certain that all essential information about the security is disclosed prior to its distribution.

The Exchange Act, on the other hand, governs dealings in securities after they have been issued. Its basic objective is to regulate securities exchanges and the securities markets in order to instill investor confidence therein. It does this by making certain that potential investors receive all relevant and material information relating to issuers of securities, in addition to prohibiting the manipulation of securities prices and the use or employment of any manipulative or deceptive devices in the purchase or sale of securities registered on national securities exchanges. In view of the remedial nature of the act, it is construed broadly by the courts both to protect investors and to maintain the integrity of the securities markets.

The Self-regulation Concept

When the Exchange Act was passed in 1934, national securities exchanges already in existence had their own detailed internal rules and regulations governing the ethical practices of their members. However, the over-the-counter market had no comparable controls, and this was a matter of concern to federal legislators. After considering the matter, the Congress decided that the best way to regulate the ethical practices of the over-the-counter securities industry was a scheme calling for a substantial degree of *self-regulation,* with the securities industry imposing acceptable ethical standards upon its own members.

Thus came into being the Maloney Act in 1938, which amended the Exchange Act by providing for registration with the SEC any association of brokers or dealers as a ''national securities association,'' which would supervise the conduct of its members under the general aegis of the SEC. The National Association of Securities Dealers (hereafter, the NASD) was established in 1939, and it became the first and only national securities association to register under the act.

In accordance with the statutory design, it was intended that the NASD would establish its own principles of fair trading and its own disciplinary procedures. A broker-member would be expelled from the organization if found in violation of any of the principles of fair trading established by the NASD. Chapter Five discusses the role of the NASD and its relationship to the SEC and the courts at length. For now, it is important that you understand it is the NASD, rather than the SEC, with which you will be most directly concerned in matters pertaining to the selling of securities.

One of the most important NASD rules provides that no member of the organization may permit any other person to manage, supervise, solicit, or handle any securities business on behalf of the member unless such person registers as a ''registered representative'' with the NASD. The rules also provide that an applicant for registration must first pass a qualifying examination, which is discussed later in this chapter.

Statutory Definitions

The Exchange Act defines the term *broker* to mean anyone engaged in the business of effecting transactions in securities for the account of others. A *dealer* is defined as "any person engaged in the business of buying and selling securities for his own account, through a broker or otherwise," but only as a part of a regular business. The distinction between a broker and a dealer set forth in the act was based on technical differences in the legal obligations and liabilities of each category under the common law prevailing in the early 1930s. That distinction has long since been blurred by the courts in securities act cases, so that today, for registration and most other purposes, the distinction between brokers acting as agents for others and brokers acting on their own behalf as dealers is no longer significant. For this reason, we will use the term *broker-dealer(s)* to encompass the activities of all who are required to register either as brokers or dealers under the Exchange Act, unless the context indicates otherwise. Banks are expressly excluded from the statutory definitions of "broker" and "dealer" under the act.

The provisions of the Exchange Act also apply specifically to two other categories: persons who are associated with a broker-dealer, and persons who either directly or indirectly control, or are controlled by, a broker-dealer. Clerical and ministerial employees are not included within the statutory definitions.

A *security* within the meaning of the Exchange Act has been defined as an equity security, a term that has been given more precise meaning by the SEC pursuant to regulation. An *equity security* includes any stock or similar security, certificate of interest or participation in any profit-sharing agreement, preorganization certificate or subscription, transferable share, voting trust certificate or certificate of deposit for an equity security, limited partnership interest, interest in a joint venture, or certificate of interest in a business trust. Warrants, rights to subscribe to or purchase securities, promissory notes, puts, calls, straddles, options, and other investment contracts all fall within the definition of "securities" under the law. State law definitions of "securities" tend to parallel those under federal law but may differ in certain respects.

In accordance with the foregoing statutory definitions, if you intend to buy, sell, or otherwise effect transactions in securities for the account of others, you must apply for and obtain the necessary securities registration under federal law. And if you are required to be registered under federal law, then you will also have to obtain a state securities license.

Selecting Your Broker-Dealer

In accordance with the statutory requirement under the Exchange Act that all brokers and dealers be registered, the financial planner who intends to sell securities must take certain prescribed steps. Your first step is to select the broker-dealer firm with which you intend to be associated, since registration is accomplished only through a formal submission made by a broker-dealer member of the National Association of Securities Dealers (NASD). You cannot apply for and obtain your securities registration in any other manner. If you have no personal contacts with broker-dealers in your local area, you can learn the names of possible choices by referring to the stock and bond broker listings in the yellow pages of your local telephone directory or, if a more comprehensive listing is desired, by referring to the NASD Manual, a copy of which should be available in every brokerage firm in the United States and in most business libraries. Copies are also available for purchase from any of the NASD regional offices at nominal cost. See Appendix C for the addresses and telephone numbers of NASD regional offices.

For the would-be planner, the selection of a broker-dealer will be of paramount importance, and not just from the standpoint of the scope and quality of investment products the broker-dealer can offer, the quality of its due diligence activities, or the efficiency of its ''back office'' staff. To be sure, those are all important considerations; but perhaps of even greater importance is the fact that you, the beginning planner, will be a *registered representative* (or legal agent) of that firm. Hence, the firm's reputation for honesty, integrity, and fair dealing with the investing public will undoubtedly play an important role in the public's perception of you and its willingness to deal with you. Like it or not, you are judged by the company you keep, so you should choose your broker-dealer carefully.

Obviously, you and your broker-dealer must first come to some preliminary understanding with respect to several important matters, such as office space, compensation and commission arrangements, access to computer services, tax, legal, and accounting specialists, and whether you intend to become a registered investment adviser or use the broker-dealer as the conduit for all investment advisory functions.

Applying for NASD Securities Registration

Once these preliminary issues have been resolved, you must make formal application for NASD securities registration. Each new applicant must complete the four-page *Form U-4, Uniform Application for Securities In-*

dustry Registration, revised as of July 1, 1985. The Form U-4, together with a passport-size photograph, a set of fingerprints, and the appropriate fees, is forwarded to the NASD in Washington, D.C., by the sponsoring broker-dealer. Currently, the NASD registration fee is $50, a fee of $12 is charged for checking the applicant's fingerprints, and a fee of $40 is charged for each examination the applicant proposes to take. These fees, together with the applicable state filing fees, are combined and transmitted to the NASD along with the Form U-4.

Assuming you intend to handle the full range of securities, you will indicate on the application that you wish to take the NASD's Series 7 examination. A Series 7 registration qualifies an individual to become a General Securities Representative, which gives him the authority to sell corporate stocks and bonds, government bonds, limited partnership interests, mutual funds, real estate investment trusts (REITs), and the full range of general securities. This registration does not authorize the securities representative to sell or deal in commodities or in certain types of options. In some cases, you may also have to take a second examination to obtain your state license, an issue which is covered more fully later.

At the present time, the Series 7 examination is being given each month by the NASD at locations throughout the United States. The same examination is given, incidentally, to qualify representatives for the stock exchanges. The examination consists of 250 multiple-choice questions covering a wide range of subjects. A passing score is 70%, or 175 correct answers. Normally, the examinee will learn the examination results within a week; the information is transmitted to his sponsoring broker-dealer by the NASD's Washington office. If it is necessary, a make-up examination can be taken whenever the monthly examinations are scheduled.

Once a person is appropriately registered with the NASD as a registered representative (salesman or agent) of a particular broker-dealer, he may represent only that broker-dealer. If he undertakes to sell securities not authorized to be sold by his broker-dealer, legally he is not acting on the latter's behalf and all such sales represent violations of the securities laws. The practical and legal consequences of making such sales (called private securities transactions) both for the registered representative and his broker-dealer, are covered in detail in Chapter Four.

A registered representative can, of course, change broker-dealers, and provided such transfer takes place within 120 days, only a partial refiling of revised Form U-4 is necessary. Should a representative wish to leave the securities field entirely (full termination of securities registration), or wish to terminate registration with a particular state or self-regulatory organization other than the NASD (called a partial termination), the broker-dealer must file with the NASD *Form U-5, Uniform Termination Notice for Securities Industry Registration,* indicating the reason(s) therefor.

If a planner who is a registered representative later wishes to become more actively engaged in the management of his broker-dealer's securities business, and wants to establish a branch office in which he assumes responsibility for supervising other representatives, he must apply for registration as a General Securities Principal and take the necessary examination, the Series 24 General Securities Principal Examination. This exam is given on the computerized Control Data Plato system and consists of 125 questions in a three-hour time allotment. The advantages and disadvantages of becoming licensed as your own broker-dealer are covered in Chapter Four.

STATE LICENSE TO SELL SECURITIES

Earlier, it was pointed out that the states actually preceded the federal government in enacting securities legislation. Hence, it is not surprising that the Congress included a number of intrastate exemptions when drafting the federal securities acts, thus recognizing and preserving the states' rights to regulate in those areas. State blue-sky laws are legally operative so long as they do not create a direct conflict with provisions of the federal securities statutes. To the extent that a blue-sky law establishes qualifications for an individual to engage in business as a securities salesperson, it has been held to be a proper exercise of the state's police power for the protection of investors from fraud. To carry out their statutory intent, state blue-sky laws are liberally construed by the courts.

Practically all the state securities laws follow the suggested language of the Uniform Securities Act, which was developed and approved by the Conference of Commissioners on Uniform State Laws and the American Bar Association in 1956. The Uniform Securities Act is divided into a number of parts: fraud provisions; registration requirements relating to brokers, dealers, and agents; registration requirements relating to securities; provisions making certain representations regarding registration unlawful; and civil liability provisions. Many provisions of the state blue-sky laws are identical with provisions of the federal securities acts, and there is a conscious effort to interpret and administer the state acts in a manner consonant with the related federal acts.

Applicability of the State Blue-sky Acts

The state securities acts generally apply to any person who sells or offers to sell a security when the offer to sell is made in the state or where the offer to buy is made and accepted in the state. State acts patterned after the Uniform Securities Act make it unlawful for any person to transact business within the particular state as a broker or dealer, or as an agent of a broker or dealer, unless the individual is registered in such capacity. It should be noted that even though an individual may be registered as an agent under the state act, such registration is not effective during any period when the individual is not associated with a particular broker-dealer who is registered under the appropriate state law. You are simply begging for trouble if you fail to heed this rule. State registration ordinarily is effective for a period of one year and must be renewed annually.

State Securities Act Definitions

Under the Uniform Securities Act, a *broker* and *dealer* are synonymous terms. This differs from the definitions contained in the federal securities acts, where a dealer is someone who buys and sells securities for his own account, while a broker is someone who acts as an agent for another in buying or selling securities. Instead, the Uniform Securities Act defines the combined term *broker-dealer* as any person engaged in the business of effecting transactions in securities for the account of others or for his own account. The definition expressly excludes an agent, an issuer, a bank, or a trust company.

An *agent* is any individual other than a broker-dealer who represents a broker-dealer or issuer of securities in making sales or purchases of securities. Although there may be cases in which it is difficult to determine whether an individual is an agent of a broker-dealer or a broker-dealer himself, the blue-sky laws generally use the terms *agent* and *salesman* to mean someone who sells securities as a representative of a broker-dealer and who is paid on a commission basis.

Prohibited Practices

As already mentioned, the state blue-sky laws follow the general pattern of the federal securities laws, with great emphasis being placed on preventing fraud in securities transactions. It is, of course, unlawful for any person to transact business within the state as a securities broker or dealer unless he has registered to do so under the state's blue-sky law. And it is likewise unlawful to transact business as an investment adviser without proper state registration. This is discussed more fully in Chapter Three.

The relevant state acts make it unlawful for any securities representative to employ any device, scheme, or artifice to defraud an investor in the offer, sale, or purchase of any security. Likewise, it is unlawful to make untrue statements with respect to material facts about securities or to omit to state material facts about such securities so as to mislead the investor. And any act, practice, or course of business conduct that operates as a fraud or deceit upon an investor is a violation of the law. By and large, the courts deciding cases under the state blue-sky laws have followed the precedents of the federal courts in deciding issues of a similar nature.

The State Registration Process

In years past, persons wishing to apply for registration as securities representatives at both the state and federal levels had to complete a series of different forms to satisfy the particular requirements of the respective authorities. Today, this tedious process is no longer necessary, now that the registration of securities professionals has become standardized and computerized on the Central Registration Depository (CRD) System operated by the NASD. Currently, the District of Columbia and all states but Hawaii have joined the CRD System, so that an applicant from a member state or the District of Columbia merely has to complete and file a single *Form U-4, Uniform Application for Securities Industry Registration* in order to register with the NASD and the specific jurisdictions in which he wishes to sell securities.

For the most part, the various state blue-sky laws contain fairly similar registration requirements. To register as a broker-dealer, agent, or investment adviser, an initial or renewal application must be filed with the appropriate state administrator, director, or commissioner of securities (utilizing the Form U-4). An applicant typically must provide information regarding his integrity, moral fitness, education, and experience in the field. Just about every state requires the applicant to appoint the secretary of state or some other state official as agent for receipt of service of process in civil actions relating to securities matters. Occasionally, character references are required to be submitted, and some states also have bonding requirements.

As pointed out earlier with respect to federal registration, the actual application process is normally handled by the broker-dealer with whom the applicant is to be affiliated. One cannot apply for a state securities license independently. Information about a particular state's securities laws can be obtained from its securities regulatory agency. Appendix G lists the state regulatory commissions and their key personnel.

In addition to the filing of the preceding information, the applicant also must have passed the NASD Series 7 examination (General Securities Representative) or the Series 6 (Investment Company/Variable Contracts Limited Representative) and the Series 22 (Direct Participation Programs Limited Representative) examinations. A number of states impose an additional examination requirement—the Series 63 (Uniform Securities Agent State Law) examination. The Series 63 is a NASD-administered, 50-question multiple-choice examination given on a computer terminal. It replaces the many individual examinations developed by the states themselves. A passing score is 70, or 35 correctly answered questions.

SUMMARY

The foregoing has been a brief exposition of the federal and state law requirements for obtaining the necessary registration(s) to engage in securities transactions. Basically, how you structure your financial planning practice will determine whether or not you need to apply for federal and state securities registration. The planner who chooses to engage in practice as a fee-only planner, taking *no part* in the plan implementation process, will not be required to become registered with the NASD as a securities representative or licensed under state law.

But there is nothing in the law that says a person has to label himself a stockbroker or securities salesperson to come within the purview of the law. One can be considered "engaged in the business" of effecting transactions in securities even if this is done only on an intermittent or part-time basis, and even if the income therefrom represents only a minor fraction of the person's total occupational income. As long as the activity is engaged in on a compensable basis sufficiently often to justify the inference it is a *de facto* part of his business, the person in question will be held subject to registration as a securities broker. Thus, the fee-only financial planner who customarily refers clients to a specific broker, and receives a referral fee from the latter for so doing, undoubtedly will be held to be "engaged in the business" of effecting securities transactions, and accordingly will be required to register as a securities broker under the state and federal laws.

As in most areas subject to regulation, there are many borderline situations that are not amenable to easy resolution. In these cases your best bet is to seek the advice of a lawyer who specializes in securities law before actually undertaking to practice without a securities license. Sometimes, the issues are so abstruse or novel that they have to be resolved by the courts. If you definitely intend to handle general securities transactions, then you must apply for registration through the broker-dealer firm with which you will be associated and must take the Series 7 examination administered by the NASD. If you are required to register under the federal law, then you will be obliged to register under the pertinent state securities act as well. Most states consider a passing grade on the NASD Series 7 exam sufficient to qualify you without any further state examination requirement.

Finally, there is the matter of registration as an investment adviser, which is discussed at length in the next chapter. Planners sometimes assume they are not required to register as investment advisers under the federal and state securities laws simply because they are appropriately registered to sell securities. *It is important to understand that there is no direct relationship between the two forms of registration.* The mere fact that you may have obtained your securities registration under the Exchange Act or under a state's blue-sky act has no bearing on your obligation to register as an investment adviser under the relevant federal and state investment adviser statutes. The financial planner who ignores this reality runs the risk of swift SEC and state disciplinary action that could seriously jeopardize his right to practice as a financial planner.

KEY POINTS TO REMEMBER

1. You cannot legally practice financial planning without first obtaining the necessary federal registration (via the NASD) and the necessary state securities licenses.

2. Your need to obtain NASD registration to sell securities will depend on whether or not you intend to implement securities recommendations to clients personally. If so, you are legally required to register with the NASD as a securities broker.

3. The NASD was the first and only national securities association ever to register as a self-regulatory organization with the SEC. For the most part, your activities with respect to securities will be more directly supervised by the NASD than the SEC.

4. Registration to sell securities is accomplished only through an NASD-registered broker-dealer. You cannot apply for and obtain your securities registration independently.

5. Choosing the right broker-dealer is one of the most important decisions you will have to make as a beginning financial planner, because the firm's reputation and

integrity will affect the way in which clients regard you and choose to deal with you.

6. You must pass the Series 7 examination given by the NASD before you can be registered to sell securities legally under federal law.

7. The General Securities Principal registration is necessary if you want to establish your own branch office. Passing the Series 24 examination is also required.

8. Many provisions of the state securities laws are nearly identical with the federal laws and are construed in the same manner by the courts.

9. If you are required to be registered under the federal securities law, then you will also have to obtain a state securities license.

10. Most states require that you pass the Series 7 NASD examination in order to be licensed by the state, and some further require your passing the Series 63 (Uniform Securities Agent State Law) examination.

SELECTED REFERENCES

Statutes

Securities Act of 1933, 15 U.S.C. §§ 77a–77aa.

Securities Exchange Act of 1934, 15 U.S.C. §§ 78a–78hh.

Uniform Securities Act, 7 Uniform Laws Annotated 691.

Historical Background

Brandeis, Louis D., *Other People's Money and How The Bankers Use It,* (Augustus M. Kelley, Fairfield, N.J., 1979; reprint of 1932 Ed.).

DeBedts, Ralph F., *The New Deal's SEC* (Columbia University Press, New York, 1964).

Loss, Louis, *Securities Regulation,* 3rd ed. (Little, Brown and Company, Boston, 1983).

State Authority To Regulate Professions

Goldfarb v. *Virginia State Bar,* 421 U.S. 773 (1975).

Barsky v. *Board of Regents,* 347 U.S. 442 (1954).

In the Matter of Walter H. Seager, Exchange Act Release No. 906 (April 6, 1984).

General

NASD Manual (National Association of Securities Dealers, Washington, D.C., 1984).

Vol. 69 AMJUR 2d, *Securities Regulation—Federal.*

Johnson, D. S., "Regulation Guideposts," *Financial Planning,* vol. 14, no. 5, 210 (May 1985).

Registration of Investment Advisers

THE INVESTMENT ADVISERS ACT OF 1940

As a financial planner, you are expected to do more than just review a client's existing financial situation; you are expected to analyze a mass of financial information and then make concrete recommendations in a number of areas, one being the important investment area. And this activity brings you squarely within the purview of several statutes you will have to deal with both at the federal and state level. The first and most significant of these is the federal *Investment Advisers Act of 1940* (15 U.S.C. §§ 80b-1—80b-2). Before discussing the ramifications of this act in detail, it would be helpful to show how and why it came into being.

Background of the Investment Advisers Act

The securities business has always tempted the unscrupulous, whether the outright confidence men whose motives are to intentionally deceive, or the bona fide investment counselors with good intentions, but lacking in honesty and integrity. The *Investment Companies Act of 1940* and the companion *Investment Advisers Act* (Title II of the same law) were two in a series of statutes designed by the Congress to eliminate various abuses in the securities industry that were believed to have contributed to the stock market crash of 1929 and the ensuing Great Depression.

The Investment Advisers Act (hereafter referred to simply as the Advisers Act) was the last in this series of statutes, and was passed with the intent to protect the public against the harmful or fraudulent conduct of persons who are paid to advise others about buying and/or selling securities. It was aimed at two categories of advisers: those who publish periodic market reports or newsletters that make recommendations regarding securities for paying subscribers, and those who give advice on securities to individual clients. One of its prime objectives was (and is) to expose all possible conflicts likely to cause the adviser to make recommendations more in his own interest than in the interests of his client(s).

Notwithstanding its intention to more effectively regulate practices in the investment advisory area, until the act was amended in 1960, it did a poor job of regulation of any sort. As originally enacted, it required registration of advisers and outlawed fraudulent or deceptive advisory practices. It also outlawed the charging of fees based on profits made by the client, as well as transactions in which the adviser was a principal, unless he so informed the client in writing. And it further prohibited the assignment of advisory contracts without the client's consent.

However, since the law had no record-keeping or reporting requirements, the SEC had no power to check on the (possibly illegal) activities of an investment adviser except in a formal investigation charging him with specific violations of the act. Nor did the SEC have any rule-making authority to interpret the terms "fraudulent and deceptive." Thus, in many respects the Advisers Act was ineffective in attempting to correct abuses.

The 1960 amendments gave the SEC needed authority to define fraudulent, deceptive, or manipulative practices and to issue rules for their prevention. At the same time, the SEC was given extensive authority to inspect the books and records of investment advisers. Perhaps most important of all, the 1960 amendments extended the scope of the statute's basic fraud provisions to *all* investment advisers, whether required to register under the law or not. This was a major change, albeit one that to this day is not fully appreciated by many investment advisers who are clearly exempt from registration, such as lawyers and accountants whose advisory services are deemed incidental to their principal activities.

The additional enforcement authority given the SEC by Congress in 1960 was deemed necessary because, unlike the securities field, there were (and still are) no self-regulatory organizations in the investment advisory field who could share these responsibilities.

What the Advisers Act Provides

The basic regulatory mechanism of the statute is the legal requirement that all persons who are deemed to be "investment advisers" within the meaning of the statute (and who are not specifically excluded or exempt) must register with the SEC and be subject to direct SEC regulation. This differs from the regulation of securities representatives who, as noted earlier, come under the direct regulation of the NASD, a self-regulatory organization. Noncompliance with the act's registration requirements can be costly. Clients of an unregistered investment adviser have the right to rescind their investment transactions and, in some cases, to obtain money damages. Moreover, a person who willfully fails to register as an investment adviser not only may be fined and enjoined from further advisory activities, but may be barred from registration forever.

It should be noted that the Advisers Act does not contain any professional or academic qualification requirements for investment advisers, based on the apparent belief (at least when first enacted) that the essential qualities of good investment advisers, sound judgment and integrity, cannot be measured by examinations or demonstrated by academic degrees.

The act contains a provision negativing any inference that registration is a badge of approval by the SEC and, in fact, section 208 makes it unlawful for any registered adviser to represent or imply that his abilities or qualifications have been passed upon by any agency of the United States.

The act also prohibits certain types of investment advisory contracts and specifically makes it unlawful to employ any device, scheme, or artifice to defraud any client or prospective client, or to engage in any transaction, practice, or course of business that operates as a fraud or deceit upon any client or prospective client—the extremely important antifraud provision, section 206. Other sections of the act deal with disclosures an investment adviser must make to avoid conflicts of interest and otherwise deal truthfully with clients.

To carry out the statutory scheme, the SEC is given a number of enforcement mechanisms, including broad investigative authority and the right to deny, suspend, or revoke registration in specific instances, subject to review by the courts. It also has the very important right to seek an injunction and close down an adviser's business literally overnight. In 1979 the Supreme Court ruled that an aggrieved investor has no private cause of action under the Advisers Act against an adviser who has violated the act's antifraud provisions, merely the right to rescind the contract and obtain restitution.

Who Is an Investment Adviser?

A wide variety of persons and organizations provide many different kinds of investment advisory services. Some, including financial planners, provide personal services geared to the needs of individual clients, while others provide impersonal advice through newspaper columns, newsletters, radio and television programs, and other forms of mass communication. Many of these persons consider themselves true professionals; others see themselves as sellers of securities whose investment advice is simply part of the technique of making the sale.

Keeping track of all these different types of investment advisers has not been an easy task for the SEC, which has the primary authority to determine who is and who is not required to register as an investment adviser in accordance with the statutory language. The pertinent provision of the Advisers Act is section 202(a)(11), which defines an "investment adviser" as:

> any person who, for compensation, engages in the business of advising others, either directly or through publications or writings, as to the value of securities or as to the advisability of investing in, purchasing, or selling securities, or who, for compensation and as part of a regular business, issues or promulgates analyses or reports concerning securities.

The statutory definition expressly excludes banks and, in addition, expressly excludes lawyers, accountants, engineers, and teachers whose performance of investment advisory services is *solely incidental* to the practice of their professions. It also specifically excludes (1) brokers or dealers whose performance of such services is solely incidental to the conduct of their business as a broker or dealer and who receive no special compensation therefrom, (2) publishers of bona fide newspapers, magazines, or business or financial publications of general and regular circulation, (3) persons whose advice relates only to U.S. Government securities, and (4) such other persons not within the intent of the statutory definition as the SEC may designate by rule or regulation.

In addition to the preceding persons who are excluded from the definition of "investment adviser," the statute also contains several specific *exemptions,* that is, persons who qualify as investment advisers but are held to be exempt from the law's registration requirements. The exemptions include (1) any investment adviser all of whose clients are residents of the state within which he maintains his principal place of business, and who does not furnish advice or issue reports concerning securities traded on any national securities exchange; (2) any investment adviser whose only clients are insurance companies; and (3) any investment adviser who during the preceding 12 months has had fewer than 15 clients and who does not hold himself out generally to the public as an investment adviser. Incidentally, the law contemplates a rolling 12-month period, so that this last exemption is necessarily limited in applicability to the circumstances prevailing during the preceding 12 months only.

At the time the Advisers Act was first enacted, the financial planning profession as we know it today had not yet come into being; thus, the early case law and administrative agency (SEC) rulings interpreting the term ''investment adviser'' do not even mention financial planners as potential registrants under the law. By the mid-1970s, however, the volume of requests for ''no-action letters'' submitted to the SEC staff seeking opinions on the applicability of the Advisers Act indicated the growing concerns of many persons who called themselves financial planners that they might be subject to the law.

The matter was resolved once and for all when the SEC issued its comprehensive *Interpretive Release No. IA-770* in August 1981. In that document (the text of which is contained in Appendix A) the SEC set forth in detail its position with respect to several categories of investment advisers, including specifically financial planners, pension consultants, sports and entertainment representatives, and others who provide investment advisory services as a normal part of their business and professional activities.

The SEC's interpretation of who qualifies as an ''investment adviser'' within the meaning of the statute, and thus is required to register with the agency, boils down to three essential components: (1) whether the person in question provides advice or issues reports or analyses regarding securities; (2) whether he is in the business of providing such services; and (3) whether he provides such services for compensation. As a general proposition, if the activities of a person providing integrated advisory services satisfy each of the elements described, he qualifies as an investment adviser within the meaning of the Advisers Act, unless he is specifically *excluded* thereunder or is *exempt* from the Act's registration requirements. To gain further insight into the SEC's approach to the matter of registration of investment advisers and to see how the law applies to financial planners, let us take a closer look at each of the qualifying elements.

Advice or analyses concerning securities.

If you are a financial planner who gives advice or makes recommendations to clients with respect to specific securities, which is what financial planners are supposed to do, without question you are an "investment adviser" within the meaning of the Advisers Act, assuming the other elements of the definition are met (i.e., your services are an integral part of a business and are performed for compensation).

Generally, one can come within the definition of the Advisers Act even if the advice given does not relate to specific securities—for example, merely by comparing the relative advantages of investing in securities as opposed to other forms of investment. In fact, the SEC has ruled that just giving an opinion regarding the choice or retention of investment advisers is itself considered to be investment "advice." Employing this rationale, the SEC has held that an insurance agent who receives a fixed fee for each client he refers to an investment adviser would be an investment adviser himself on the ground that the act of making such referral inherently involves advising the client that investing in securities is desirable. The issue of paying finders' fees is taken up later in this chapter.

By way of summary, almost any type of analyses or reports that incorporate the writer's judgments about securities are considered to be investment "advice" by the SEC. Note, however, that advice need not be rendered in written form to bring one within the statutory definition. A financial planner who gives seminars, makes audio or video tapes, or appears regularly on a radio or television program dealing with financial matters would be considered to be giving investment "advice" within the meaning of the law, whether or not written materials are made available as part of his presentation. The fact that advice may be given, however, will not by itself bring a person within the statutory definition. All three key determinants of the statutory definition must be satisfied.

The definition of securities in the Advisers Act is identical to the definition in the Securities Act of 1933 and almost identical to the definition in the Exchange Act of 1934. Thus, a *security* includes notes, common and preferred stocks, bonds and other debt instruments, money market and other mutual funds, CDs, commercial paper, fractional interests in gas, oil, or other mineral rights, limited partnership interests, and investment contracts of many kinds.

Just what constitutes an *investment contract,* and hence a security, was established rather precisely by the Supreme Court in *S.E.C.* v. *T. W. Howey Co.,* 328 U.S. 293 (1946). In that case the court ruled, "The test is whether the scheme involves an investment of money in a common enterprise with profits to come solely from the efforts of others." Using this benchmark, just about every investment that a planner would recommend as suitable for a passive investor would qualify as a security. The typical limited partnership interest purchased by an investor is a prime example of an investment contract.

In legal decisions interpreting the term *securities* under the Securities Act and the Exchange Act, insurance contracts, real estate contracts, commodities futures contracts and contracts for the purchase or sale of collectibles such as rare coins, gemstones, or other tangibles have been held not to be securities. It is especially important to note that even if a security is exempt from registration under the Securities Act (e.g., a private placement under SEC Regulation D, or an intrastate offering), it does not thereby lose its character as a security for purposes of the Advisers Act.

Engaged in "the business of advising others" regarding securities. The second element of the three-part definition is the "business" standard. One cannot be an investment adviser within the meaning of the statute unless the giving of investment advice is part of his regular business. This does not mean it has to be his sole or principal business activity, or even any specific percentage of his principal business activity. But the giving of investment advice cannot be an incidental activity —for example, giving advice on a single occasion. One must be "in the business" of giving such advice as a normal activity for the statute to apply.

In accordance with Interpretive Release IA-770, the SEC considers anyone who provides financial services that include investment advice, and who charges therefor, as being "in the business" of providing investment advice, *unless such advice is solely incidental to a noninvestment-advisory business of such person, is nonspecific, and is not specially compensated.* This interpretation certainly covers the activities of the typical financial planner or, for that matter, anyone who advertises investment advisory services. Incidentally, the SEC has ruled that the solicitation of clients is an integral part of the activity of an investment adviser, and thus, a person just starting in the investment advisory business must register with the SEC *before* using the mails or other interstate facilities to advertise for initial clients.

Undoubtedly, there are some persons who, notwithstanding the fact they call themselves financial planners, would not be considered investment advisers by the SEC. Take the case of a person who calls himself a financial planner but who spends most of his time helping his clients prepare their tax forms. Let us assume this hypothetical person has no securities license and does not buy or sell securities, although occasionally he is asked for his opinion regarding the merits of specific investments in a client's portfolio from the tax-shelter standpoint.

Would the giving of advice in this context make our hypothetical tax preparer an investment adviser within the meaning of the Advisers Act? Not likely, since he is not "in the business" of giving investment advice, notwithstanding the fact he holds himself out to be a financial planner. And if he receives no special compensation for rendering advice in this manner, then it is highly unlikely he would have to register under the act.

What about a person who writes an occasional financial article or book that includes references to investing in securities? The SEC has held that the definition of an investment adviser would not include the author or publisher of

> any book, pamphlet, or article (1) which does not contain recommendations, reports, analysis or other advisory information relating to specific securities or issuers, and (2) which is not one of a series of publications by such person or intended to be supplemented or updated, *provided that* the author or publisher has not and does not intend to engage in any other activities which would bring him within the definition of investment adviser. [ADV-563, 1977.]

The matter of compensation.   To be considered an investment adviser under the Advisers Act, the individual must receive compensation therefor. The SEC has indicated in Release IA-770 that the compensation element is satisfied by the receipt of "any economic benefit, whether in the form of an advisory fee, some other fee relating to the total services rendered, commissions, or some combination of the foregoing."

The SEC has also pointed out that it is not necessary for the compensation to be paid by the person actually receiving the investment advice, merely that the adviser receives compensation from *some* source for the services rendered, including benefits from other transactions. To illustrate, let us assume you were to review a client's situation and prepare a financial plan that includes specific investment and insurance recommendations. Even though you do not charge a fee for preparing the plan, as long as you receive a commission on any insurance products or securities recommended to the client, you will have provided advisory services "for compensation" within the meaning of the Advisers Act.

Preparing a plan without charge in order to generate additional brokerage commissions would be another form of compensation that would bring you under the act. This was precisely the situation that the

SEC ruled on in a relatively recent "no-action" letter. A financial planning firm in St. Louis sought an exemption from the SEC's "brochure rule," which mandates that the adviser furnish to each investment advisory client detailed information disclosing key facts about the adviser's methods of operation, its key personnel, and all possible conflicts of interest. The planning firm set forth the salient facts as follows in its letter of inquiry:

> We charge no fees to any existing clients. . . . We charge no fees to any prospective clients. . . . We enter into no contracts to provide any services. Likewise, a client or prospective client has no contract or any obligation to do business with us.
>
> We offer to do a financial analysis for a prospective client with the objective of bettering his financial plan. We explain to each prospective client that we do not charge a fee for this and that he is under no obligation whatsoever. We tell him that if he implements recommendations in our financial plan we may earn a commission on those products and that we of course would like him to implement the plan with us. . . .

In replying to the financial planning firm's letter of inquiry, the SEC noted that all the persons who worked for and owned the firm were registered representatives of a specific broker-dealer (First Affiliated Securities, Inc.), even though in giving their financial planning and investment advice none of the planners were under the broker-dealer's supervision and control. The SEC held:

> In light of these representations, we would treat these persons [financial planners/registered representatives] and Adviser [the planning firm] as identical and deem compensation paid to these persons [from securities commissions] as paid to Adviser for the purposes of the Investment Advisers Act of 1940. . . . Accordingly, Adviser is subject to the Act and the rules thereunder such as Rule 204-3, also known as the brochure rule. [First Affiliated Securities, Inc., No-Action Letter, Feb. 16, 1984, ¶ 77,609, CCH Federal Securities Law Reporter, 4-25-84.]

Bear in mind that all three elements of the statutory definition of investment adviser must be met before a person is considered subject to the act. And also bear in mind that if there is any possible legal basis for finding a person to be an investment adviser, the SEC will do so. Interpretive Release IA-770 gives additional examples of activities that the SEC claims will bring a person within the statutory definition. It should be noted that the views of the SEC, as expressed in releases of this nature, do not take precedence over actual court decisions, but they do have considerable persuasive effect as guidelines for compliance with the law.

Statutory Exclusions

Earlier, reference was made to the enumerated categories of persons who are specifically excluded from the definition of investment adviser: banks, certain professionals (lawyers, accountants, engineers, teachers), broker-dealers, newspaper publishers, and persons whose advice relates to U.S. Government securities. What is important to understand is that one who falls within a stated *exclusion* is, by definition, not considered an "investment adviser" under the act, and hence is not subject to the act's registration requirements. Perhaps of even greater significance is the fact that someone who is not legally an investment adviser is not subject to the antifraud provisions of the Advisers Act. By contrast, an investment adviser who is merely *exempt* from registering under the act is very much subject to the antifraud provisions.

The SEC construes all the exclusions and exemptions very strictly, and unless you can meet the precise statutory tests for exclusion or exemption, you will not avoid the law's applicability. To get a better idea of how they work, let's look at the two exclusion categories that are most directly related to persons providing financial planning services.

Professional persons. The professional exception category is available only to the four professions specifically mentioned in the law: lawyers, accountants, engineers, and teachers. By and large, a professional person in one of the enumerated classes who does not hold himself out to the public as a financial adviser will not be considered an investment adviser merely because he may, as an incident to the practice of his profession, give investment advice to others. Estate planning attorneys, for example, commonly have to consider and suggest various investment alternatives to their clients as an integral aspect of their overall estate planning services. This activity does not make the estate attorney an "investment adviser" for purposes of the Advisers Act. Similarly, accountants occasionally review prospect uses for clients to assess their tax implications, and this, too, would be considered an incidental activity.

In a 1984 no-action letter, the SEC held that a registered representative who teaches education courses in investments at an accredited educational institution would likewise come within the professional person exclusion since any investment advice rendered under such circumstances would be solely incidental to the conduct of his normal securities activities.

And in the same no-action letter the SEC held that a registered representative who regularly appears on television, conducts radio programs, or writes columns for local newspapers about financial matters, would not be an investment adviser because of the exemption provided publishers of bona fide news, business, or financial publications of general and regular circulation. [Baker, Watts & Co., SEC No-action letter, May 11, 1984, ¶ 77,667, CCH Federal Securities Law Reporter, August 1, 1984.]

On the other hand, a person who is clearly within one of these professional categories but who specifically holds himself out to the public as providing financial planning, pension consulting, or other financial advisory services would not qualify for the statutory exclusion since his investment advisory services would no longer be deemed "incidental" to the practice of his profession. By way of illustration, it is not likely that an accountant would qualify for the solely incidental exclusion, and would thus have to register as an adviser, if he (1) advertises his financial planning services, (2) charges fees for giving investment advice, (3) makes detailed evaluations and comparisons of investment alternatives, (4) recommends specific tax shelters, or (5) directs clients to investment advisers.

And, finally, it is clear that the statutory exclusion was not intended to permit a professional person whose entire business consists of rendering investment advice to claim he is not an investment adviser just because he happens to give his advice in the form of instruction, such as correspondence courses, seminars, books, tapes, or other forms of instruction. For example, someone in the professional exception category who teaches investment strategies at a stock market school will not qualify under this exemption if the school lacks the attributes normally associated with educational institutions and if the primary focus of the school is not the providing of general knowledge about the financial markets but detailed practical instruction in how to make profitable security investments.

Broker-dealers. The SEC has taken the position that broker-dealers commonly give a certain amount of investment advice to their customers in the course of their regular business, and that it would be inappropriate to bring them within the scope of the Advisers Act merely because of this aspect of their business. Thus, the statutory exclusion has been held to apply to a broker-dealer who distributes to its customers periodic market reports or analyses containing investment advice, without making any special charge therefor, *as long as the rendering of such advice is solely incidental to the conduct of the broker-dealer's securities business.*

Whether investment advice is or is not "solely incidental" to the conduct of the broker-dealer's business must be determined by the facts in each case. But the SEC has ruled that it is not considered solely incidental to a broker-dealer's business to assist clients in choosing an investment adviser and to monitor his performance thereafter on a continuing basis, particularly where the adviser is given discretionary management authority over client funds and is required to funnel all securities transactions through the broker-dealer in question. Such conduct, according to the SEC, represents a "very significant activity outside the scope of normal brokerage operations," and could not be considered solely incidental thereto. *FPC Securities Corp.,* [1974–1975 Transfer Binder] ¶ 80,072, CCH Federal Securities Law Reporter (September 9, 1974).

Even if investment advice clearly is incidental to the broker-dealer's business, it is the SEC's position that once "special compensation" is received for its advisory services, even if uniform in amount and charged only to those customers to whom specific investment advice is given, the broker-dealer will be considered an investment adviser and cannot claim the statutory exclusion. Moreover, should the broker-dealer agree to actively solicit clients for a registered investment adviser (i.e., become a *finder*), *the receipt of any portion of the adviser's fee will make the broker-dealer an investment adviser subject to the law's registration requirements.*

The broker-dealer exclusion applies to all the registered representatives of a broker-dealer who, as such, render investment advisory services that are *solely incidental* to their conduct as registered representatives and who receive no special compensation therefor. The typical stockbroker/account executive in most national stock exchange wire houses presumably would come within this category. Note, however, that if a registered representative is not acting under the supervision of a broker-dealer in providing investment advice, but is acting on his own (say he publishes his own financial newsletter or owns and manages his own financial planning firm) he would not come within the statutory exclusion and must register separately as an investment adviser.

At one time, the SEC took the position that a registered representative of a broker-dealer could not individually register with the SEC as an investment adviser because all of his securities recommendations would necessarily involve a potential conflict of interest. That position has long since been altered, and now such individual registration is permitted, *provided the broker-dealer gives written approval and thereby assumes the requisite supervisory control.* If a broker-dealer chooses not to assume this supervisory responsibility and does not give its approval, the registered representative/investment adviser would seem to have little choice but to locate a broker-dealer who is willing to accept this responsibility.

At the outset of their practices, the majority of financial planners with securities licenses find it more practical to affiliate with broker-dealers who have themselves become registered investment advisers, with the broker-dealer entering into the formal contracts with clients and sharing the fees for the investment advice rendered (by the planner) on some agreed-upon basis. As time passes, however, many planners begin to think about making more practical arrangements both to avoid the circuitous process involved as well as to increase their income. The relative merits of offering advisory services through a broker-dealer or as a solo practitioner are discussed later in this chapter.

The Registration Process

Section 203 of the Advisers Act provides that it is unlawful for an investment adviser to use the mails or any means or instrumentality of interstate commerce to conduct his business unless he has registered with the SEC or is specifically exempted from registration under the law. As earlier noted, since the SEC considers the act of advertising oneself as being an investment adviser an integral part of the ''business'' of an investment adviser even if he has no clients as yet, one who is just starting in the investment advisory business must be sure to register *before* he uses the mails or other interstate facilities to solicit clients.

Registration is accomplished by filing an application directly with the SEC in Washington, D.C., on *Form ADV,* along with a $150 registration fee. In this case, you do not apply through your broker-dealer, assuming you have one. The fee, incidentally, is nonrefundable. Form ADV, which has just been revised for joint use by the states and the SEC, is a questionnaire in two parts, along with several schedules, which allows the applicant to amplify or clarify the data provided in Parts I and II. It asks for information regarding the applicant's name, form and place of organization, nature of business activities, scope of authority with respect to client funds and accounts, information concerning any convictions or injunctions arising out of securities transactions and related matters (including similar information with respect to any person associated with the applicant), educational background, and business affiliations for the past ten years.

Any applicant who has or expects to have custody or possession of client funds or securities or who requires or expects to require clients to prepay advisory fees six months or more in advance (and in excess of $500 per client) must file a balance sheet audited by an independent public accountant.

Reasons for Denial of Registration

The SEC may deny an application for registration for any of the following reasons:

- Willful filing of false or misleading information in the Advisers Act application or any registration proceeding before the SEC.
- Failure to state in an application or proceeding any material fact required to be stated therein.
- Conviction within the previous ten years of certain crimes that relate to securities or arise out of the conduct of the business of a broker, dealer, municipal securities dealer, investment adviser-bank, insurance company, or fiduciary.
- Willful violation of the Securities Act of 1933, the Securities Exchange Act of 1934, the Investment Company Act of 1940, or the Advisers Act.
- Aiding or abetting violation of these acts by any other person.
- Failure to reasonably supervise another person who violates any of these acts if that person was subject to supervision.

The Advisers Act has been criticized because it does not require an investment adviser to have any minimum education, training, or experience, nor does it require any qualifying examination. It is not surprising, therefore, to learn that the SEC has granted registrations to many persons whose occupations are not normally associated with investment advice, including booking agents, dress designers, dentists, physicians, and so on. In 1975, the SEC transmitted a bill to Congress that proposed various amendments to the Advisers Act, including one that would have granted specific authority to the SEC to prescribe qualifications and financial responsibility standards for investment advisers. Unfortunately, this particular amendment was not adopted. Several of the states, however, do regulate the competence of investment advisers at the present time.

In accordance with the law and regulations, the SEC has 45 days to review and deny an application for registration. Unless the SEC institutes proceedings prior to that time, the application is automatically effective at the end of the 45-day period. As mentioned earlier, registration under the Advisers Act does not represent any sort of endorsement by the SEC, and any representation otherwise is a violation of the law. The mere fact of registration (i.e., calling oneself a registered investment adviser) is permissible, provided the statement is true.

Statutory Exemptions from Coverage

In addition to the earlier mentioned categories of persons who are excluded from the definition of investment adviser, the Advisers Act also contains three specific exemptions from the requirement that an investment adviser register with the SEC:

1. Any investment adviser all of whose clients are residents of the state within which the adviser maintains his principal office and who does not furnish advice with respect to securities listed on any national exchange.

2. Any investment adviser whose only clients are insurance companies.

3. Any investment adviser who during the preceding 12 months has had fewer than 15 clients and who does not hold himself out to the public generally as an investment adviser.

A person who qualifies under one of the enumerated exemptions does not have to register as an investment adviser under the law. Note, however, that, unlike the *excluded* persons mentioned earlier (those not considered "investment advisers" within the meaning of the statute), an *exempt* person is still considered to be an investment adviser and accordingly subject to the act's antifraud provisions.

The intrastate exemption is of limited applicability and will be of little help to the typical financial planner, since it restricts investment advice to securities not listed or admitted to unlisted trading privileges on any national securities exchange. This automatically eliminates advice regarding stocks, bonds, mutual funds, many real estate investment trusts, and a wide variety of other investments normally reviewed and recommended by financial planners. Also, *exemption from registration under the federal act will not necessarily affect the adviser's obligation to register under state law.*

To illustrate how the exemption might apply, the SEC indicated in a 1974 "no-action letter" that a California estate and tax planning service, all of whose clients were California residents, would quality for exemption under the Advisers Act in view of the fact that it restricted its investment advice to the benefits of investing in real estate, cattle, beaver, manufacturers, restaurants, mining, oil and gas, and films, all in the form of partnerships, joint ventures, or privately owned corporations within the state.

The exemption for investment advisers whose *only* clients are insurance companies needs no elaboration. If you happen to be a financial planner within this rather narrow category, you are not required to register as an investment adviser, but you will still be subject to the law's antifraud provisions.

Someone seeking to take advantage of the under-15-client exemption not only must have had 14 or less clients during the preceding 12 months (and this is a rolling 12-month period), but also must not hold himself out to the public as an investment adviser. According to the SEC, "holding oneself out to the public as an investment adviser" includes (1) maintenance of a listing as an investment adviser in a telephone or business directory, (2) expressing willingness to accept new clients, and (3) use of a letterhead indicating any activity as an investment adviser. For all practical purposes, this exemption is limited to persons who give investment advice to members of their families or close friends and who do not offer their services as advisers to the public generally.

In the final analysis, the exemptions from registration as an investment adviser apply only in limited circumstances to persons who provide the services normally offered by financial planners. And anyone seeking to come within a statutory exemption will find that the SEC construes the exemptions very strictly. A person who is exempt not only does not have to register as an investment adviser, but is not subject to the record-keeping and reporting requirements of section 204 of the law, or to section 205, which regulates investment advisory contracts.

Legal Obligations of Investment Advisers

The financial planner who is an investment adviser, and the typical planner will be, assumes thereby a number of important legal obligations. Some of these are statutory in nature, while others arise out of common law principles enunciated by the courts over the years. Here is a rundown on the most significant of these obligations.

Registration. The basic statutory obligation requires the adviser to register under the federal Investment Advisers Act, in the manner noted previously. And once the applicant has been accepted for registration, he is required to file with the SEC each year a supplemental *Form ADV-S*, which is described next.

Record-keeping and reporting requirements. Under its broad rulemaking authority, the SEC has imposed extensive record-keeping and reporting requirements. All investment advisers must keep their registrations with the SEC up to date by filing amendments to their Form ADV as circumstances may require, as well as filing a brief report annually on Form ADV-S to keep the SEC advised with respect to whether the adviser is still in business or if any significant changes have taken place that might affect information submitted on the original Form ADV. The filing of the ADV-S also gives the adviser-registrant the opportunity to submit a current balance sheet to the SEC.

SEC Rule 204-2 provides that every adviser who uses the mails or any interstate facility in connection with his business shall keep, preserve, and have ready for inspection certain specified books and records. This particular rule, by the way, applies to *unregistered* as well as registered advisers, unless they are exempt from registration. The basic records required to be kept are those normally maintained by the typical advisory business, such as invoices, logs, confirmations, journals, checkbooks, bank statements, and the usual financial statements.

Today, many investment advisers maintain the better part of these records in computerized formats, although this is not a legal requirement. When SEC examiners make periodic inspections, they generally indicate whether an adviser's accounting and record-keeping system is adequate or inadequate.

Investment advisory contracts. An adviser is prohibited from entering into any investment advisory contract (1) if such contract provides for compensation to the adviser on the basis of a share of the capital gains or capital appreciation of the client's funds, (2) if the contract fails to provide that it can only be assigned with the client's consent and approval, and (3) where the adviser is a partnership, if it fails to notify the other party to the contract of any change in the membership of such partnership.

Brochure rule. In accordance with SEC Rule 204-3, every registered investment adviser, when entering into an advisory contract, must deliver a written disclosure statement (the "brochure") to the prospective client. This statement must disclose information about the adviser's background, education, experience in the investment advisory field, types of services offered, investment techniques employed, and other relevant information.

The brochure itself can be either a copy of the entire Part II of Form ADV submitted to the SEC or a narrative statement summarizing all the entries on Part II. In either case it must disclose all the information required by law. Many planners choose to furnish their clients with actual copies of Part II of Form ADV, rather than a specially prepared brochure. One thing is certain: the SEC takes the brochure rule seriously and will not tolerate attempts to circumvent its requirements. The reader will recall the SEC's no-action letter in the First Affiliated Securities case discussed earlier in this chapter. Incidentally, Rule 204-3 further provides that a current copy of the brochure must be offered to each advisory client annually.

Use of the term "investment counselor." The Advisers Act makes it unlawful for any investment adviser to represent that he is an investment counsel or to use the term "investment counsel" as descriptive of his business unless (1) his principal business consists of acting as an investment adviser, and (2) a substantial part of his business consists of rendering investment supervisory services.

The term *investment supervisory services* is defined by the SEC to mean "the giving of continuous advice as to the investment of funds on the basis of the individual needs of each client." A person who is registered under the Advisers Act but who is not an investment counsel within the meaning of that Act should be careful in his advertising and on his letterhead not to refer to himself as an investment counsel.

Paying finders' fees. In accordance with the Advisers Act and the rules issued by the SEC, registered investment advisers are permitted to make cash payments to persons who solicit clients for the adviser ("finders"), provided all the conditions outlined in SEC Rule 206(4)-3, relating to cash payments for client solicitations, are followed precisely. These guidelines provide that (1) there be a written agreement between the adviser and the solicitor, (2) the solicitor must present to the prospective client not only a copy of the adviser's disclosure brochure, but a *separate* disclosure statement outlining in detail the arrangement between the solicitor and adviser, including the exact nature of the compensation to be paid by the adviser to the solicitor for finding new clients, as well as whether or not the client will also be charged for this service in addition to any advisory fee paid.

The rule further provides that each prospective client must sign and date an acknowledgment of receipt of the adviser's brochure from the solicitor before any advisory contract can be entered into. And finally, the rule provides that it is the adviser's responsibility to ensure that all legal requirements are met by the solicitor he has engaged.

The financial planner who chooses this method of obtaining new clients must be prepared for rigorous enforcement oversight by the SEC, which has never looked favorably upon this practice. This means there is little room for error, under penalty of prompt disciplinary action. In addition, many states have enacted laws relating to the solicitation of clients and the payment of finder's fees, making compliance just that much more burdensome.

Fiduciary responsibility. At the time the Advisers Act was under consideration, leading investment advisers emphasized the importance of the relationship of trust and confidence between advisers and their clients, and the Congress accordingly gave emphasis to this concept in enacting the legislation. Thus, section 206 of the Advisers Act, the antifraud section, details various types of conduct the lawmakers deemed to be violative of the delicate fiduciary nature of the investment advisory relationship. Specifically, section 206 prohibits "any act, practice, or course of business which is fraudulent, deceptive, or manipulative." The U.S. Supreme Court gave further meaning to the concept in the landmark case of *SEC* v. *Capital Gains Research Bureau*, 375 U.S. 180 (1963), observing therein:

> Courts have imposed on a fiduciary an affirmative duty of utmost good faith, and full and fair disclosure of all material facts, as well as an affirmative obligation to employ reasonable care to avoid misleading his clients.

It is the SEC's position, as expressed in *Interpretive Release IA-770*, that the duty of a planner-investment adviser to refrain from fraudulent conduct includes the affirmative obligation (1) to disclose to each client all material facts regarding any potential conflicts of interest so that the client can make an informed decision whether to enter into or to continue a formal relationship with the planner, (2) to disclose fully the nature and extent of any interest the planner-adviser may have in any particular recommendation (including any compensation he might receive from his employing broker-dealer), (3) to inform clients of their right to execute recommended investment purchases through other broker-dealers, (4) to disclose if his personal securities transactions are inconsistent with advice given to his clients, and (5) in general, not to engage in any conduct that could result in preferring his own interests to those of his advisory clients.

The financial planner's liability for engaging in conduct that violates his fiduciary responsibility to his clients is dealt with in more detail in Chapter Six. Once again, it bears repeating that the antifraud provisions of the Advisers Act apply to any person who is an investment adviser as defined in the act, *whether or not such person is required to be registered with the SEC as an investment adviser.* Hence, although persons who are excluded from the definition of investment adviser are not subject to the act's antifraud provisions, those who are merely exempt from registration are clearly covered.

Securities Registration and Investment Advisers Registration Compared

The foregoing has been a rather detailed analysis of the Investment Advisers Act of 1940, showing how it applies to the conduct of persons who provide investment advice as a normal part of their business activities. Planners sometimes assume they are not required to register with the SEC as investment advisers simply because they already have their Series 7 securities representative registrations, or because they are associated with a broker-dealer who is exempt from registration under the Advisers Act. This can be a dangerous assumption, since there is no direct relationship between the two forms of licensing.

As we have seen, being an investment adviser does not necessarily obligate an individual to effect transactions in securities for others, and, thus, there may be no need to obtain securities registration. By the same token, being registered to buy and sell securities does not ipso facto qualify one to provide investment advice without being appropriately registered to do so. The prudent financial planner will seriously consider the need for having both registrations and should consult legal counsel for specific advice if he still has doubts with respect thereto.

One thing you can bank on: the SEC and the NASD are now devoting more attention than ever to the vigorous enforcement of the securities laws, and particularly on matters of licensing and registration. Even though the SEC considers financial planners to be investment advisers within the meaning of the Advisers Act, relatively few planners have voluntarily chosen to comply with the law's registration requirements. As a professional planner, you owe it to yourself to make sure you are in compliance with all the applicable laws.

STATE REGULATION OF INVESTMENT ADVISERS

The discussion thus far has centered on the financial planner's legal obligation to register as an investment adviser under federal law. But the financial planner required to register as an investment adviser under federal law almost invariably must register as an investment adviser under the law of the state in which he practices. And sometimes even if he is exempt under federal law, state registration may be legally required.

From the very beginning, the pertinent statutes have made it clear that the federal government had no intention of preempting this area of activity. Thus, Section 222 of the Advisers Act specifically states that

> Nothing in this subchapter shall affect the jurisdiction of the securities commissioner (or any agency or officer performing like functions) of any state over any security or any persons insofar as it does not conflict with the provisions of this subchapter or the rules and regulations thereunder.

It is also clear, however, that nothing in a state law can relieve an adviser of his duties under the federal law. Moreover, the terms used in the federal Advisers Act are required to be interpreted according to federal law, not state law.

At the present time, 38 states, Puerto Rico, and Guam require the registration or licensing of investment advisers, while several others, although not requiring registration, have statutory provisions dealing with fraud by advisers. (Appendix B indicates the basic requirements for each of the states.)

As pointed out earlier, most of the states have patterned their blue-sky laws after the Uniform Securities Act, which allows great flexibility in the area of state control of investment advisers. Fraudulent practices by investment advisers are dealt with under the Uniform Securities Act in three ways: (1) by generally outlawing fraudulent practices, (2) by placing restrictions on the types of investment advisory contracts that may be entered into, and (3) by providing for restrictions upon the obtaining of custody of a client's securities. Of the states that have enacted blue-sky laws based on the Uniform Securities Act, about three-fourths have included antifraud provisions relating to investment advisory activities.

Who Is an Investment Adviser under State Law?

If you qualify as an investment adviser under the federal Advisers Act, you will also qualify under any state blue-sky law that conforms to the Uniform Securities Act. The latter makes it unlawful for any person to transact business in the state as an investment adviser unless he is registered as an investment adviser, with essentially the same exceptions contained in the federal law. An investment adviser is defined in the Uniform Securities Act as any person who, for compensation, engages in the business of advising others, either directly or through publications or writings, as to the value of securities or as to the advisability of investing in, purchasing, or selling securities. It also includes persons who, for compensation as a part of a regular business, issue analyses or reports concerning securities.

A person is not subject to the investment adviser provisions of the Uniform Securities Act if he has no place of business within the state and if his only clients within the state are other investment advisers, broker-dealers, banks, savings institutions, trust companies, investment companies, pension or profit-sharing trusts, or other financial institutions. In addition, a person is not subject to the investment adviser provisions of a state blue-sky law if his place of business is out of state and he does not, during any 12-month period, direct business communications into the state to more than five clients (other than the types of clients mentioned previously).

State Registration Procedure

The registration requirements of the states that currently require advisers to register are far from uniform. Accordingly, the SEC and the North American Securities Administrators' Association (NASAA) have been considering for some time the development of a uniform investment adviser registration form for use both by the SEC and the states, as well as the development of a central registration system for investment advisers similar to the one used for broker-dealers. These efforts have been productive, and in mid-1985 NASAA adopted a revised ADV form permitting simultaneous registration as an investment adviser in the states and with the SEC utilizing a uniform registration form. If adopted by the SEC (which is anticipated), the revised ADV form will become effective January 1, 1986.

At present, state registration as an investment adviser in those states that have patterned their laws after the Uniform Securities Act consists of submitting a separate application form together with filing fees and a financial statement, posting a surety bond, and—in 24 states at the present time—taking an examination. The examinations generally focus on the applicant's basic knowledge of securities law, but also test his knowledge of specific provisions of the state's blue-sky law.

Many states waive the examination requirement if the applicant has already passed the NASD's Series 7 examination. Others require that the applicant pass not only the Series 7 examination, but also a separate state examination. The NASD Series 63 examination (called the *Uniform Securities Agent State Law Exam*) meets the requirements of most states and is the exam most commonly employed. It is a one-hour, 50-question test given on a computer terminal. A passing score is 70%, or a minimum of 35 correct answers.

Legal Obligations under the State Acts

Much like the federal Advisers Act, the various state investment adviser acts require fairly detailed record-keeping requirements. Just about all the states have adopted antifraud provisions virtually identical to the Advisers Act language, and here, again, the antifraud provisions of the state acts apply to investment advisers who are exempt from registration, as well as those who are not.

Investment advisory contracts generally have to be in writing to comply with the state acts, and these contracts must make it clear that the adviser's fee is not predicated on any capital gain or appreciation of client funds. As under the federal law, advisory contracts cannot be assigned without the client's consent.

On a more practical level, states that permit (or require) registered securities representatives to be registered investment advisers typically oblige the representative's broker-dealer to formally accept supervisory responsibility for the investment advisory activities of their registered representatives as a *sine qua non* for granting state registration as an investment adviser.

Denial or Revocation of Registration

The Uniform Securities Act gives the state administrator or commissioner of securities the authority to deny, suspend, or revoke the registration of an investment adviser if he finds such action to be in the public interest. The law also extends to applicants for registration. By and large, the grounds for denial, suspension, or revocation parallel those under the state's securities licensing authority, that is, questions of an applicant's moral fitness, technical competence, and financial stability.

The common grounds for denial, suspension, or revocation of an investment adviser's registration (or application therefor) are incomplete, false, or misleading statements in the application and evidence of prior criminal convictions, prior injunctions, noncompliance with securities statutes or rules, unethical practices, insolvency, inexperience or lack of knowledge, failure to supervise agents or employees, and nonpayment of filing or registration fees.

The appropriate state official is empowered to conduct investigations into an applicant's reputation and character, to make certain that the granting of an investment adviser's license or registration will be in the interest of the investing public.

In general, the states are tightening up on their regulation of investment advisers, and this should be welcomed by planners and their industry spokesmen since it is bound to instill greater investor confidence and thus enhance the credibility of the financial planning profession as a whole.

REGISTRATION AS AN INVESTMENT ADVISER: SOME PRACTICAL CONSIDERATIONS

Up to now, the emphasis has been on the legal requirements for registering as an investment adviser under both federal and state laws. But even if it is clear that you are required to register as an investment adviser, several alternative methods are available for accomplishing this, and it is important that you understand what they involve and how they might apply to your personal situation.

The form of business you choose for your financial planning practice (which includes, of course, how you plan to provide investment advisory services), generally will depend on several factors: (1) the extent of your personal liability for business losses, (2) the income tax advantages of your form of doing business, (3) the management and administrative advantages, and (4) the effect of the form of your business on your personal legal liability and your regulatory obligations. Obviously, all these are important considerations that you must address without regard to the single issue of how to register as an investment adviser. Still, it may be useful at this point to review the issues you should be thinking about before it is time to register. The principal advantages and disadvantages of each of the three basic modes of registration are discussed next.

Individual Registration

The first method is to register with the SEC as an individual, a method many financial planners have adopted. Under this approach, you are an independent professional whose services include the giving of investment advice to your financial planning clients. And you do so for compensation. You are your own boss and can decide for yourself what types of financial plans to prepare, what investment recommendations to make, and what you will charge for your services.

With this total autonomy, however, comes total (and individual) legal responsibility for the manner in which you conduct your business. If you also have a securities license and typically assist your clients in implementing investment recommendations with securities that will net you a commission, you must be absolutely candid and disclose to them the nature of the dual role you are playing. This means you must clearly disclose the potential conflict of interest in recommending specific investments that will result in sales commissions.

Affiliation with a Broker-Dealer

Earlier, it was pointed out that a registered broker-dealer is excluded from the definition of investment adviser if the broker-dealer's investment advisory services are solely incidental to the securities activities and no special charge is made for such services. Many broker-dealers in recent years have sought to expand their normal activities to include financial planning and investment advisory services, and to accomplish this they have taken the necessary steps to register as investment advisers under the pertinent federal and state laws. Financial planners affiliated with such firms may be obliged to write all their financial plans under the aegis of their broker-dealers, since most will not permit their registered representatives to have dual licenses as securities representatives and investment advisers. At present, there appears to be nothing in the law or SEC regulations that specifically permits (or prohibits) this practice.

Under this system, the planner prepares the financial plan and the accompanying investment advice, but all the billing is done through the broker-dealer. One advantage to this type of arrangement is that the overall financial plan will be reviewed by a principal of the firm, or at least should be. This not only helps to produce a better plan, but gives the planner an added layer of protection in the event of later litigation. Not that he cannot be sued when something goes wrong; but his broker-dealer undoubtedly will be joined in the litigation, and will not only be required to defend the suit, but more than likely will have to share in the payment of any damages awarded. An obvious drawback to this type of arrangement is the fact that the planner must forfeit a percentage of his planning fees to the broker-dealer.

Broker-dealers that do permit their registered representatives to become registered investment advisers and to give written investment advice to their clients invariably require prior written permission to do so. And, as noted earlier, some states will not grant registration as an investment adviser to a registered representative of a broker-dealer unless the latter formally accepts supervisory responsibilities over the adviser's activities.

Incorporation as an Investment Adviser

A growing number of financial planners have chosen to handle the registration problem by forming their own closely held corporations and then having the corporation register as the investment adviser. By utilizing this mechanism, the planner can achieve a number of objectives, including the ability to separate his financial planning and investment advisory functions from his securities representative functions, which is one way of avoiding the conflicts of interest that might otherwise occur.

Under this arrangement, the client is charged a fee by the financial planner (acting through his corporation) for a plan that includes investment advice and recommendations. If the client chooses to implement any of the recommended investment strategies by purchasing investment products through the same person (now acting as a licensed securities representative), so much the better. If he chooses to implement the securities recommendations elsewhere, then the planner at least will have been compensated for his planning and investment advice.

A corporate form of doing business as an investment adviser may also offer some desirable administrative and tax advantages not available under the other modes of doing business. But do not assume you can shield yourself from personal legal liability or can avoid other legal and regulatory responsibilities merely by adopting the corporate form of doing business. Neither the securities laws, the regulatory agencies, nor the courts permit insulation from legal and regulatory obligations so easily.

KEY POINTS TO REMEMBER

1. The Investment Advisers Act of 1940 was passed to assure the public greater honesty and integrity in the investment advisory field.

2. As enacted, the law requires all who qualify as investment advisers to register with the SEC and comply with all SEC regulations.

3. The law also contains strict antifraud provisions designed to thwart attempts to defraud investors in securities transactions.

4. An investment adviser is defined in the law as anyone who advises others as to the value of or the advisability of purchasing or selling securities, provided this is done "for compensation" and "as a part of a regular business."

5. Most financial planners automatically qualify as investment advisers in the eyes of the SEC and, accordingly, must register with the SEC, unless otherwise specifically exempt or excluded by the law.

6. Broker-dealers whose investment advice is solely incidental to their securities business are excluded under the law; so are publishers of investment newsletters and other similar publications.

7. A person is exempt from the law's registration requirements (and does not have to register) if he has had no more than 14 clients within the preceding 12 months and does not hold himself out as being an investment adviser. Few planners will qualify for this exemption.

8. The compensation receivable by an investment adviser need not come in the form of a direct fee, but may be tied in with commissions on investments recommended or other sources of remuneration, in order for the Advisers Act to apply.

9. Although a lawyer or accountant who gives financial planning advice solely as an incident to his professional services is excluded from the law and does not have to register, registration *is* required if the lawyer or accountant has arranged to refer clients to a specific planner and split fees with him.

10. The broker-dealer exclusion from the Advisers Act applies to all registered representatives of the broker-dealer as long as their advisory services are solely incidental to their securities business and they receive no special compensation therefor.

11. Registration as an investment adviser is accomplished by filing Form ADV directly with the SEC, and not through a broker-dealer. The form has just recently been revised.

12. All investment advisers are required to furnish each client with an initial copy and an annual updated copy of the adviser's brochure, which discloses his educational and business background and other pertinent information.

13. Advisers who utilize the services of solicitors (finders) to obtain new clients must comply with the strict requirements of SEC Rule 206(4)-3 in order to avoid disciplinary action.

14. As a fiduciary, an investment adviser is held to the highest standard of personal trust and confidence under the law.

15. The mere fact that a planner has a securities license does not mean he does not have to register as an investment adviser, and vice versa.

16. If you qualify as an investment adviser under the federal act, you will generally qualify as such under most state investment adviser laws, and you must register thereunder accordingly.

17. Forming your own corporate investment advisory firm and separating your financial planning/investment advisory functions from your securities function may help avoid some of the potential conflicts of interest that would otherwise arise.

Chapter Three

SELECTED REFERENCES

Statutes

Investment Advisers Act of 1940, 15 U.S.C. §§ 80b-1—80b-21.

Uniform Securities Act, 7 Uniform Laws Annotated 691.

Historical Background

SEC, Investment Trusts and Investment Companies, Supplementary Report on Investment Counsel, Investment Management, Investment Supervisory and Investment Advisory Services, H.R. Doc. No. 477, 76th Cong., 2d Sess. (1939).

Hearings on S. 3580 before subcommittee of the Senate Committee on Banking and Currency, 76th Cong., 3d Sess. (1940).

Frankel, Tamar, *The Regulation of Money Managers: The Investment Company Act and the Investment Advisers Act,* Vol. 1 (Little, Brown and Company, Boston, 1978).

Requirement to Register

Federal: 15 U.S.C. § 78o (a)(1).

State: See *Registration Requirements for Investment Advisers,* a state-by-state survey conducted by the ICFP (Denver, April 1984).

S.E.C. v. *Myers,* 285 F.Supp. 743 (D.C. Md. 1968).

Schuder, C. C., "State Regs: The Basics," *Financial Planning,* vol. 13, no. 5, 118 (May 1984).

Who Is an "Investment Adviser"?

Loss, Louis, *Fundamentals of Securities Regulation,* 733 et seq. (Little, Brown and Company, Boston, 1983).

Lovitch, Fred B., "The Investment Advisers Act of 1940—Who Is an 'Investment Adviser'?" 24 *U. Kan. L. Rev.* 67 (1975).

SEC Release No. IA-770, Interpretive advice of the SEC staff on the Investment Advisers Act of 1940, August 13, 1981 (see Appendix A).

Annotation, "Construction and Effect of Investment Advisers Act of 1940, as Amended," 5 ALR Fed 246.

Exemption of Attorneys from Registration

Sullivan v. *Chase Investment Services, Inc.*, 434 F.Supp. 171, (N. D. Cal. 1977).

Brochure Rule

SEC No-action letter, First Affiliated Securities, Inc., ¶ 77,609, *CCH Federal Securities Law Reporter* (April 25, 1984).

Record-keeping Requirements

Gohlke, G. A., "Required Records," *Financial Planning*, vol. 13, no. 8, 43 (August 1984).

Finder's Fees

Hallihan, J. H., "The Finders Headache," *Financial Planning*, vol. 14, no. 5, 39 (May 1985).

Private Cause of Action versus Right of Rescission

Transamerica Mortgage Investors, Inc. v. *Lewis*, 444 U.S. 11 (1979).

Enforcement Authority of the SEC

S.E.C. v. *Wall Street Transcript Corp.*, 422 F.2d 1371 (2d Cir. 1970).
Charles W. Steadman v. *S.E.C.*, 603 F.2d 1126 (5th Cir. 1979).

chapter four

Registering as a Broker-Dealer

If your financial planning activities routinely include the implementation of investment strategies that call for buying or selling securities on behalf of your clients, you fall within the statutory definition of a "broker" and must be registered and licensed as such under the federal and state laws. Although most full-time financial planners with securities licenses are registered representatives affiliated with other broker-dealers, the bulk of their professional time is spent in developing financial plans for clients and other related activities. Still, as a planner acquires more experience and clients, the extent of his securities activities normally increases, and this often prompts his consideration of whether or not to become his own broker-dealer.

It is beyond the scope of this book to explore in depth all the legal and administrative ramifications of registering as a broker-dealer or choosing one form of registration over another. But, for the benefit of those planners who may be contemplating forming their own broker-dealerships, this chapter will give a brief rundown of the relevant considerations and outline the process itself. The discussion is intentionally limited to the registration of broker-dealers under the federal Securities Exchange Act; but even though no reference will be made to the registration requirements under state blue-sky laws, the reader should not forget that they also apply.

REASONS FOR REGISTERING
AS A BROKER-DEALER

The legal requirements for a planner to register as a securities representative have already been reviewed, but it may be helpful to repeat a few salient points. The term *broker* under the Exchange Act means any person engaged in the business of effecting transactions in securities for the account of others. A *dealer* is any person engaged in the business of buying and selling securities for his own account. As has been pointed out, these distinctions have long since become blurred, and it is now common to utilize the general term *broker-dealer* to refer to legal entities engaged in the securities brokerage business, and to their securities sales personnel as *registered representatives.*

The Exchange Act requires that a broker-dealer, unless his business is exclusively intrastate or his security transactions are executed only on a national securities exchange, must register with the SEC if (1) the broker or dealer is not a natural person, or (2) the broker or dealer is a natural person not associated with a broker or dealer that is not a natural person.

The first clause is simple enough to understand; the second refers to individual brokers who are not subject to the control or supervision of any other broker doing business other than as a natural person (e.g., a corporation). What this means in practical terms is that, if you no longer wish to have your securities activities subject to the supervision and control of a NASD registered broker-dealer, or if you want to buy and sell securities for your own account (i.e., be a "dealer"), you must be registered as a NASD broker-dealer yourself.

There are some obvious advantages of registering as your own broker-dealer, including the following:

1. The opportunity to enjoy an equity participation in your own brokerage business.

2. The opportunity to have a greater voice in the management of your own business and freedom from supervision by your controlling broker-dealer.

3. The opportunity to select and handle a wider range of security products.

4. The opportunity to become a dealer in various securities offerings and a co-general partner in other investment issuances.

5. The opportunity to give better service and thereby attract a wider range of clients.

6. The very important advantage of retaining all commissions earned on securities bought or sold and, thus, of increasing your income.

Notwithstanding these various advantages, owning and managing a broker-dealership is not as simple as it may appear, and it may well create more problems than it is worth. This is especially true for the securities salesperson who is simply looking for a bigger slice of the commission pie. Being one's own boss and retaining all the commissions are undoubtedly attractive reasons for becoming a broker-dealer, but there are a number of negative factors that a would-be broker-dealer must also consider:

1. The burden of filing itself.

2. The attorneys' fees involved, both initially and on a continuing basis.

3. The necessity for preparing and filing annual reports.

4. Meeting the statutory minimum capital and financial requirements.

5. The burden of everyday compliance activities, as well as periodic NASD and SEC audits.

6. The need to hire competent clerical help to handle all the additional paper work.

7. The legal responsibility to closely supervise all representatives and employees.

8. The legal responsibility to perform due diligence activities not only for yourself, but for your registered representatives as well.

9. The vastly increased liability exposure.

Of all of these, three stand out as major drawbacks to forming your own broker-dealership: the frightening amount of compliance paperwork; the enormous responsibility to handle due diligence on new and existing products; and the enormously increased legal liability exposure of a broker-dealer. These are by no means the only factors to consider, and one should not come to any final decision without first seeking the advice of other broker-dealers and planners as well as legal counsel experienced in securities matters.

In view of the time and complexities involved, to say nothing of the financial resources required, it is highly unlikely that the beginning planner with little or no practical experience in the securities industry will choose to register as his own broker-dealer, nor should he want to. On the other hand, the planner with more experience, with growing numbers of clients, and with sufficient financial resources may well want to consider becoming a NASD-registered broker-dealer, or perhaps join with other planners as members of a broker-dealer co-op, a movement that has begun to attract a number of experienced planners recently. The material that follows reviews the procedures involved in becoming a broker-dealer.

THE BROKER-DEALER REGISTRATION PROCESS

The process of registration as a broker-dealer is initiated by the filing of SEC *Form BD* and all accompanying exhibits with the SEC in Washington, D.C. The form is submitted in triplicate, with all three copies being manually signed. There is no filing fee. Beginning in 1984, Form BD has been revised to permit a single form to be used for filing with the state regulatory agencies, the self-regulatory organizations, and the SEC. The revised forms are now compatible with the Central Registration Depository (CRD) System, which is a computer data base maintained by the NASD and used by nearly all the states.

Prior to 1984, a broker-dealer who did not choose to join a registered securities exchange or the NASD was required to register directly with the SEC, thereby placing himself under direct SEC supervision, the SEC-only (SECO) program. In 1983, however, the Exchange Act was amended to eliminate direct regulation by the SEC. Now, all broker-dealers seeking authority to engage in the over-the-counter (OTC) securities business are required to register with the NASD, unless otherwise exempt from registration. Revised Form BD is used for this purpose.

Form BD consists of five pages of basic information and numerous backup schedules. The larger your organization (in terms of overall size and the number of personnel you plan to supervise), the more schedules you are required to file. The basic application requests information on a host of items that relate to your proposed manner of doing business and prior activities in the securities field. If not completed precisely in the manner and detail indicated, it will be deemed unacceptable. The SEC has made it clear that carelessness and negligence in preparing the application may be deemed evidence of willfulness, since it is likely to frustrate the fundamental objective of the statute. Moreover, *intentional misstatements or omissions of fact may be grounds for criminal prosecution.* Obviously, the manner in which you prepare Form BD is not something to be taken lightly.

The most extensive item calls for detailed information concerning the past history and background of the persons who are to be the principals, directors, officers, or controlling shareholders of the applicant. Registration may be denied if the applicant makes any false or misleading statement in the application, has been convicted within the previous ten years of a felony or misdemeanor arising out of a securities violation, or has been involved in any prior activity reflecting negatively on his moral fitness and integrity to engage in the securities business. Incidentally, where the SEC denies the application because of inaccuracies, the applicant is not allowed to withdraw or cancel his application. In other words, once you file Form BD with the SEC, you have agreed to submit yourself to the SEC's jurisdiction and will be legally bound by everything you have said, even if you decide not to proceed further.

Form BD must be accompanied by a statement of financial condition showing the nature and amount of the applicant's assets, liabilities, and net worth. It must also include figures showing all indebtedness and information regarding the capital, financing, and facilities contemplated to run the business. The purpose of this information is to gauge the applicant's financial ability to meet all customers' claims for cash and securities, should the circumstances so require.

The SEC's review process usually takes 45 days, although it is theoretically possible to expedite the process. Upon its receipt, the SEC reviews the application against information in its headquarter files in Washington, D.C., and by memorandum asks for comments from the appropriate regional office concerning any information it may have regarding the applicant's principals. In some cases, corrective amendments may be necessary before an application is deemed acceptable. But, in general, if the record is clean and all accompanying exhibits are in order, the application will be declared effective 45 days after its receipt.

While the registration process is not inordinately difficult, an applicant must complete all forms with painstaking care. If the paper work is not done properly or if the SEC has additional questions they want answered, the process can go on seemingly forever. Some applicants prefer to hire turn-key licensing consultants who, for fees starting at $2,000, will handle the registration process with the SEC, the NASD (discussed next), and all necessary state filings. These consultants will prepare all the required forms, see to it that the papers are sent to the right places, give advice on how to handle the NASD preacceptance interview and how to set up your books, and in general handle all the myriad details for registration on your behalf. Although at first paying for this service may seem an unwarranted expense, all in all it may prove a wise way to proceed when one considers the many headaches avoided, as well as the extra time made available to service existing clients or solicit new ones.

Once registration has become effective, a new registrant is authorized to engage in all activities that require statutory registration. Thus, within the limits of the antifraud provisions of the Exchange Act, he may engage in business as both a broker and a dealer.

The registration of a broker-dealer has no effect on the registration of its sales personnel. As discussed at length in Chapter Two, anyone who intends to buy or sell securities for the account of others under the aegis of a broker-dealer must apply for registration with the NASD as a general securities representative, using Form U-4 for this purpose. The sponsoring broker-dealer handles the actual submission.

THE NASD MEMBERSHIP REQUIREMENT

All registered broker-dealers in the over-the-counter (OTC) market must be members of the NASD. There is no longer any option to stay out of the NASD and choose direct SEC regulation. Since the 1983 amendments to the Exchange Act, all prior SECO broker-dealers have had to apply for NASD registration or else cease operations in the securities business. Thus far, 465 SECO broker-dealers have chosen to come under NASD supervision. Even though a broker-dealer remains subject to the SEC's overall jurisdiction, it is the NASD that will assume primary authority for monitoring the firm's activities. A broker-dealer whose securities business is confined to effecting securities transactions on national exchanges need not register with the SEC or become a member of the NASD.

There are two levels of qualification for NASD membership: one for registered principals (management personnel), and one for registered representatives (sales personnel). The NASD has established six categories for registration as a principal and three categories for registration as a registered representative, with separate examinations for each category.

With the exception of sole proprietorships, all new applicants for NASD membership must have at least two officers or partners who are qualified to become registered as General Securities Principals (the Series 24 examination) and one who is qualified to register as Limited Principal–Financial Operations and Investments (the Series 27 examination). Under recent changes in the rules, any person required to be registered as a principal whose supervisory responsibilities will be limited to securities sales activities and the training of sales personnel may register as a Limited Principal–General Sales Supervisor. This category of registration reduces the burdens on principals of general securities firms who would otherwise have to meet more stringent qualifications.

Finally, under SEC Rule 15c3-1, the Uniform Net Capital Rule, every broker-dealer is required to maintain a minimum ratio of liquid assets to total indebtedness. Unless you intend to do your own securities clearing, more than likely you will begin operations as an *introducing broker,* one who forwards all customer funds and securities to a separate clearing broker who handles the actual trades. The minimum net capital required of an introducing broker is $5,000, although it can go higher. It is in dealing with issues such as deciding the method of securities clearing and the minimum net capital requirements that the financial planner who wishes to become his own broker-dealer would be wise to seek the advice of an experienced securities lawyer.

The application for NASD membership must be accompanied by a fee of $500, plus $40 for each separate examination that is to be taken by principals or associates of the firm. See Chapter Two for details concerning the registration process for registered representatives.

An important part of the application process is the premembership interview at the regional level. This gives the NASD staff an opportunity to elicit information personally from you to determine if you have the necessary knowledge, experience, and ability to run a brokerage firm, as well as the necessary financial resources. At this interview, you will be questioned about your proposed compliance activities and your clearing agreement with the brokerage organization that will actually handle your orders and execute all trades. Incidentally, it will pay to inquire of other recently registered broker-dealers about who they selected as their clearing brokers so you can ascertain who might be willing to accept your business, what they normally charge, and how well they have performed their clearing services in the past.

Once you become registered as a broker-dealer, you will have to join the Securities Investor Protection Corporation (SIPC), the nonprofit federally chartered organization that protects customer accounts at failed brokerage firms. When a SIPC member goes bankrupt, SIPC applies to the courts for a trustee who returns to the customers all fully paid and excess margin securities held by the firm. SIPC also advances any money necessary to reimburse customers up to $500,000 per customer, not more than $100,000 of which can be for a cash claim.

A reminder about state broker-dealer registration. Every state has its own registration requirements, and even though the use of Form BD has made the registration process somewhat easier than in the past, many states impose additional filing requirements, so you must check with the appropriate state licensing authority for all the current requirements. Appendix G lists all the state regulatory agencies, including the names of key personnel and their phone numbers. Incidentally, the NASD has prepared a booklet entitled "How to Become a Member of the NASD," available without charge from NASD headquarters and regional offices, which discusses most of the state requirements, but here, again, many new applicants may find it easier to utilize the services of a turn-key registration consultant. Note also that all your securities representatives must apply for registration with each state in which you plan to operate before they can engage in sales activities on your behalf.

LEGAL OBLIGATIONS ARISING OUT OF REGISTRATION

A broker-dealer is legally responsible for meeting all statutory requirements of the pertinent federal and state laws governing the conduct of his securities business. Many of these laws govern broker-dealer behavior in fairly narrow areas; others, like SEC Rule 10b-5 (discussed later), apply to a broad spectrum of broker-dealer actions designed to prevent fraudulent activities or deceptive practices likely to harm innocent investors. Clearly, a member of the NASD also must agree to abide by all applicable NASD rules and regulations. Generally speaking, there are two types of NASD rules: (1) those that have as their primary purpose the direct protection of the investing public—rules designed to prevent fraudulent conduct and help ensure the integrity of the securities markets, and (2) housekeeping rules designed to regulate the technicalities of the broker's day-to-day business activities, many of which are codified in the NASD's Uniform Practice Code.

Article III, Section 1 of the NASD Rules of Fair Practice, one of the rules in the first category, has served as the basis for a large number of disciplinary actions against recalcitrant broker-dealers, as well as some private legal actions against brokers by dissatisfied customers. It reads:

> **Business Conduct of Members.** A member, in the conduct of his business, shall observe high standards of commercial honor and just and equitable principles of trade.

Another very significant rule governing the conduct of broker-dealers is Article III, Section 2 of the Rules of Fair Practice, the *suitability rule.* It reads:

> **Recommendations to Customers.** In recommending to a customer the purchase, sale or exchange of any security, a member

shall have reasonable grounds for believing that the recommendation is suitable for such customer upon the basis of the facts, if any, disclosed by such customer as to his other security holdings and as to his financial situation and needs.

Many private legal actions against brokers over the years have included allegations that the NASD suitability rule was breached, and there is an abundance of case law on the subject, including some decisions by the Supreme Court itself. The suitability rule and its potential impact on planners are examined in detail in Chapter Six.

Importance of Supervision

Exercising appropriate supervision over employees to assure their compliance with all pertinent securities laws is one of the most difficult and time-consuming tasks of the broker-dealer. Anyone who becomes a registered NASD broker-dealer will soon appreciate the importance of Article III, Section 27 of the NASD Rules of Fair Practice. This is the rule that requires brokers to "establish, maintain, and enforce appropriate supervisory procedures with respect to their personnel." It is derived from Section 15(b)(4)(E) of the Exchange Act, which provides for SEC sanctions if a broker-dealer fails to reasonably supervise against securities violations by employees.

One of the offshoots of this rule provides that a broker-dealer must never permit a person to buy or sell securities as agent for the broker-dealer unless such person is duly licensed as a general securities representative with the NASD. The failure of a broker-dealer to register an employee who should be registered is grounds for swift disciplinary action, since it is considered not only a violation of Article III, Section 27, but "conduct inconsistent with just and equitable principles of trade" under Article III, Section 1 of the Rules of Fair Practice.

A broker-dealer will be held accountable for all violations of the federal securities laws committed by any person employed by the firm in any capacity, including the giving of investment advice by registered investment advisers under its supervision. This form of vicarious or secondary liability, called the *controlling person* liability, has its roots in statutory as well as common law. Section 20(a) of the Exchange Act states:

Every person who, directly or indirectly, controls any person liable under any provision of this title or any rule or regulation thereunder, shall also be liable jointly and severally with and to the same extent as such controlled person to any person to whom such controlled person is liable. . . .

Pursuant to this provision, brokerage firms have been held vicariously liable for a multitude of sins committed by their registered representatives, including downright fraudulent conduct and other direct violations of the securities acts. The common law doctrine of *respondeat superior* is yet another basis of liability. Under that doctrine, an employer is held absolutely liable for the harmful acts of his employees committed within the scope of their employment, without regard to the reasonableness of the broker-dealer's efforts to exercise proper supervision over such employees. There is a vast body of case law surrounding the controlling-persons and *respondeat superior* theories of broker-dealer liability (see Chapter Six).

Private Securities Transactions

The NASD has been particularly concerned about one area of supervision, that relating to *private securities transactions*. These are transactions in which a registered representative or other associated person of a broker-dealer sells securities to private investors without the participation of the broker-dealer (sometimes referred to as *selling away* or engaging in *off-book transactions*). The problem presented in cases of this sort is that the securities are sold without the benefit of any supervision or oversight by the broker-dealer, even though the investor commonly is led to believe otherwise. Often he assumes that the representative's broker-dealer has analyzed the security from a due diligence standpoint and stands behind the product, when in fact this is not the case. He is also likely to assume that the broker-dealer has approved the investment from the suitability standpoint when this, too, is not the case.

But the fact that a broker-dealer has not exercised such supervision or oversight over a private securities transaction in no way diminishes the broker-dealer's derivative liability to an investor who later sues to recover losses suffered because due diligence was not exercised or because the investment was not suitable considering his circumstances. And, in fact, a number of broker-dealers have been held liable for malfeasances committed by their registered representatives in executing private securities transactions even though they were totally unaware of the transactions.

Because this has proved to be one of the most troublesome areas for the NASD and has led to a growing number of disciplinary actions, that self-regulatory body recently amended its Private Securities Transaction

Interpretation under its rules and issued a revised interpretation containing new and stiffer requirements. The earlier interpretation merely required advance written notification by the securities representative to his broker-dealer of his intention to engage in a private securities transaction. The new rule goes much farther and not merely requires written notification, but gives the broker-dealer the option to approve or disapprove of the private securities transaction if any selling compensation is to be received by the representative. If approval is given, the rule now requires (1) that the broker-dealer treat the transaction as a transaction of the firm, (2) that the transaction be recorded on the firm's books, and (3) that the broker-dealer supervise the representative's participation in the transaction to the same extent as if the transaction were executed on behalf of the firm. *If approval is not given, the representative may not participate in the transaction in any manner.*

In the past, the NASD has found that many representatives who have engaged in private securities transactions have acted primarily out of ignorance, believing that they had no need to inform their broker-dealers of their selling-away activities because the issuers or their legal counsel had advised that the products in question were not securities—usually by claiming they were exempt from registration under some specific exemption under the Securities Act. More often than not, such advice has been erroneous (i.e., the product legally was a security); but even exemption from registration of a security does not alter the representative's clear-cut legal obligation now not only to inform his broker-dealer *in writing* before undertaking to handle such transactions, but to obtain the firm's formal approval in writing to do so.

Responsibilities under SEC Rule 10b-5

Section 10(b) of the Exchange Act granted broad regulatory authority to the SEC to govern the actions of broker-dealers, and over the years that section, as codified by the SEC under its Rule 10b-5, has become the most widely litigated provision in the federal securities laws. Under 10b-5, broker-dealers may be held accountable for various acts or omissions that are uniquely applicable to persons acting in a fiduciary capacity. The broker-dealer's liability as a fiduciary was highlighted by the court in *Hughes* v. *S.E.C.,* 174 F.2d 969 (D.C. Cir. 1949), where a broker-dealer who was also the plaintiff's investment adviser had her license revoked by the SEC for not selling securities to her client at the best obtainable price. The court of appeals affirmed the license revocation in an opinion that duly noted the broker-dealer's dual role of investment adviser and broker-dealer, observing:

> petitioner acted simultaneously in the dual capacity of investment adviser and of broker or dealer. In such capacity, conflicting interests must necessarily arise. When they arise, the law has consistently stepped in to provide safeguards in the form of prescribed and stringent standards of conduct on the part of the fiduciary.

Higher standards of conduct are imposed on a broker-dealer simply by virtue of being in business, the so-called "shingle theory" of liability. From the moment he hangs out his shingle to engage in business, a broker-dealer represents that he will deal fairly with the public in accordance with the highest standards of the profession. The shingle theory received judicial approval in *Charles Hughes & Co.* v. *S.E.C.*, 139 F.2d 434 (2d Cir. 1943), in which the court affirmed the SEC's revocation of a broker-dealer's license for selling stock to customers at prices substantially in excess of OTC market quotes and without disclosing the mark-up. The court held that the broker-dealer was under a special duty, in view of its expert knowledge and proffered advice, not to take advantage of its customers' ignorance of market conditions.

The shingle theory implies that the broker-dealer will deal fairly with his clients at all times and will not exploit their trust and ignorance to gain an unwarranted profit. As evolved by the courts, it now encompasses a host of additional obligations and representations. Thus, a broker-dealer is deemed to represent that he has an adequate basis for his recommendation to buy or sell a security, that any recommended security is suitable for the specific investor, and that he has not concealed any material facts in recommending a security. It also holds the broker-dealer legally responsible for manipulating the market, engaging in excessive trades (*churning*), delaying execution of trades, selling or pledging securities without authority, misappropriating clients' funds, and other malfeasances.

A broker-dealer's responsibilities under statutory and common law are rather considerable, to say the least. Most of these issues are touched upon only briefly in this book, since they are less related to the activities of financial planners than they are to the activities of stockbrokers and brokerage firms not expressly involved in financial planning. Those issues that are particularly germane to financial planners are addressed in later chapters.

Miscellaneous Obligations

In addition to those just outlined, the NASD registered broker-dealer must meet a number of miscellaneous statutory and regulatory obligations. You must, of course, register as a broker-dealer with all appropriate state regulatory authorities, and as noted earlier you must join the Securities Investors Protection Corporation (SIPC). You are also subject to rigorous bookkeeping requirements which can prove quite burdensome, including a mandatory annual audit by a public accountant. In addition, you must be prepared to be subjected to frequent and unannounced audits and inspections by the SEC, the NASD, and your own state's securities regulatory commission. You may as well get used to the idea that administrative headaches and constant monitoring of your activities will be a way of life as long as you remain in the securities business.

KEY POINTS TO REMEMBER

1. Becoming your own broker-dealer has both advantages and disadvantages, which the planner should consider carefully before taking this important step.

2. The opportunity to manage your own brokerage business and to substantially increase your income from securities commissions are two principal advantages of becoming your own broker-dealer.

3. The enormous administrative burdens and the additional legal liabilities assumed are two important disadvantages.

4. The registration process calls for the filing of Form BD with the SEC in Washington, D.C. It is a long and complicated form calling for a vast amount of personal, financial, and business information about the applicant.

5. All broker-dealers in the over-the-counter (OTC) market are now required to register with the NASD, unless they are exempt from registration for some statutory reason. The former SECO (SEC-only) direct SEC registration program has been abolished by law.

6. Failure to complete the Form BD carefully will not only delay the registration process, but can have serious legal ramifications, including even possible criminal prosecution.

7. The SEC review process normally takes 45 days, assuming all papers are in order. An application normally is filed with the NASD at the same time, as well as with the appropriate state securities authorities.

8. Some applicants will find it advantageous to utilize the services of registration consultants to handle all the details associated with SEC, NASD, and state filing requirements.

9. The registration of a broker-dealer does not cover the registration of the firm's securities sales personnel. Separate U-4 applications must be filed for each proposed registered representative.

10. The NASD's preacceptance interview is an important part of its review process. It is handled by the NASD regional office having jurisdiction over the proposed broker-dealer-member.

11. The statutory and common law obligations arising out of broker-dealer registration are significant, having been developed specifically to prevent fraudulent conduct in the securities business.

12. The NASD's Rules of Fair Practice mimic the federal securities law prohibitions and go even further in establishing standards of fairness in dealings with investors.

13. The NASD's suitability rule is an important guideline that must be followed if the broker wishes to avoid disciplinary action by the NASD or possible legal action by the aggrieved investor.

14. Being a broker-dealer requires constant supervision of all securities personnel, and the failure to supervise carefully can lead to significant legal liability.

15. Under the so-called "shingle theory," the moment he hangs out his shingle a broker-dealer represents that he will deal fairly with the public and in accordance with high professional standards.

16. SEC Rule 10b-5 is the basis for most private legal actions against registered representatives and their employing broker-dealers. It prohibits all forms of fraudulent conduct and recognizes the broker's fiduciary duty to his clients.

SELECTED REFERENCES

Statutes

Securities Investors Protection Act, 15 U.S.C. §§78aaa et seq.

Registration of broker-dealers, 15 U.S.C. §78o(a)(1).

State registration of broker-dealers, Uniform Securities Act, §§210(b), 204.

Rationale for Becoming a Broker-Dealer

Seglin, J. L., "The Producers' Revolution," *Financial Planning,* vol. 13, no. 10, 135 (October 1984).

Freeman, P., and Hernacki, M., "Breaking Away," *Registered Representative,* vol. 8, no. 6, 42 (June 1984).

Process of Registration

Jaffe, S., *Broker-Dealers and Securities Markets,* Chapter 3 (Shepard's, Inc., Colorado Springs, Colo., 1977).

Weiss, E., *Registration and Regulation of Brokers and Dealers* (Bureau of National Affairs, Washington, D.C., 1965).

Bill, A. H., "Regulation Landmarks," *Financial Planning,* vol. 13, no. 3, 125 (March 1984).

Seglin, J. L., "Prospecting for Planners," *Financial Planning,* vol. 13, no. 11, 135 (November 1984).

Right to Withdraw Broker-Dealer Application

Fontaine and Investors Overseas Services, Inc. v. *S.E.C.,* 259 F.Supp. 880 (D.C.P.R. 1966).

Peoples Securities Co. v. *S.E.C.,* 289 F.2d 268 (5th Cir. 1961).

Broker-Dealer as a Fiduciary

Hughes v. *S.E.C.,* 174 F.2d 969 (C.A. D.C., 1949).

S.E.C. v. *Capital Gains Research Bureau,* 375 U.S. 180 (1963).

Mansbach v. *Prescott, Ball & Turben,* 598 F.2d 1017 (6th Cir. 1979).

Rolf v. *Blyth, Eastman Dillon & Co.,* 424 F.Supp. 1021 (S.D.N.Y. 1977).

Private Securities Transactions

NASD Notice to Members No. 85–21, Proposed Rule on Private Securities Transactions (March 29, 1985).

Shingle Theory of Liability

Charles Hughes & Co. v. *S.E.C.*, 139 F.2d 434 (2d Cir. 1943).

Kahn v. *S.E.C.*, 297 F.2d 115 (2d Cir. 1961).

S.E.C. v. *R. J. Allen & Associates*, 386 F.Supp. 866 (S.D. Fla. 1974).

Broker-Dealer's Responsibilities under Rule 10b-5

Globus v. *Law Research Services, Inc.*, 418 F.2d 1276 (2d Cir. 1969).

Van Gemert v. *Boeing Co.*, 520 F.2d 1373 (2d Cir. 1975).

See generally, Bloomenthal, H. S., *Securities and Federal Corporate Law,* Vol. 3A (Clark Boardman Co., New York, 1972).

Jaffe, S., *Broker-Dealers and Securities Markets,* op. cit., Chapter 7.

See generally, Jacobs, A. S., *Litigation and Practice under Rule 10b-5* (Clark Boardman Co., New York, 2d Ed., 1981).

chapter five

Regulatory Enforcement and Sanctions

Becoming registered and licensed as a securities representative, investment adviser, or broker-dealer is only the first step in the formal legal process that will directly affect the day-to-day conduct of the typical financial planner throughout his or her entire career. It is merely an introduction to the complex regulatory environment of the securities industry, probably the most highly regulated industry in the country. As we have seen in the preceding chapters, the federal and state laws that were passed to protect innocent investors from being defrauded by unscrupulous securities salespeople and investment advisers are exacting in their application to everyone in the securities business. Exceptions, exclusions, and exemptions are few in number and granted only grudgingly.

The courts have been zealous in carrying out the intent of the lawmakers, and at every opportunity they have made it clear that the securities laws are there for good reason and must be interpreted liberally to achieve their stated purposes. Note the sweep of the court's language in the early case of *Archer* v. *S.E.C.*, 133 F.2d 795, 803 (8th Cir. 1943):

> The business of trading in securities is one in which opportunities for dishonesty are of constant recurrence and ever present. It engages acute, active minds, trained to quick apprehension, decision and action. The Congress has seen fit to regulate this business. Though such regulation must be done in strict subordination to constitutional and lawful safeguards of individual rights, it is to be enforced notwith-

standing the frauds to be suppressed may take on more subtle and involved forms than those in which dishonesty manifests itself in cruder and less specialized activities.

In this chapter we take a closer look at the role of the principal governmental and self-regulatory organizations to see how they function and how their enforcement activities can play a critical role in the life of the financial planner. We also look at the manner in which the principal financial planning professional bodies, the International Association for Financial Planning (IAFP) and the Institute of Certified Financial Planners (ICFP), exercise disciplinary authority over members who violate their respective ethical codes.

Perhaps it would help at this point to remind the reader of the two distinctly different types of liability a financial planner can incur: (1) the liability to governmental authorities for failing to comply with all pertinent statutes and regulations, generally resulting in a fine, suspension, or revocation of his securities license, and (2) the liability to his clients for failing to meet his legal responsibilities under statutory or common law, generally resulting in his payment of money damages. Our attention in this chapter will be devoted principally to the first type of liability—that arising out of the planner's obligations to comply with federal and state laws regulating securities transactions or the giving of investment advice. We will also review the procedures for handling violations of the ethical standards of conduct promulgated by the IAFP and ICFP. Chapter Six will deal with the planner's liability to his client for negligent or wrongful professional conduct, also referred to as malpractice.

THE SELF-REGULATORY ORGANIZATIONS

Because of the pervasive role played by self-regulatory organizations (SROs), it is important to understand how they began. Following enactment of the major federal securities laws in the early 1930s, both the Congress and the Executive Branch were dissatisfied with the manner in which the national securities exchanges (the New York Stock Exchange, the New York Curb Exchange, and the Detroit and Chicago stock exchanges) had been dealing with the ethics of their members. Congress had granted special privileges to these organizations and in return imposed important enforcement responsibilities on them. They were given the opportunity to clean up their own houses with a bare minimum of federal intervention, all within the framework of the federal securities laws.

Just when the exchanges were exhorting the government to give them more freedom in these matters, an incredible incident came to light. The brokerage firm of Richard Whitney, a former president of the New York Stock Exchange, was suspended by the Exchange after it was discovered (quite by chance) that his firm had been insolvent for over three years as a result of his personal speculations in ventures he financed by embezzling funds from clients' accounts. To make matters worse, it appears that the Exchange's leaders knew what was going on all the time, but did nothing about it. They chose to observe the unwritten "code of silence" aimed at protecting the reputation of a member from adverse publicity rather than concern themselves with the rights of defrauded investors.

The ensuing investigation and public hearings mobilized action on the part of the Exchange as no government edict could have accomplished. Before long, a new constitution was adopted by the New York Stock Exchange and an entirely new administrative mechanism was set in place, designed to put teeth into the Exchange's determination to regulate its membership far more closely and to encourage ethical practices. The other major exchanges instituted similar reforms during the same period.

Self-regulation by the Exchanges

The Exchange Act provides that no registration as a national securities exchange shall be granted or allowed to remain in force unless the rules of the exchange include provisions for expelling, suspending, or disciplining a member for conduct inconsistent with just and equitable principles of trade. The SEC is given specific authority to apply sanctions to an exchange for its failure to enforce compliance by a member with the Exchange Act.

All the major stock exchanges have registered under the Exchange Act and all now require their members to adhere to strict codes of ethics and fair dealing with clients. If a stock exchange fails to enforce its rules in this respect, it not only may suffer SEC sanctions, but may be sued for damages by a person who has been harmed financially as a result of such lack of enforcement.

There are a multitude of rules and regulations applicable to the conduct of the national securities exchanges and their members, but since they affect persons who are primarily engaged in the day-to-day handling of securities transactions as stockbrokers rather than financial planners, no further attention will be directed to the self-regulatory responsibilities of the stock exchanges.

Self-regulation by the Over-the-Counter Market

Throughout the period of the 1930s, the over-the-counter (OTC) market for securities not listed or traded on one of the exchanges had no administrative structure comparable to that of the major exchanges, thus making self-regulation impossible for OTC broker-dealers. It was this deficit that prompted the Congress to enact the Maloney Act in 1938. This important amendment to the Exchange Act provided for the registration of "national securities associations," which would perform the same self-regulatory functions for the OTC market as the stock exchanges did for their markets.

The Maloney Act granted special privileges to qualifying national securities associations, including extensive disciplinary powers, with the SEC remaining in the background but given the authority to oversee matters of discipline and to act as an appellate authority should the circumstances so require. The act provides that the rules of such national associations must be designed to prevent fraudulent and manipulative acts and practices, must provide safeguards against unreasonable profits or unreasonable fees or commissions, and in general must look to the protection of investors and the interests of the general public.

The NASD is the only national securities association ever to apply for registration under the Maloney Act, and today the organization is comprised of some 2,800 member firms. In general, the NASD has received great praise for the manner in which it has carried out its authority, even by some who originally doubted that this type of industry self-regulation could ever succeed.

Direct Regulation by the SEC

Over the years, the vast majority of broker-dealers in the OTC market chose to become members of the NASD and submit to its scheme of self-regulation. But a significant minority of firms that were actively engaged in the securities business chose not to join either the NASD or one of the major exchanges, and this lack of control over the ethics and business practices of these broker-dealers disturbed the SEC. The net result was an amendment to the Exchange Act in 1975, which made these broker-dealers subject to direct SEC control.

Until the act was amended again in 1983, SECO (meaning SEC-only) broker-dealers were required to register with the SEC and were subject to the SEC's direct control as regards qualifications for engaging in the securities business. The SEC was given authority (under the earlier law) to adopt rules designed to promote ''just and equitable principles of trade'' and to enforce compliance with its standards of training, experience, and competence and all other qualifications it deemed necessary in the public interest and to protect investors. SECO broker-dealers and their associated persons were required to take and pass qualifying examinations, generally the same examinations administered by the NASD to its prospective members and their registered representatives.

By 1983, only 12% of the active OTC broker-dealers had chosen the SECO alternative, but even this small number created administrative burdens for the SEC, which was having difficulty enforcing the many technical SECO rules because of its limited sanction authority. By comparison, the NASD has long had the power, through disciplinary proceedings, to levy fines on its members for rules violations. Accordingly, Congress chose to relieve the SEC of the burden of direct supervision called for by the 1975 amendments. P.L. 98-38, enacted in 1983, made it obligatory for all new broker-dealer applicants to apply for registration with the NASD, and further required all existing SECO broker-dealers to become NASD members as well. Thus, the SECO program is no longer in existence.

Self-regulation by Investment Advisers

As far back as 1963, the SEC had recommended that investment advisers take steps to develop some form of self-regulatory organization (SRO) that could adopt substantive rules for more effectively governing the conduct of members of that profession. Then, as now, the SEC was experiencing great difficulty in enforcing the law in this rapidly developing area of the securities industry and was hoping that investment advisers would help share that burden.

Thus far, however, investment advisers as a class have not created such a self-regulatory body with authority comparable to that of the NASD. This may be due in part to the fact that investment advisers do not comprise a homogeneous class of persons, with their interests varying widely depending upon the services they provide and the clientele they cater to. Some, such as financial planners, provide personal services to individual clients, while others provide impersonal advice through newsletters and other publications. Some are money managers with discretionary control over clients' assets, while others exercise no such control. Some consider themselves true financial professionals whose main occupation is giving investment advice, while others consider themselves primarily sales personnel who mix occasional investment advice with sales talk.

With the exceptional growth of the financial services industry in recent years, it does not seem likely that investment advisers as a class will be able to avoid some form of regulation indefinitely, and self-regulation may be the preferred choice, if only to ward off the threat of more direct governmental regulation. Legislators in a number of states have become quite serious about regulating financial planners, investment advisers of all kinds, and the entire financial planning industry. Various recommendations have surfaced, including the establishment of a self-regulatory organization (SRO) for financial planners and investment advisers under the general jurisdiction of the SEC as one mode of dealing with the issue. At the moment, however, only the SEC, the stock exchanges, and the NASD have direct authority over the actions of planners insofar as securities transactions and investment advice are concerned, along with the respective state regulatory authorities, of course.

HOW THE NASD REGULATES

Organization

Although the overall management of the NASD is in the hands of a Board of Governors that sets policy nationally, the day-to-day implementation of such policy is left to each of the 13 geographical districts, which are managed by District Committees of not more than 12 members who are elected to serve staggered three-year terms by vote of the district membership. (Appendix C lists the states included in each NASD district.) The District Committees, in turn, each appoint District Business Conduct Committees, which have the basic authority to hear complaints, exercise discipline, and in general to enforce the NASD Rules of Fair Practice. All the persons elected to be governors or committee members serve without compensation.

Rules and Practices

Becoming a member of the NASD brings with it privileges as well as obligations. Clearly, one of the major privileges is the opportunity given NASD member firms to participate in the investment banking and OTC securities business on a preferential basis, since a cardinal rule of the NASD is that no member may deal with a nonmember except on the same terms as the member would accord the general public. Another NASD rule requires that no member may permit any other person to manage, supervise, solicit, or handle any securities business on behalf of the member unless such person first registers as a registered representative with the NASD. And when an individual becomes a registered representative, he is bound by the NASD's rules and is subject to the same grounds of disqualification as a member. He also has the same rights as a member on matters of discipline, meaning the right to a hearing and the right to appeal an adverse decision to the SEC.

As was pointed out in Chapter Two, an applicant for registration as a securities representative also must pass a qualifying examination (the Series 7 exam).

Of all the NASD rules, Article III, Section 1 of the Rules of Fair Practice is the one that most directly affects the financial planner who is a registered securities representative or a registered principal. You will recall it reads as follows: "A member, in the conduct of his business, shall observe high standards of commercial honor and just and equitable principles of trade." Just about every practice prohibited under the federal securities acts would also constitute a violation of the NASD's Rules of Fair Practice, and Article III, Section 1 is the principal rule that lays down the applicable ethical standard. This general rule is buttressed by a number of specific rules, relating to such matters as the following:

1. Business conduct of members

2. Recommendations to customers

3. Charges for services performed

4. Fair prices and commissions

5. Use of information obtained in a fiduciary capacity

6. Use of fraudulent practices or devices

7. Manner of supervision of employees and agents

Under its operating rules, the NASD has established a Code of Procedure for Handling Trade Practice Complaints arising out of any alleged violations of the Rules of Fair Practice. It has also established a Uniform Practice Code applicable to all securities transactions between members, dealing with such matters as confirmations, delivery of securities, handling of funds, and other securities transactions.

Handling of Disciplinary Matters

If you are a registered securities representative or a registered securities principal, it is essential that you understand the NASD's rules and regulations regarding disciplinary matters and procedures. Under the NASD rules, any person may file a complaint against a member (or an "associated person") with the District Business Conduct Committee. The complaining party may be a member of the general public (e.g., a client), a fellow member of the NASD, or an associated person. In addition, the District Business Conduct Committee can initiate proceedings on its own after conducting an investigation into an alleged unethical practice or other violation of the Rules of Fair Practice.

The complaint must be in writing and must specify in reasonable detail the nature of the charges and the NASD rule or rules allegedly violated. The person complained of (called the *respondent*) is given ten business days within which to answer the complaint in writing and to request a hearing, if he so desires. If the respondent does not answer the complaint, the allegations of the complaint are deemed admitted.

Hearings ordinarily are held at the office of the District Committee entitled to hear the complaint, generally the committee whose jurisdiction encompasses the geographical area closest to the respondent's principal place of business. At the hearing, the respective parties are entitled to be represented by legal counsel; and even though a record of the proceedings is kept, the emphasis is more on the substance of the complaint rather than on procedural form. The committee is not bound by the formal rules of evidence in court cases and may even receive and consider hearsay evidence.

Generally, the respondent and other witnesses are interrogated by the committee or its counsel, and then the respondent is allowed to cross-examine the witnesses and present rebuttal evidence. Often, the respondent chooses simply to explain in narrative fashion the reason or reasons for his conduct.

Under NASD rules, the committee is not required to find that the violation in question was willful or even unlawful. All that is required is a finding that the respondent violated a specific NASD rule and that the acts or omissions complained of represent "conduct inconsistent with just and equitable principles of trade." Since in many disciplinary cases there is no dispute as to the fact a violation has occurred, the committee often directs most of its attention to ascertaining the reasons for the respondent's actions to see if there were any mitigating circumstances. Thus, the respondent's prior conduct as a securities representative is very important to the committee in deciding the type and severity of any sanctions to be imposed.

The penalty assessed may consist of censure, a fine of not more than $1,000 for each violation, suspension, or expulsion from the NASD. Costs may also be assessed.

It should be noted that NASD officials exercising disciplinary authority under NASD rules are absolutely immune from prosecution for personal liability for acts within the scope of their official duties, an issue that was recently reaffirmed by the 5th Circuit Court of Appeals. [*Austin Municipal Securities, Inc.* v. *National Association of Securities Dealers* (decided April 15, 1985).]

If the committee finds that no violation has occurred, it will dismiss the complaint and notify the parties of its decision in writing.

If a respondent wishes to cut short the proceedings, he may at any time submit a formal offer of settlement in writing to the District Committee in which he must set forth proposed findings of fact and a proposed penalty, while agreeing to waive all rights of appeal either to the SEC or the courts. Occasionally, a District Business Conduct Committee will file a summary complaint against an individual where it appears the facts are not in dispute and the committee believes that following the regular complaint procedure is not warranted. In a case of this type, the committee may offer the respondent an opportunity to waive a hearing and accept a summary complaint procedure. Under the summary complaint procedure the respondent admits the violation, agrees to accept the penalty imposed, and waives all appeal rights to the Board of Governors. The maximum penalty in a summary complaint procedure cannot exceed censure and/or a fine of $1,000.

Review and Appeals Procedures

There are several levels of review and appeal in a disciplinary action brought against an NASD member. These are required both by federal law (the Exchange Act) as well as the rules of the NASD.

The final action of the District Business Conduct Committee, whether for or against the respondent, is subject to review by the Board of Governors of the NASD on its own motion within 45 days or upon application filed by the respondent (or any party aggrieved by the decision) within 15 days. The Board of Governors, on the basis of the record before the District Committee and any other evidence it deems relevant, has the complete power to affirm, modify, or reverse the decision by the District Committee, including the power to increase, reduce, or cancel the penalty or to remand the case to the District Business Conduct Committee for further proceedings.

SEC review. The Exchange Act provides that any final decision of the NASD is reviewable by the SEC either on its own motion or on application filed by any aggrieved party (generally the respondent) within 30 days. Before the 1975 amendments to the Exchange Act, the filing of an application for SEC review of an NASD decision acted as an automatic stay of any sanctions imposed. The automatic stay was eliminated by the 1975 amendments; thus, any penalties imposed may be effective immediately, although the SEC does have the authority to grant a stay in appropriate cases.

The SEC's authority to review a decision of the NASD is limited to two matters: (1) determining if the record of the NASD hearing supports its findings of the violations alleged, and (2) determining if the sanction imposed is excessive, oppressive, imposes an unnecessary or inappropriate burden on competition, is inconsistent with the public interest, or represents an unjust application of NASD rules.

In the first instance, the SEC is limited to setting aside the decision if it finds that the evidence does not warrant the NASD's finding of violation of its rules. In the second instance, the SEC may reduce, modify, or cancel the sanction imposed. It may not find a violation where the District Committee has not found one, nor may it increase any penalty imposed. If the SEC agrees with the findings of the NASD, the proceedings are dismissed, and the respondent can then appeal to the courts for review within 60 days of the date of entry of the SEC's order. The SEC's separate investigative and hearing authority is discussed later.

Court review. A person aggrieved by an order of the SEC may obtain a review of such order by filing an appeal within 60 days after the entry of such order in the United States Court of Appeals having jurisdiction of the circuit within which such person resides. No such appeal will be considered unless the appealing party previously objected to the SEC's order when it was first entered.

In reviewing a decision of the SEC in a disciplinary matter, the only question before the Court of Appeals is whether the SEC's findings in the case are supported by substantial evidence; if so, such findings are conclusive. The appeals court has no authority to hear the case *de novo*. In limited instances, additional evidence may be presented to the Court of Appeals if either party applies to the court for permission to adduce such additional evidence, can show that such evidence is material, and can show that there were reasonable grounds for failing to obtain such evidence in the SEC hearing.

The judgment or decree of the Court of Appeals affirming, modifying, or setting aside the order of the SEC is final and appealable only to the United States Supreme Court, upon proper certification thereto. The Court of Appeals may also issue an injunction or restraining order to prevent further violations of the securities laws, in addition to issuing a writ of mandamus to enforce compliance with specific provisions of the securities acts or any SEC order issued pursuant thereto.

SEC ENFORCEMENT AUTHORITY

Apart from its statutory authority to review NASD disciplinary cases, the SEC has independent legal authority to conduct investigations and to hold hearings to determine whether a person has violated or is about to violate some provision of the federal securities acts. The Commission's authority is broad and powerful and consists of three elements. First, it is empowered to conduct investigations of past, present, or impending violations. Second, it may make application to a federal district court for a temporary or permanent injunction whenever it appears to the Commission that a person is engaged or about to engage in harmful practices prohibited by the securities acts or the antifraud rules of one of the self-regulatory organizations. And, finally, it can authorize direct criminal prosecution by the Department of Justice for willful violations of the federal securities acts. By and large, the courts have been more than cooperative with the SEC and responsive to their insistence that meaningful sanctions be imposed on violators.

In carrying out its investigative activities, the Commission or officers designated by the Commission may administer oaths, subpoena witnesses and documents, take evidence, and inquire into all matters deemed relevant to such investigations. Even if the SEC is motivated by nothing more than official curiosity in conducting an investigation, its issuance of a subpoena is legally enforceable as long as it can demonstrate that (1) its investigation is relevant to a legitimate statutory purpose, (2) it does not already possess the information it seeks, and (3) it has followed all required administrative steps.

If an investigation uncovers violations by a broker-dealer or investment adviser, the SEC may, of course, institute disciplinary proceedings. The vast majority of disciplinary cases are disposed of by settlement, pursuant to SEC Rule of Practice 8(a). Those that are contested result in hearings, which typically are heard and first decided by a hearing officer, usually an Administrative Law Judge, in accordance with SEC rules of practice and the Administrative Procedure Act. SEC hearings are similar to those held before other government agencies and, in general, follow the format of a trial, with the parties being represented by legal counsel and entitled to subpoena witnesses, present formal arguments, file briefs, and so forth.

Although depositions and interrogatories are permitted, the rules do not permit formal discovery. Under the rules, official records must be kept of the proceedings, at the conclusion of which the hearing examiner must render an Initial Decision containing findings of fact, conclusions of law, and appropriate sanctions to be imposed against the respondent.

In general, the legal standards applied by the SEC in an administrative hearing are those imposed either by statute or derived from common law principles. Where alleged statutory violations are involved (e.g., violation of the antifraud provisions of the law), the SEC must show that the respondent acted "willfully" or that he "willfully" aided and abetted the violation of another. The Supreme Court has held that the standard of proof required of the SEC to sustain a finding of a statutory violation is the "preponderance of the evidence" standard—a burden of proof far less demanding than the "clear and convincing evidence" standard urged by many respondents and applied by the courts in some of the earlier cases.

Based on the outcome of a hearing, the SEC may impose appropriate sanctions. Under the pertinent statutes, the SEC's sanctions may include censure, limitations on the violator's activities, suspension of the violator's SEC registration for up to a year, or total revocation of the violator's SEC registration. In all cases the sanctions imposed by the SEC must be appropriate to the circumstances and "in the public interest." The courts have held that the public interest is served whenever the sanction furthers the fundamental purpose of the securities laws, meaning it will tend to ensure the maintenance of fair and honest securities markets. Usually, the SEC takes into consideration the nature of the violation, the respondent's prior record and reputation, the amount of money and number of investors involved, and the respondent's attitude toward the offense and willingness to reform.

A fairly recent SEC disciplinary action illustrates the SEC's philosophy in applying sanctions. It barred a broker-dealer's registered representative from further association with any broker or dealer based on his conviction for federal income tax evasion. He had pleaded guilty to the taking of a false oath, the making of a false report, and perjury. At the disciplinary hearing before the SEC Administrative Law Judge, the registered representative argued that, since his conviction for income tax evasion did not involve any securities violations, his expulsion from the securities industry would be too severe a penalty.

The judge's Initial Decision noted that the 1975 amendments to the Exchange Act expanded the scope of Section 15(b)(4)(B) by adding, as grounds for expulsion, conviction for a felony or misdemeanor involving the taking of a false oath, the making of a false report, bribery, perjury, and other similar offenses. He then commented: "There is no doubt that respondent's plea of guilty to the two counts of tax evasion bring him within the perjury provision of Section 15(b)(4)(B) of the Exchange Act and thus make him subject to sanction by the Commission." Citing *United States v. Levy*, 533 F.2d 973 (5th Cir. 1976), the judge observed that "perjury is one of the most serious offenses known to the law," and cited as precedent for the broker's expulsion the reasoning in an earlier SEC case where the parties involved were barred from the securities industry:

> Irreparable injury to the petitioners (brokers) is urged on the ground that they are excluded from the securities business and thus from earning their livelihoods in their chosen vocation. Serious as this personal injury may be, it is not of controlling importance as primary consideration must be given to the statutory intent to protect investors. Exclusion from the securities business is a remedial device for the protection of the public. [*Associated Securities Corp. v. S.E.C.*, 283 F.2d 773 (10th Cir. 1960).]

Determining the sanction to be appropriate under the circumstances, the judge remarked, "The purpose of such severe sanctions must be to demonstrate not only to petitioner but to others that the Commission will deal harshly with egregious cases." [*In the Matter of Bruce Paul*, Administrative Proceeding File No. 3-6271 (Feb. 1, 1984).]

Procedurally, the Initial Decision of an Administrative Law Judge becomes the final decision of the SEC unless the SEC chooses to review the decision on its own or any party thereto files a petition for review within 15 days. The SEC is authorized to impose greater sanctions than those ordered by the hearing examiner, but this is not a common occurrence. As in all SEC final decisions, any person aggrieved by such decision may obtain a review thereof by appealing to the United States Court of Appeals within 60 days after the entry of the SEC's order. Unless the appellant raised a specific issue before the SEC itself, the Court of Appeals will not consider it. As mentioned previously, the judgment of the Court of Appeals affirming, modifying, or setting aside the SEC's order is final and subject to review only by the Supreme Court.

In actual practice, very few proceedings are initiated by the SEC under its statutory disciplinary authority. Its normal practice is to refer directly to the NASD for appropriate disciplinary action any facts it may have acquired about a member's possible violation of law or the NASD's

Rules of Fair Practice and allow the matter to proceed as an NASD disciplinary action.

STATE ENFORCEMENT PROCEEDINGS

The financial planner who is licensed as a securities representative and/or investment adviser under state law will find that an entirely separate regulatory agency is now looking over his shoulder, one that in recent years has become much more aggressive in its enforcement activities.

State securities law administrators (or persons with comparable titles and authority) have broad powers to make public or private investigations to determine whether any person has violated or is about to violate any provision of the state's blue-sky law. And, just as in the case of the federal securities laws, for purposes of such investigation the administrator is authorized to administer oaths, to subpoena witnesses, and to compel the production of any documents, records, and papers deemed relevant to the inquiry at hand.

Like its federal counterpart, the state securities commission is empowered to enjoin and restrain any act or practice and to enforce compliance with the state's blue-sky law or any rule or regulation issued thereunder. This is particularly useful where the respondent has engaged in a pattern of fraudulent practices in the sale of securities. In addition to injunctive relief, the state administrator may refer such evidence as is available concerning violations of the act to the state attorney general for appropriate criminal proceedings. In all important respects, state courts follow federal legal authorities on matters of securities law, including definitions of securities, what constitutes fraud, and the like.

Hearings before state securities authorities are conducted in much the same manner as hearings before the SEC, with the parties being permitted to be heard in person and through legal counsel, and with the final decision and any penalties assessed required to be in writing.

States that follow the language of the Uniform Securities Act permit review of the final order of the state securities administrator in a specified state court within 60 days after entry of the order. The court in question has exclusive jurisdiction to affirm, modify, enforce, or set aside the order. And here, again, the findings of the state administrator with respect to facts, if supported by substantial evidence, are deemed conclusive and not subject to review *de novo* by the appeals court. Appeal to the next higher stage of appellate review in the state is generally allowed, but this does not normally operate to stay the order being appealed. At this level of appeal, a court will set aside the administrator's holding only where it finds his action to have been arbitrary, oppressive, or unreasonable.

PROFESSIONAL ORGANIZATION REGULATION

Various professional organizations currently sponsor advanced educational programs designed to upgrade the skills of men and women seeking to become more intimately involved in the financial planning process. The most notable of these are the College for Financial Planning, which issues its Certified Financial Planner designation, and the American College at Bryn Mawr, which issues the Chartered Life Underwriter (CLU) certificate and the Chartered Financial Consultant (ChFC) certificate. Both organizations are dedicated to inculcating the highest degree of professionalism in their graduates, and candidates for degrees must meet and pledge to adhere to strict ethical requirements throughout their professional careers.

On the professional organization front, there is little doubt that the most aggressive leadership in advocating effective self-regulation of the financial planning industry has come from the International Association for Financial Planning (IAFP) and the Institute of Certified Financial Planners (ICFP). Leaders of both organizations are acutely aware that the future success of the financial planning industry will be in large part dependent on the public's perception of financial planners as truly qualified individuals with experience, education, and a commitment to ethical conduct and professionalism. Such perception can easily be tarnished by the conduct of those individuals who are attracted to the field primarily for the financial rewards they hope to achieve and have little concern for ethical issues.

One approach to greater professionalism, that adopted by the IAFP, led to the establishment of the IAFP's Registry of Financial Planning Practitioners in 1983. Since that time, several hundred financial planners have qualified for the program, which sets minimum standards and qualifications for persons desiring to provide top-quality financial planning services.

Recognizing the inherent dangers associated with phenomenal growth in any profession, both the IAFP and ICFP have made an all-out commitment to ethical conduct and have gone to great pains to instill in their respective members the importance of ethical practices in all their dealings with clients. Both organizations have promulgated codes of ethics and have established disciplinary procedures for hearing and resolving complaints against members, which are described briefly next.

IAFP Regulation of Ethical Conduct

The Code of Professional Ethics first created by the IAFP in 1969, and subsequently revised in 1982, was designed to establish and enforce the minimum ethical conduct expected of its members as financial planning professionals. The Code of Professional Ethics is in three sections: Canons, Rules, and Guidelines. The Canons are general statements of ethical goals, the Rules are more specific standards of a mandatory and enforceable nature derived therefrom, and the Guidelines are intended to assist in interpreting the Canons and Rules when a planner is faced with a practical ethical problem.

Matters pertaining to ethical conduct are brought to the attention of IAFP members in a variety of ways, including publication of recent Ethics Committee decisions in the organization's newsletter, special panels on ethics at IAFP annual and mid-year conventions, and so forth. Local IAFP chapters are encouraged to disseminate headquarters opinions on ethical matters (especially those prepared by the general counsel for the organization) in their respective chapter newsletters, as well as in regional seminars.

Financial planners who are members of the IAFP are expected to practice in accordance with the Code of Professional Ethics or face disciplinary action by the organization. The handling of disciplinary matters is a relatively straightforward process. Complaints against IAFP members may be made by other members or their clients, by the general public, or by official agencies. All complaints must be in writing and must be forwarded to the organization's headquarters for resolution by the National Ethics Committee. The Ethics Committee, which may initiate a complaint on its own, meets quarterly to review all pending cases, after having given each person charged with conduct alleged to be in violation of the code 30 days within which to respond thereto in writing. The member-respondent does not appear personally.

The range of sanctions applicable to an individual found in violation of the IAFP Code includes (1) a written reprimand, with specific recommendations with respect to correcting the violation found, (2) suspension from all IAFP activities and receipt of mailings for a given period, or (3) removal from IAFP membership. The IAFP does not apply fines or have the legal authority to restrict an individual's right to practice financial planning.

ICFP Regulation of Ethical Conduct

In November 1984, the ICFP's Ethics Committee proposed a new Code of Ethics for Certified Financial Planners designed to upgrade the existing code and put teeth into the entire disciplinary review procedure. The new code subsequently was approved by the ICFP's Board of Directors and by the Board of Regents of the College for Financial Planning.

The new ICFP Code contains six primary articles dealing with the following issues: (1) parameters, a general set of principles, (2) client relationship, the acceptance of clients, (3) responsibilities to clients, (4) responsibilities to employers, (5) responsibilities to partners, and (6) responsibilities to subordinates, competitors, and the like. A series of practical interpretations as to what these code provisions mean and how they will be applied will be developed by the Ethics Committee and disseminated to ICFP members periodically.

Complaints brought under the Ethics Code are handled in a manner similar to the process set up by the IAFP. The complainant must submit the complaint in writing to the Ethics Committee at the organization's Denver headquarters, including therewith all relevant letters, contracts, and other documents. If the committee believes additional information is necessary, it may request the complainant or respondent to provide such information in a personal interview.

The new code calls for one of three sanctions to be levied against an offending member: (1) private censure or admonishment, (2) public censure or admonishment, and (3) removal of the Certified Financial Planner (CFP) designation. Private censure consists of a letter sent to the offending member describing the conduct found to be in violation of the code and warning that any further unethical conduct may lead to more severe sanctions. Public censure consists of publishing in the organization's official *Digest* a statement naming the offending member and describing the unethical conduct in question. Finally, the names of all members who have been removed from CFP status also will be published in the *Digest*.

The texts of the ethics codes promulgated by the IAFP and ICFP are set forth in Appendixes D and E, respectively.

KEY POINTS TO REMEMBER

1. A financial planner can incur liability to governmental authorities for failure to comply with all pertinent laws and regulations relating to selling securities or giving investment advice.

2.   The self-regulatory organizations (SROs) play an important role in governing the conduct of their members and aid the SEC in carrying out its basic statutory responsibilities.

3.   All the major stock exchanges have established strict rules and regulations to assure that their members deal fairly with clients.

4.   The NASD is the SRO set up to regulate and monitor the activities of brokers in the OTC market. It is the only national securities association ever to register under the Exchange Act.

5.   Broker-dealers who formerly elected to come under direct SEC regulation (the SECO program) now must join the NASD or one of the major exchanges. The SECO program was terminated by P.L. 98–38.

6.   Thus far, investment advisers as a class have not set up any SRO, although efforts to impose greater regulation on investment advisers may well stimulate movement in that direction.

7.   The NASD is under the overall direction of a 12-member Board of Governors, which sets policy nationally. It is governed at the local level by District Committees, each of which has a set geographical jurisdiction.

8.   NASD members are not allowed to deal with nonmembers, nor may anyone handle business on behalf of a member unless officially registered with the NASD as a registered representative.

9.   Article III, Section 1 of the NASD Rules of Fair Practice is the basic rule governing all members. It requires that they observe high standards of commercial honor and just and equitable principles of trade.

10.   Disciplinary matters under NASD rules are handled by District Business Conduct Committees, which have the authority to investigate and discipline members for alleged violations of NASD rules. In so doing, they are immune from personal liability in retaliatory suits brought by disciplined members.

11.   Sanctions for members found guilty in disciplinary cases may include censure, fines of not more than $1,000 per violation, suspension, or expulsion from the NASD.

12.   Both the SEC and the courts can hear appeals of final NASD decisions, but SEC administrative review must come first.

13.   The SEC can initiate investigations on its own and has broad statutory authority for this purpose. It may apply for a temporary injunction against an alleged violator, and it can authorize criminal prosecution by the Department of Justice for willful violations of the securities acts.

14.   If deemed advisable, the SEC can initiate its own disciplinary hearings, the final decisions of which are appealable to the various U.S. Courts of Appeals.

15. The two financial planning professional organizations that have taken the lead in establishing educational and ethical standards for financial planners are the IAFP and the ICFP. Both have promulgated strict ethical codes governing their members. The College for Financial Planning and the American College at Bryn Mawr also require their graduates to adhere to strict ethical standards.

SELECTED REFERENCES

Statutes

Maloney Act [Sec. 15A(a), Securities Exchange Act], 15 U.S.C. § 78o-3.

Concept of Self-Regulation

Sen. Rept. No. 1455, 75th Cong., 3rd Sess. (1938).

Remarks of William O. Douglas, Chairman of S.E.C., published in 83 Cong. Record (75th Cong., 3rd Sess., at Appendix p. 68 (1938).

Loss, L., *Securities Regulation,* Vol. II, Ch. 8, 2d ed. (Little, Brown and Company, Boston, 1961).

Self-Regulation by the Stock Exchanges

Silver v. *New York Stock Exchange,* 373 U.S. 341 (1963).

See generally, Weiss, E., *Registration and Regulation of Brokers and Dealers,* Chapter 23 (Bureau of National Affairs, Washington, D.C., 1965).

Termination of SECO Program

P.L. 98-38, 15 U.S.C. § 78o(b)(7).

Exchange Act Release No. 20409 (Nov. 1983).

NASD Rules, Practices, and Procedures

NASD Manual (NASD, Washington, D.C., 1984).

See generally, Jaffe, S., *Broker-Dealers and Securities Markets,* Chapter 11 (Shepard's, Inc., Colorado Springs, Colo., 1977).

NASD Disciplinary Proceedings

S.E.C. v. *Waco Financial, Inc.,* 752 F.2d 831 (6th Cir. 1985).

Merrill Lynch, Pierce, Fenner & Smith, Inc. v. *NASD,* 616 F.2d 1363 (5th Cir. 1980).

SEC Review of NASD Disciplinary Actions

69 AMJUR 2d, Securities Regulation—Federal, Section 413.

General Securities Corp. v. *S.E.C.,* 583 F.2d 1108 (9th Cir. 1978).

SEC Investigative Authority

Sections 19(b) and 20(a), Securities Exchange Act, 15 U.S.C.77s(b), 15 U.S.C. § 77t(a).

See generally, Bloomenthal, H., *1983 Securities Law Handbook,* Chap. 24 (Clark Boardman Co., New York, 1983).

Scope of SEC Subpoena Power

S.E.C. v. *Kaplan,* 397 F.Supp. 564 (E.D.N.Y. 1975).

S.E.C. v. *Brigadoon Scotch Distributing Co.,* 480 F.2d 1047 (2d Cir. 1973).

Standard of Proof Required to Convict Broker-Dealer

Herman & Maclean v. *Huddleston,* 103 S.Ct. 683 (1983).

Seaton v. *S.E.C.,* 670 F.2d 309 (D.C. Cir. 1982).

Charles Steadman v. *S.E.C.,* 450 U.S. 91 (1981).

Applicability of Federal Law to State Law Violations

United States v. *Namer,* 680 F.2d 1088 (5th Cir. 1982).

Ethical Standards Applicable to Financial Planners

Hanly v. *S.E.C.,* 415 F.2d 589 (2d. Cir. 1969).

IAFP Code of Professional Ethics [see Appendix D].

ICFP Code of Ethics for Certified Financial Planners [see Appendix E].

chapter six

Professional Liability
of the Financial Planner

When a financial planner violates federal or state securities laws, he incurs liabilities to the respective state and federal regulatory authorities for which he can be fined, have his registration suspended or revoked, and in some instances even be subjected to criminal prosecution. Unquestionably, these are serious consequences and should not be taken lightly. But there is another form of liability that can have equally serious and possibly even greater consequences, the planner's liability to his client in a civil suit for damages.

The legal liability of the financial planner to his client is a subject that relatively little has been written about. Undoubtedly, this is because financial planners are only slowly being perceived by the public as a distinct category of professionals who can be sued for acts amounting to professional negligence, or malpractice. Thus far, nearly all suits against financial planners have been based on violations of the securities acts, the types of claims that investors have been asserting against negligent or fraudulent stockbrokers for years.

Case law governing the liabilities of financial planners is virtually nonexistent. The profession is simply too new to have generated a body of appellate decisions, although this is likely to be only a temporary phenomenon. With the growing sophistication of the investing public and with the financial planning profession as a whole striving for, and gradually achieving, greater respect as providers of specialized professional services, it is only reasonable to assume that the number of lawsuits by clients against planners based on common law negligence doctrines will steadily increase.

Financial planners can find themselves the targets of professional liability (or malpractice) litigation in dozens of ways that go beyond the liabilities of a typical stockbroker. This is because of the nature of the financial planning process itself. The prototype financial planner, as you will recall, routinely will perform a number of functions as a part of the financial planning process. As set forth in the standards established by the IAFP Registry of Financial Planning Practitioners, he will (1) collect and assess all relevant data, (2) identify financial goals and objectives, (3) identify financial problems, (4) provide written recommendations and alternative solutions to the identified problems, (5) coordinate the implementation of recommendations, and (6) provide periodic review and plan updates. The written recommendations outlined in step 4 (i.e., the financial plan) will include a discussion of a wide range of subjects: cash flow management, tax planning, risk management (insurance planning), retirement planning, estate planning, and so on. The legal booby traps in dealing with such a wide range of technical subjects are enormous, as we shall see.

This chapter addresses the issue of the financial planner's liability for negligent conduct. We will look at the planner-client relationship itself, the applicable legal standards of care, and some specific types of negligent conduct, as well as the legal consequences thereof. To a lesser extent, we will look at the vicarious or derivative liability of financial planners who are broker-dealers for the wrongful acts of persons whom they supervise.

TORT VERSUS CONTRACT LIABILITY

Since financial planners generally enter into express or implied contracts with their clients at the time their services are procured, it would be helpful at this point to note the differences between the planner's contract liability and tort liability. Technically, a tort is a civil wrong, other than a breach of contract, for which a court will provide a remedy in the form of a civil action for money damages. On a more practical level, a tort is simply a legal wrong committed by one person against the person or property of another. A tort may be either an *intentional* wrong, such as assault, battery, libel, slander, malicious prosecution, or invasion of privacy, or an *unintentional* wrong, such as ordinary negligence.

All torts have certain characteristics in common. First, they represent a breach of duties the common law imposes upon persons generally, and the duties in question are those owed to all persons as a matter of social policy rather than to any person in particular. For example, when a person drives an automobile down the street, the common law imposes upon him the obligation to drive with reasonable care for the safety of all persons, and if he fails to do so and causes injury, he can be held liable for having committed a tort. Note that this obligation requires no prior consent or understanding between the driver and those likely to be harmed by his unsafe conduct. The second common characteristic of a tort is that the harm caused must be capable of being compensated in a legal action seeking money damages.

Thus, we see that tort liability protects the interest of everyone in freedom from various kinds of harm and does not depend on the will or intention of the parties. Contract liability, on the other hand, is imposed by law for the protection of individuals to assure them that the promises of others will be performed. Contract obligations arise out of the mutual consent of the parties and are owed only to the specific persons who are parties to the contract.

Occasionally, there are circumstances in which both contract liability and tort liability may be applicable. By way of illustration, the courts have held that one who provides professional services pursuant to an express contract impliedly agrees to possess and exercise appropriate skill and care, and that the failure to meet this implied obligation will be a breach of the implied contract. Hence, two separate bases of liability—implied contract and tort—may arise out of the identical duty to exercise due care, and this occasionally raises the tactical question on the part of a plaintiff as to which legal action to bring. In actual practice, most plaintiffs would prefer to bring a tort action rather than a contract action, since the damages recoverable in tort are almost always greater. For this reason, it is likely that most suits brought by clients of financial planners will be bottomed on tort theories (primarily negligence), along with possible violations of the federal and state securities acts. We turn now to the specific legal obligations of planners to their clients under common-law negligence principles and related tort doctrines.

THE PLANNER-CLIENT RELATIONSHIP

Before any of the duties owed by a planner to his client become operative, a special legal relationship, the planner-client relationship, must exist between the parties. The planner-client relationship is consensual in nature; it results from a meeting of the minds, a legally enforceable understanding that the client wishes to engage the services of the planner to undertake specified tasks, and the latter's consent to do so. The legal consideration (or *quid pro quo*) may be explicitly spelled out (e.g., $75 per hour or $500 for a plan) or legally implied; but the end result is nothing less than a legally binding contract.

Clearly, not all discussions between financial planners and would-be clients automatically establish a planner-client relationship. For example, many financial planners routinely sponsor public seminars and offer attendees at such seminars a financial planning consultation without charge or further obligation. The mere discussion of general planning goals and strategies at such a consultation session would not, by itself, create a legally cognizable planner-client relationship. By the same token, if a planner suggests specific investment strategies to a public audience, he cannot later be held liable to someone in the audience who acts on one or more of those suggestions to his detriment, since no planner-client relationship was formally established.

Because the planner-client relationship is a consensual one, it cannot be created indirectly or by implication. For example, if you were engaged to prepare a detailed financial plan for a client and needed some specialized tax help, the mere fact that you might seek the advice of another planner who is a tax expert, even with the client's knowledge, would not thereby create a separate planner-client relationship between your client and the tax expert. Such a relationship could be established, of course, but only if the client were to engage the services of the second planner on his own, with the latter's consent and for the necessary legal consideration.

It goes without saying that as a planner you are always free to choose your clients and may legally refuse to assume professional responsibility toward any individual. But once you have entered into that professional relationship, you are obliged to continue your services until they are no longer reasonably required, unless you are expressly discharged by the client or there is mutual agreement between you to terminate the relationship.

STANDARDS OF CARE

At law, every person is always responsible for conducting himself in a reasonable and prudent manner whether he is a layman or a professional and whether he is engaged in the most simple or most complex type of activity. When a person fails to conduct himself in this required manner and causes harm to another, we say he is legally "negligent," and he can be held liable in damages for the harm caused.

Professional persons in general, and those who undertake any work calling for special skill, are required not only to exercise reasonable care in what they do, but also to possess a standard minimum of special knowledge and ability. Thus, while a financial planner is also expected to exercise reasonable care in carrying out his professional duties, because the planner holds himself out as a person possessing special skills and learning in the financial planning field, the law says that the reasonableness of his conduct must be measured against that of other reasonably prudent members of the financial planning profession given the same or similar circumstances. Again, the failure to meet the required legal standard of care is professional negligence, or malpractice. In view of the fact that financial planning deals extensively with securities that are sold and purchased on an interstate basis (and thus subject to federal regulation), the same standards of conduct logically should apply to planners throughout the United States, since all are subject to the same federal statutes, which were enacted to bring uniformity to the field of securities regulation.

In addition to the negligence standard arising out of tort law, several other sources of legal standards are also applicable: (1) prior SEC and court cases, (2) national securities exchange rules, (3) NASD regulations, (4) SEC regulations, and (5) professional organization standards. A court may rely on one or more of these sources as the basis for establishing the planner's proper conduct. The NASD's Rules of Fair Practice, for example, have served as the governing standard in numerous cases. As the court observed in *Cash* v. *Frederick & Company, Inc.,* 57 F.R.D. 71 (E.D. Wis. 1972), "The alleged violation of the NASD Rules of Fair Practice is relevant [in the instant case] not to form the basis of an action, but to suggest what duty the defendant had to the plaintiff."

In general, a cause of action in negligence requires the following elements:

1. A legal duty to conform to a certain standard of conduct

2. A failure to conform to that standard

3. A reasonably close causal connection between the conduct and the resulting harm

4. Actual loss or damage

What actually constitutes conduct leading to liability will depend, of course, upon the facts of each individual case.

LIABILITY-PRODUCING CONDUCT

Earlier, mention was made of the numerous legal booby traps that financial planners face in their daily practices. Now we shall focus on some of the specifics to see just how extensive the planner's liability to his client can be.

Breach of Fiduciary Duty

One of the key functions of a financial planner is the giving of investment advice, and in carrying out this responsibility the planner obligates himself to meet the most rigid of legal standards, those applicable to the fiduciary. You will recall that, at the time the Advisers Act of 1940 was under consideration, securities industry witnesses stressed the importance of the relationship of trust and confidence between investment advisers and their clients. When the law was enacted, section 206 thereof specifically prohibited "fraudulent, deceptive, or manipulative" practices. Moreover, section 206 was made applicable to *all* investment advisers, whether or not they were required to be registered with the SEC.

As we have seen, the SEC has made it abundantly clear in Release IA-770 that financial planners fall within the statutory definition of investment advisers and that an investment adviser "is a fiduciary who owes his clients an affirmative duty of utmost good faith, and full and fair disclosure of all material facts." The quoted language is from the U.S. Supreme Court's landmark decision in *S.E.C.* v. *Capital Gains Research Bureau,* 375 U.S. 180 (1963).

In the broadest sense, a fiduciary relationship is one founded upon trust or confidence reposed by one person in the integrity and fidelity of another, especially where the person in whom such confidence is reposed is in a position to exercise considerable influence or control over the affairs of the other. The fiduciary then, in equity and good conscience, is bound to act in good faith and with due regard to the interests of the party imposing the confidence.

The law regards the duty of a fiduciary as a very high one, higher than the negligence standard applicable to most of the planner's other legal obligations. As stated by the court in *Kohler* v. *Kohler Co.,* 319 F.2d 634, 642 (7th Cir. 1963), "A defendant must exercise a higher standard of care when he knows or has reason to know that the plaintiff has relied almost exclusively upon his advice." And the courts consider breach of the fiduciary duty as tantamount to constructive fraud, making the planner liable for violation of the pertinent provisions of the federal and state securities acts, as well as liable in a common law action for fraud.

The planner who charges a fee for his planning services and also receives commissions on investments and insurance products he has recommended to the client is extremely vulnerable to a claim of breach of fiduciary duty if he fails to inform the client of the potential conflict(s) of interest. The SEC has made it clear that an investment adviser has an affirmative duty to disclose fully the nature and extent of any interest the adviser may have in any recommendation, including any compensation that would be received should the client act on the recommendation. Moreover, the SEC requires disclosure in writing of all fees, compensation, and possible conflicts at the time of entering into the investment advisory agreement.

With increasing frequency, many product sponsors have been offering various sales incentives such as cash bonuses or other gifts to financial planners who achieve specified production goals—trips to Hawaii and other exotic locations being favorite forms of sales incentives. Although no court cases have thus far discussed this issue, there is little doubt that the receipt of such gifts, trips, or bonuses often violates specific NASD rules (Article III, Sections 26 and 34, Rules of Fair Practice), as well as state securities laws and regulations dealing with such matters. They certainly tend to compromise the planner's fiduciary responsibility to exercise his independent and objective judgment in the best interests of his client. For this reason, you lay yourself wide open to a charge of breach of fiduciary duty unless you candidly disclose to your client the existence and nature of specific product sales incentives (if relevant to particular investment recommendations) and explain the potential conflict of interest they represent.

Negligent Planning Diagnosis

Much like the physician who must take the patient's history and order baseline tests before he can diagnose the patient's condition and institute a treatment regimen, the financial planner must obtain relevant financial data and make appropriate tax and other calculations before he can diagnose the client's financial situation and then prepare a plan or strategy for dealing with the key issues.

From the legal standpoint, a planner need only exercise reasonable care, that is, do what other reasonably prudent planners would do under the same or similar circumstances. This means you must utilize the standard techniques and tools of the financial planning profession in diagnosing your client's situation and in making recommendations for dealing therewith. Note that even if a planner's conclusions and recommendations happen to differ from those of his colleagues, and his client suffers losses, he will not be deemed negligent on that ground alone as long as he exercised the requisite degree of prudence and care in arriving at those conclusions and recommendations. All this assumes, of course, that the recommended investments meet the test of client suitability, which is discussed more fully later.

When a planner fails to employ commonly accepted diagnostic tools and techniques in analyzing his client's situation and making recommendations, he can be held liable to the client in damages for the losses sustained. Recommending an investment because of its touted tax benefits, only to have them subsequently disallowed by the IRS because of the alternative minimum tax—a circumstance the planner either overlooked or chose to ignore—would be an example of the sort of negligence in diagnosis that would lead to liability. Failing to inquire about the client's will or existing estate plans, leading to wholly inappropriate investment recommendations, would be another example. Failing to inquire about the client's existing pension or retirement plan and options he may (or should) have exercised thereunder would be still another example of negligence in diagnosis for which a planner would be held liable in damages to his client. The list is virtually endless, but the point is clear: If you intend to provide professional financial planning services, you had better meet the standards established by your colleagues and by the principal standard-setting organizations in the field if you want to avoid making errors likely to generate a lawsuit.

Failure to Disclose Material Facts

When a planner recommends a specific investment vehicle to a client, he has a legal duty to disclose all relevant and material information about the proposed investment. A person who fails to meet the legal duty of disclosure will be deemed negligent and accordingly held liable in damages to the client. The client is almost always at a disadvantage when it comes to judging the merits of a proposed investment and must rely substantially on the planner's explanation of the investment's objectives, risks, and potential returns, and how it ties in with the client's financial needs and objectives. In this sense the duty to disclose and inform is simply an offshoot of the planner's overall fiduciary responsibility to his client.

But the duty to disclose and inform has a statutory basis, as well. SEC

Rule 10b-5 states in pertinent part that it shall be unlawful, in connection with the sale of a security, for any person "to make any untrue statement of a material fact or omit to state a material fact necessary in order to make the statements made, in the light of the circumstances under which they were made, not misleading." Just what constitutes the type of "omission of a material fact" that will give rise to liability was discussed by the U.S. Supreme Court in *TSC Industries, Inc.* v. *Northway, Inc.* 426 U.S. 438, 96 S.Ct. 2126 (1976). The objective standard established by the court in that case requires

> a showing of a substantial likelihood that, under all the circumstances, the omitted fact would have assumed actual significance in the deliberations of the reasonable shareholder. Put another way, there must be a substantial likelihood that the disclosure of the omitted fact would have been viewed by the reasonable investor as having significantly altered the "total mix" of information made available.

The essence of the legal requirement of disclosure is not the perfunctory dispensing of a mass of technical information, but an honest-to-goodness explanation of the advantages and disadvantages of the investment, especially the risks, in language the client can understand. This does not mean a planner has to give a full-scale lecture explaining all there is to know about each and every recommended investment. The nature and scope of the duty to inform will vary according to the type of investment under consideration and the client's age, education, and relative degree of investment sophistication. The less complex the investment and the more sophisticated the investor, the less information need be furnished. Conversely, the more complex the investment and the less sophisticated the investor, the more information that need be furnished and the more detailed the explanation that must be given.

Assuming you are dealing with a security, there is absolutely no substitute for full and complete disclosure to your client. This means presenting the prospectus to him, indicating the investment's stated objectives, and discussing how they relate to his overall financial goals. You should also discuss the track record of the investment's promoters and make a practice of pointing out the downside potential of every investment.

Misrepresentation

Many familiar forms of negligent conduct may be said to involve an element of misrepresentation, which literally means giving a false, improper, or imperfect representation. As a distinct tort, however, misrepresentation is most closely identified with the common law action for deceit.

The essential elements of a legal action for deceit are as follows:

1. A false representation by the defendant.

2. Knowledge on the part of the defendant that the representation is false, or the defendant's lack of a sufficient basis of information to make the representation.

3. An intention by the defendant to induce the plaintiff to act or refrain from acting in reliance on the misrepresentation.

4. Justifiable reliance by the plaintiff in acting or refraining from acting.

5. Resultant damages to the plaintiff due to such reliance.

Misrepresentation is a legal booby trap that can cause a planner inestimable harm, resulting not only in legal liability to the client, but possible loss or suspension of your securities license. It is most likely to arise when outlining the characteristics of a particular investment, when one may be tempted to exaggerate the anticipated yield, tax benefits, or overall economic potential of the investment while failing to disclose its potential risks or other material facts. The decided cases make it clear that conduct of this nature constitutes reckless behavior sufficient to satisfy the "scienter" requirement of common law fraud or deceit. Any words or acts that create a false impression or cover up the truth are deemed to be a form of misrepresentation and will form the basis of an actionable liability claim.

Hanly v. *S.E.C.,* 425 F.2d 589 (2d Cir. 1969), illustrates the type of conduct likely to result in liability. In *Hanly,* four securities salesmen were permanently barred by the SEC from further association with any broker or dealer for fraudulent conduct. "The fraud in this case," said the SEC in its decision, "consisted of optimistic representations or recommendations [made] without disclosure of known or reasonably ascertainable information which rendered them materially misleading." The Commission then held that "a salesman must not merely avoid affirmative misstatements when he recommends the stock to a customer; he must also disclose material adverse facts of which he is or should be aware."

The stock the salesmen had touted was an electronics company that, from its inception, had operated at a deficit and, during the entire period it was being recommended, was insolvent. Among the affirmative misrepresentations made by the brokers in question were statements that the company was a winner and would make money, that it had a fabulous potential and would double or triple, that it would make Xerox look like a standstill, that the broker had purchased the stock for himself and he would be able to retire and get rich on it, that it had possibilities of skyrocketing and would probably double in price within six months, and so on. None of the firm's financial problems was mentioned.

The appeals court affirmed the permanent expulsion of the brokers from the securities industry, and in so doing it stated:

> When a securities salesman fraudulently violates the high standards with which he is charged, he subjects himself to a variety of punitive, compensatory, and remedial sanctions. . . . Brokers and salesmen are under a duty to investigate, and their violation of that duty brings them within the term "willful" in the Exchange Act. Thus, a salesman cannot deliberately ignore that which he has a duty to know and recklessly state facts about matters of which he is ignorant. . . . Where the salesman lacks essential information about a security, he should disclose this as well as the risks which arise from his lack of information.

Certainly, no conscientious planner should ever use the word "guaranteed" in discussing tax benefits, yields, anticipated capital gains, or profits on an investment. It is a representation you cannot possibly substantiate and violates all ethical standards of the profession. What is worse, nothing is more likely to fuel a client's exaggerated expectations regarding the outcome of his investment (or to furnish a better motivation for suing) than your indiscriminate use of the word "guaranteed."

Recommending Unsuitable Investments

The financial planner has an affirmative duty not to recommend investments that are unsuitable for a client in light of his financial objectives, his overall financial situation and needs, his comprehension of investment risk, and other relevant factors. This obviously calls for some basic information gathering with respect to these factors—in effect, a due diligence inquiry regarding the client's suitability for a particular proposed investment—before recommending it. Given the wide differences between clients in their financial needs, goals, and levels of risk tolerance, it goes without saying that what may be a perfectly suitable investment for one client may be entirely unsuitable for another.

Since securities brokers traditionally are compensated by commissions that are directly in proportion to sales, the motivation and opportunity to take advantage of a client is always present. To counteract any tendency to do so, the NASD, the SEC, and the various stock exchanges have imposed the clear-cut obligation on securities representatives to ascertain the suitability of all investments recommended to their clients.

Article III, Section 2, of the NASD's Rules of Fair Practice is the rule that requires members of that association to recommend or sell only those securities that are appropriate to their clients' needs and to know relevant facts about their clients before making such recommendations. It reads as follows:

> In recommending to a customer the purchase, sale or exchange of any security, a member shall have reasonable grounds for believing that the recommendation is suitable for such customer upon the basis of the facts, *if any,* disclosed by such customer as to his other security holdings and as to his financial situation and needs. [Emphasis added]

The NASD has taken the position that this rule is not a legal requirement but simply an ethical precept to encourage fair dealing with investors. And based on this interpretation, it has often cited the suitability rule as grounds for disciplining brokers who have sold speculative securities to uninformed purchasers of modest financial means and to brokers who have engaged in excessive trading activity, or churning. But the NASD has steadfastly maintained over the years that its suitability rule—with the limiting words "if any" contained therein—does not obligate securities representatives to make any general inquiry regarding the suitability of an investment for a particular client except in the case of speculative, low-priced securities.

A literal interpretation of the NASD rule would appear to encourage the securities representative to learn as little as possible about his client's financial needs and goals. The SEC believes otherwise, however, and in reviewing NASD disciplinary actions predicated on suitability rule violations, it has effectively eliminated the "if any" from the NASD rule.

A number of courts have concurred with the SEC's position that the broker's obligation to ascertain investment suitability is not a conditional one. Thus, in *Plunkett* v. *Dominick & Dominick, Inc.,* 414 F.Supp. 885 (D. Conn. 1976), the court referred to the NASD suitability rule as imposing duties "identical to what is at least imposed at common law." In *Clark* v. *John Lamula Investors, Inc.,* 583 F.2d 594 (2d Cir. 1978), the court found that the knowing recommendation of unsuitable securities was not only a violation of the NASD suitability rule, but a *per se* violation of the anti-fraud provisions of SEC Rule 10b-5.

The suitability concept in the eyes of the SEC is not merely an ethical precept, but a rule of law. In 1967, the SEC adopted its own suitability rule (Rule 15b10-3) to govern the conduct of SECO brokers. Unlike the NASD rule, it imposed an affirmative obligation on the broker to make a "reasonable inquiry" concerning a customer's situation and needs. In the commentary issued when the SECO suitability rule was first adopted, the SEC indicated that the broker's obligation included obtaining "information concerning the customer's marital status, the number and age of his dependents, his earnings, the amount of his savings and life insurance, and his security holdings and other assets. . . ." Since the termination of the SECO program in 1983, pursuant to P.L. 98-38, the SECO suitability rule is no longer in effect, but the SEC still views the obligations of brokers to make only suitable recommendations as an affirmative legal requirement.

Most legal commentators agree that Rule 405 of the New York Stock Exchange, the "Know Your Customer" rule, also imposes a suitability requirement, even though it was not originally promulgated for that purpose. It provides in pertinent part that

> Every member organization is required . . . to use due diligence to learn the essential facts relative to every customer, every order, every cash or margin account accepted or carried by such organization and every person holding power of attorney over any account accepted or carried by such organization.

In *Rolf* v. *Blyth, Eastman Dillon & Co., Inc.* 424 F.Supp. 1021 (S.D.N.Y. 1977), the court held that a violation of NYSE Rule 405 would give rise to a private cause of action where the broker's actions were tantamount to fraud. The court further held that the obligation to learn all essential facts is not lessened merely because the client happens to be an investment adviser acting on behalf of others.

Most financial planners will routinely obtain all the essential information about their clients in the initial data-gathering process. But the suitability doctrine requires the planner to obtain essential information about the proposed investment, as well. Clearly, this calls for something more than mere reliance on self-serving statements contained in the issuer's prospectus and accompanying sales literature. The SEC has indicated that a securities representative is under an affirmative duty to make "an adequate independent investigation in order to ensure that his representations about a security have a reasonable basis." Accordingly, the prudent planner will routinely acquire fundamental information about the investment's degree of speculativeness, its ability to produce income, and its chances for growth or capital appreciation. If the client's concern is for specific tax relief, then the inquiry should also cover that aspect of the investment.

Prior to 1979, the majority of courts held that an investor could bring a private legal action against a securities broker who violated the NASD's suitability rule or a stock exchange's suitability rule. The U.S. Supreme Court ruled otherwise in two major decisions in 1979, and the cases decided since then have generally denied such private right of action where the case has been brought on that ground alone. Nevertheless, plaintiffs continue to assert NASD and other self-regulatory organization suitability rule violations when bringing lawsuits based on specific securities act violations, and proof of such violations is usually deemed admissible as evidence of fraudulent or deceptive conduct.

The financial planner who recommends investments that are unsuited to his client's needs and goals runs the risk of being sued on at least two additional grounds: (1) for breach of his fiduciary duty to act in his client's best interests, and (2) for his failure to exercise reasonable care (i.e., negligence) in portfolio design and plan implementation. At the very least, it is clear that the suitability rule establishes the standard of conduct required of a securities representative; and even if a breach thereof does not *ipso facto* give rise to a distinct federal cause of action, many courts still allow proof of suitability rule violations as evidence of negligence on the part of the broker-planner.

Failure to Seek Consultation

Comprehensive financial planning involves the application of knowledge peculiar to many diverse fields, among them law, accounting, insurance, pension and retirement planning, real estate, and business organization. Understandably, the law does not require the planner to be an expert in each of these fields; it merely requires that he possess the degree of knowledge, skill, and judgment possessed by other reasonably prudent financial planning practitioners.

But when a planner is faced with a specific technical issue or problem that is clearly beyond his personal competence, the law *does* insist that he seek the aid of a consultant with the requisite degree of expertise or, alternatively, refer the client directly to such a specialist. Indeed, one of the important functions of a financial planner is to recognize the need for such specialized help and to act as liaison with other professionals on behalf of the client.

Legally, the failure to consult a specialist when the circumstances so require is deemed to be negligent conduct and a clear-cut basis for liability. Incidentally, great care should be exercised when selecting or recommending a specialist with purported expertise. If that individual gives advice that proves harmful to your client's interests, or commits an error that would not have been made by other reasonably competent specialists in his field, you as the referring planner can be held personally liable if it is later shown that you did not use reasonable care in selecting that specialist.

Negligent Case Management

When a planner enters into a contract with a client to provide financial planning services, one of the implied obligations he assumes is the duty to follow through on all required implementation functions in an efficient and effective manner. Among other things, this includes:

1. Contacting and arranging to meet with other specialists.
2. Obtaining necessary information from third parties such as banks, lawyers, tax preparers, realtors, insurers, employers, and the like.
3. Making due diligence inquiries regarding potential investments.
4. Handling the normal paper work that is associated with opening and maintaining a client's account.
5. Placing orders for securities and double-checking to make sure they have been properly filled.

With respect to the last item, the court in *Ceka* v. *Beckman & Co.*, 28 Cal.App.3rd 5 (1972) specifically held that a broker who was negligent in executing orders for securities is of course liable to his customer in damages.

Critical time factors are involved in all of these activities, and the planner who is too busy to give them appropriate attention may find that important tax deadlines are missed, necessary insurance coverage is not obtained, vital legal documents are not prepared, recommended investments are not made on time, and various financial opportunities are lost forever. A client who can demonstrate compensable economic loss as a result of such negligence has a good chance of recovering damages in a suit brought against the negligent planner.

Failure to Keep Current

It is a fundamental principle of tort law that one who holds himself out to the public as a professional in a specific field of endeavor has the legal duty to keep reasonably abreast of current practices and knowledge in that field. So it is with financial planning. Buttressing the common law obligation are the ethical codes of the IAFP and the ICFP (see Appendixes D and E). Canon 2 of the IAFP Code of Professional Ethics provides that "Members should seek continually to maintain and improve their professional knowledge, skills, and competence." The ICFP's Code of Ethics for Certified Financial Planners contains similar language:

> A Certified Financial Planner should observe the profession's general and technical standards and strive continually to improve his competence and the quality of his services. . . . Moreover, since published general and technical standards can never cover the whole field of financial planning, he must keep broadly informed.

A planner's failure to keep abreast of current knowledge in the field will most likely come to light in a malpractice suit alleging negligent diagnosis of the client's situation or alleging erroneous or inappropriate tax or investment recommendations. The only defense to such a charge would be evidence of seminars, continuing education courses, and other similar activities undertaken by the planner designed to keep him abreast of developments in all relevant planning areas.

In a somewhat related aspect of the planner-client relationship, financial planners have a continuing duty to keep their clients informed of all significant changes in the tax laws, as well as any significant developments likely to have a negative impact on their existing investments. If, for example, one or more clients have invested in a real estate limited partnership, the planner is obligated to make periodic checks to ascertain whether the general partner has encountered unusual problems with renting the property, has incurred excessive operating losses, has found it difficult to borrow money at anticipated interest rates, or has run into other problems likely to affect the profitability of the partnership. If so, the planner has a legal obligation to bring these matters to the attention of the concerned clients.

Abandonment of the Client

Abandonment of a client is the unilateral severance of the planner-client relationship by the planner without reasonable notice at a point in time when the planner's services are still required and his premature withdrawal of services is likely to prove harmful to the client's interests. Where abandonment can be shown to have occurred and also shown to be the proximate cause of damages suffered by the client, such conduct represents a clear failure to meet the required standard of professional care. On the other hand, where the client has been properly notified and arrangements have been made for substitution of a new planner, a charge of abandonment will not prevail.

To illustrate a case of abandonment, let us assume a planner were to agree to review a client's portfolio and make appropriate tax calculations prior to advising the client whether to retain or to sell certain securities before the end of the current year in order to take maximum advantage of the tax laws. By mid-December the planner still has not made the necessary calculations, despite the client's repeated requests for the needed information. To make matters worse, the planner does not even return the client's insistent telephone calls.

Ultimately, the client makes no change in his portfolio, and this proves to have disastrous tax consequences. Had he received the information he had contracted to receive from the planner, but never obtained, he might have avoided altogether the payment of additional taxes—the very reason for engaging the planner's services. The client in this hypothetical case will have little difficulty in proving a case of abandonment, as well as ordinary negligence.

A lawsuit alleging abandonment necessarily must be founded on the existence of a valid planner-client relationship. Thus, there must be clear proof that the planner and the client actually entered into a contractual arrangement calling for the planner to undertake specified duties for a specific consideration and that the arrangement was not otherwise legally terminated.

Legal termination normally takes place (1) when the client discharges the planner, with or without cause, either orally or in writing, (2) upon the planner's death, or (3) when the planner withdraws for reasons of his own and gives notice thereof to the client in writing. The client's total lack of cooperation or his nonpayment of the planner's bill for services rendered would be examples of possible reasons for a planner to withdraw his services. More often than not, personality conflicts between planner and client will prove to be the real basis for terminating the relationship.

In any event, the planner who chooses to take this course of action should make sure the client is given proper notice—always in writing—and ample opportunity to find a qualified substitute planner. To the extent possible, the withdrawing planner may even assist in this process, and he will not be liable for any harm suffered by the client thereafter as long as the substitute recommended was selected with reasonable care.

Failure to Supervise Subordinates

The delegation of duties to staff subordinates is a necessary and integral part of managing a successful financial planning practice, but it is not without its legal hazards. As a general rule, everyone is held legally responsible for his own negligent conduct, but as a practical matter, a client who has suffered loss because of an error committed by the planner's employee is hardly likely to sue the employee. His lawsuit will be directed instead against the employer on the ground that the latter was negligent in failing to exercise proper supervision of the employee.

Under the common law doctrine known as *respondeat superior* ("let the master answer"), an employer is held strictly liable for the wrongful acts of his employees that cause injury to others provided the acts in question occur while acting within the scope of their employment. Thus, when a planner delegates tasks to subordinates, he must do so carefully or else suffer the legal consequences.

Liability arising out of failure to exercise adequate supervision takes on added significance as more and more financial planners begin to utilize the services of specially trained paraplanners, persons whose activities occasionally approximate those of the planner himself. Among their many functions, paraplanners commonly obtain basic client financial and personal data, provide ongoing client service and support, analyze specific investments, research tax code provisions, obtain data about new financial products, and in general assume responsibilities for tasks that permit their employers to spend more time on professional financial planning matters.

In carrying out these activities, a paraplanner may act, or fail to act, in any number of ways that might result in eventual harm to a client. For example, furnishing outdated or erroneous tax information to the employing planner may lead to an erroneous assessment of the client's tax status and inappropriate advice regarding existing or proposed investments. Thus, regardless of the degree of training an employee may have, prudent practice necessitates the regular and close supervision of all staff members. Such supervision becomes all the more important when the planner is a broker-dealer and the persons being supervised are registered securities representatives. The broker-dealer's derivative liability in these circumstances is discussed in the following section.

The careful financial planner will institute necessary office procedures to make sure that all staff members carry out their delegated responsibilities with due care. The process begins with careful attention to the hiring of capable persons and then making sure they are given the necessary formal and informal training. They must be told exactly what is expected of them, as well as the limitations of their authority. Under no circumstances should a financial planner permit a nonlicensed subordinate, such as a paraplanner, to give investment advice to a client or become directly involved in the buying or selling of securities.

Finally, since securities transactions necessarily involve money transfers, all aspects of money handling in the planner's office must be structured so that the pertinent NASD and SEC regulations are rigorously followed. The failure to comply with all applicable regulatory guidelines for the processing of security transactions and the handling of clients' funds, assuming losses are thereby suffered, will not only give rise to potential liability, but may well prompt disciplinary action by the NASD or the SEC.

The Broker-Dealer's Added Liability

When the planner is a broker-dealer who employs and supervises other registered securities representatives, his derivative liability for their wrongful acts takes on an entirely different character because of special provisions of the federal securities acts. Basically, there are two legal theories available for holding a broker-dealer liable for securities act violations committed by his registered representatives in the handling of securities transactions: (1) *respondeat superior* and (2) the controlling-person doctrine. The difference between them, from a practical standpoint, is fairly significant.

Where the injured plaintiff is allowed to assert the doctrine of *respondeat superior,* the broker-dealer will be held strictly liable for the misdeeds of his agents and employees—specifically, for negligently or recklessly failing to establish an adequate system of supervision and internal control. This doctrine makes him, in effect, an insurer. Under the controlling-person theory, on the other hand, the broker-dealer is not held strictly liable and, in fact, may escape liability altogether if he can establish the legal defenses of good faith and due care. *Respondeat superior* is a common law doctrine, while the controlling-person doctrine is based on specific provisions of the federal securities acts. Invariably, the courts that have addressed the issue have focused on whether these two doctrines can be applied concurrently (i.e., coexist) or whether the statutory controlling-persons doctrine is the exclusive remedy and displaces the common law doctrine. Notwithstanding the great number of decided cases over the years, the courts are still divided in their views, and the Supreme Court has yet to rule on the question.

Section 15 of the Securities Act provides that a "controlling person" (such as a broker-dealer) shall be free from liability for the acts of "controlled persons" (such as his registered representatives) only if he can demonstrate no knowledge or reasonable ground to believe in facts from which liability to a third party may be predicated. Section 20(a) of the Exchange Act provides that the controlling person shall *not* be liable if the broker-dealer acted in good faith and did not directly or indirectly induce the wrongful acts in question. Obviously, a broker-dealer would prefer to assert one or both of these defenses since, in the absence of his culpable participation or acquiescence in the wrongful conduct of his registered representative, he will not be held liable. Note, however, that once it is established that a broker-dealer is a controlling person, the burden shifts to him to prove that he did in fact act in good faith and did not directly or indirectly induce the fraudulent transaction.

In *Marbury Management, Inc.* v. *Kohn*, 629 F.2d 705 (2d Cir. 1980), a brokerage firm's trainee defrauded his customers by misrepresenting himself as a "portfolio management specialist" when in fact he was not even licensed to sell securities and had no authority to do so. The court ruled that even though what he did was contrary to the standing instructions of the firm, everything he did was done solely in the firm's interests. For this reason, it held the broker-dealer liable under *respondeat superior* for failing to supervise him more closely.

Rochez Bros., Inc. v. *Rhoades,* 527 F.2d 880 (3d Cir. 1975), is the leading case for the opposite point of view, championing what is called the "exclusivity doctrine." The court there noted that, since the securities laws generally impose liability only on those who to some degree are culpable, if it were to allow *respondeat superior* to apply, the good faith defense of section 20(a) of the Exchange Act would be rendered meaningless. Significantly, this case did not involve the derelictions of a registered representative, but an officer of the firm acting as an individual for his own account.

At the moment, the majority of federal circuit courts that have considered the issue have taken the position that liability for the acts of a broker-dealer's registered representative may be found either under the common law *respondeat superior* doctrine *or* under the controlling-persons sections of the federal securities acts. This trend toward expanding the secondary liability of broker-dealers appears to be attributable to the expressed need of the courts to protect the investing public from the predatory practices of unethical securities brokers.

Miscellaneous Acts of Negligence

In addition to the various legal duties outlined, the planner assumes a number of other legal responsibilities that may give rise to liability if reasonable care is not exercised. For example, once a planner-client relationship has been established, the planner assumes the duty (1) to maintain accurate and complete records, (2) to exercise ongoing due diligence with respect to investments, (3) to implement recommendations promptly and properly, and (4) to maintain the confidences of his clients and assure the privacy of their records. Any of these items can become significant factors in a lawsuit brought by an aggrieved client, and all should be regarded as potential sources of litigation.

KEY POINTS TO REMEMBER

1. Over and above his liability to the regulatory authorities, the planner's civil liability to his client can have serious economic consequences.

2. Because a planner routinely performs many complex technical functions, his risk of committing negligent acts is enormous.

3. Tort liability arises out of the law's concern that the interests of everyone be protected from various kinds of harm. Contract liability arises out of the mutual consent of the parties.

4. The special legal obligations owed by a planner to his client do not arise until and unless there is a legally recognized planner-client relationship, a consensual agreement that the planner is to provide specified services to the client for a specific *quid pro quo.*

5. Everyone is legally required to act with reasonable care to avoid harming others, but the reasonableness of the conduct of a financial planner must be measured against that of other reasonably prudent financial planning practitioners, rather than ordinary laymen.

6. Standards of care in the financial planning field are set by court cases, NASD and SEC regulations, and professional organizations.

7. Breach of fiduciary duty is one of the most likely grounds for liability of a planner, and it will arise whenever the planner fails to disclose to his client all potential conflicts of interest. Receiving fees from commissions on recommended in-

vestments and cash bonuses or other gifts as sales incentives are examples of such conflicts.

8. A planner must utilize all commonly accepted diagnostic tools in analyzing his client's situation, and his failure to do so will lead to liability if the client suffers compensable losses.

9. The failure to disclose all material facts about an investment, including its risks and downside potential as well as its anticipated advantages, is grounds for common law as well as statutory liability.

10. Knowingly misrepresenting the true nature of a recommended investment to induce the client to purchase it is a clear basis for liability.

11. A planner must recommend to his client only investments that are deemed suitable, given the client's financial situation, risk tolerance level, and overall financial objectives.

12. The suitability doctrine requires the planner to make inquiry regarding his client's personal situation and needs, as well as a due diligence inquiry regarding the proposed investment(s).

13. The law requires a planner to seek the advice of consultant-specialists whenever a technical problem is beyond his competence.

14. Proper case management calls for careful attention to the myriad details of financial planning practice, particularly with respect to items that have critical deadlines or require follow-up actions.

15. Keeping abreast of current knowledge and practices is a fundamental legal requirement for all financial planners.

16. The unilateral severance of the planner-client relationship by the planner will result in a charge of abandonment for which he can be held liable.

17. When a planner supervises others, he can be held absolutely liable for their acts of negligence under the legal doctrine of *respondeat superior,* without regard to his personal involvement.

18. Because of this vicarious or derivative form of liability, the careful planner will exercise the greatest possible care in supervising clerical personnel, paraplanners, and all others he employs in his practice, paying special attention to the manner in which securities transactions are handled.

19. The derivative liability of a broker-dealer is even greater than that of the planner who is not a broker-dealer because of specific provisions of the securities laws.

20. The broker-dealer's liability for supervision is absolute where *respondeat superior* is applicable. Under the statutory controlling-person doctrine, however, he may escape liability for the wrongful act or acts of subordinates by showing that he

acted in good faith and did not directly or indirectly induce the wrongful acts in question.

SELECTED REFERENCES

Statutes and Regulations

SEC Rule 10b-5, 17 Code of Federal Regulations, § 240.10b-5.

Tort versus Contract Liability

Prosser, W., *Handbook of the Law of Torts,* 4th Ed. (West Publishing Co., St. Paul, Minnesota, 1971).

Applicable Standards of Care

McLean v. *Alexander,* 599 F.2d 1190 (3d Cir. 1979).
Sundstrand Corp. v. *Sun Chemical Corp.,* 553 F.2d 1033 (7th Cir. 1977).

Broker's Duty to Investigate

In the Matter of Waldron & Co., Inc., SEA Release No. 34-17945 (1981).
Hiller v. *S.E.C.,* 429 F.2d 856 (2d Cir. 1970).

Failure to Disclose Material Facts

TSC Industries, Inc. v. *Northway, Inc.,* 426 U.S. 438 (1976).
Piper, Jaffray & Hopwood, Inc. v. *Ladin et al.,* 399 F.Supp. 292 (S.D. Iowa, 1975).
Affiliated Ute Citizens of Utah v. *United States,* 406 U.S. 128 (1972).
S.E.C. v. *Capital Gains Research Bureau,* 375 U.S. 180 (1963).

Acceptance of Sales Incentives

Article III, Sec. 34 (Appendix F), *NASD Manual* (NASD, Washington, D.C., 1984).
NASD Notice to Members No. 84-28, Adoption of Amendments to Appen-

dix F Concerning Sales Incentives for Direct Participation Programs (May 1984).

NASD Notice to Members No. 84-40, Compensation Arrangements with Respect to Sale of Mutual Funds (July 1984).

Misrepresentations

Nye v. Blyth, Eastman Dillon & Co., 588 F.2d 1189 (8th Cir. 1978).

Walsh v. Sherrerd, 452 F.Supp. 80 (E.D. Pa. 1978).

Hanly v. S.E.C., 415 F.2d 589 (2d Cir. 1969).

Richard J. Buck & Co., SEA Release No. 84826 (Dec. 1968).

Suitability Rule Violations

NASD Suitability Rule, Article III, Sec. 2, Rules of Fair Practice.

New York Stock Exchange, "Know Your Customer Rule," Rule 405, 2 NYSE Guide, CCH ¶ 2405.

Clark v. John Lamula Investors, Inc., 583 F.2d 594 (2d Cir. 1978).

Rolf v. Blyth, Eastman Dillon & Co., 424 F.Supp. 1021 (S.D.N.Y. 1977).

Hecht v. Harris, Upham & Co., 283 F.Supp. 417 (N.D. Ca. 1968).

See generally, Roach, A. "The Suitability Obligations of Brokers: Present Law and the Proposed Federal Securities Code," 29 *Hastings L.J.* 1067 (1978); Mundheim, R., "Professional Responsibilities of Broker-Dealers: The Suitability Doctrine," 1965 *Duke L.J.*, 445 (1965).

Suitability under State Law

Twomey v. Mitchell, Jones, & Templeton, Inc., 262 Ca. 2d 690 (1968).

See generally, Comment: "Investor Suitability Standards in Real Estate Syndication: California's Procrustean Bed Approach," 63 *Calif. L.Rev.* 471 (1975).

No Implied Private Action to Enforce NASD or Exchange Rules

Klitzman v. Bache Halsey Stuart Shields, 499 F.Supp. 255 (S.D.N.Y. 1980).

Jablon v. Dean Witter & Co., 614 F.2d 677 (9th Cir. 1980).

Touche Ross & Co. v. Redington, 442 U.S. 560 (1979).

Parsons v. *Hornblower & Weeks-Hemphill, Noyes,* 571 F.2d 203 (4th Cir. 1978).

Duty to Supervise Subordinates

In the Matter of Mabon, Nugent & Co., Exchange Act Release No. 19424 (Jan. 1983).

Financial Estate Planning, et al., S.E.C. Release No. 34-14984 (1978).

S.E.C. v. *First Securities Co. of Chicago,* 463 F.2d 981 (7th Cir. 1972).

Article III, Sec. 27, *NASD Manual* (NASD, Washington, D.C., 1984).

Liability under *Respondeat Superior*

Kravitz v. *Pressman, Frohlich & Frost, Inc.,* 447 F.Supp. 203 (D. Mass 1978).

S.E.C. v. *Geon Industries,* 531 F.2d 39 (2d Cir. 1976).

S.E.C. v. *Management Dynamics, Inc.,* 515 F.2d 801 (2d Cir. 1975).

See generally, Reininger, S., "Exclusive or Concurrent—The Role of Control and Respondeat Superior in the Imposition of Vicarious Liability on Broker-Dealers," 9 *Sec. L.J.* 226 (1981).

Annotation, *Civil Liability of Employer for Violation by Employee of Securities Exchange Act Sec. 10(b),* 32 ALR Fed. 714 (1977).

chapter seven

Civil Litigation Against the Planner

Most claims by aggrieved clients against financial planners will be based on alleged violations of the federal and state securities acts. On the other hand, many claims will also include alleged violations of the NASD's Rules of Fair Practice, common law breach of fiduciary duty, professional negligence, and other nonsecurities-related violations. The choice of the proper legal forum for resolving these various legal issues presents procedural problems for plaintiffs and defendants alike.

In this chapter we examine briefly the principal modes by which plaintiffs can assert claims against financial planners: arbitration and civil litigation. Although procedural matters normally are left to the lawyers for the respective parties to decide, it is important for the planner to have at least a general understanding of how they work and how they can affect the outcome of the claim(s) asserted.

ARBITRATION VERSUS LITIGATION

Arbitration of claims for damages, as opposed to civil litigation, has long been encouraged by the courts and legislatures as a preferred means of resolving disputes of all kinds. It is a policy that is reflected in the enactment of the Federal Arbitration Act (9 U.S.C., sec. 1–14, 1970), as well as in various state arbitration acts. It is also a policy that has been looked upon with favor by the securities industry. For many years broker-dealers have required their customers to agree to arbitrate any disputes they might have with them when entering into margin and cash account agreements for brokerage services.

The arbitration clause most widely used by brokerage firms is one prepared by the Association of Stock Exchange Firms. It reads in pertinent part:

> ARBITRATION. It is agreed that any controversy between us arising out of your business or this agreement shall be submitted to arbitration conducted under the provisions of the constitution and rules of the Board of Governors of the New York Stock Exchange, Inc. or pursuant to the Code of Arbitration Procedures of the National Association of Securities Dealers, Inc. as the undersigned may elect.

As can be seen, this clause was designed to encompass almost any dispute that might arise between an investor and his broker. Since the courts favor the application of arbitration clauses, they generally have interpreted them broadly.

But the securities industry's longstanding practice of arbitrating customers' claims encountered a major obstacle with the Supreme Court's decision in *Wilko* v. *Swan,* 346 U.S. 427 (1953). The Supreme Court held that an arbitration clause in a broker's margin agreement was unenforceable since it impermissibly waived an investor's right to have his federal securities act claims decided by a court. The Court reasoned that since section 22(a) of the Securities Act specifically provides for a judicial forum for the enforcement of rights arising under the act, an agreement to arbitrate future disputes is, in essence, a stipulation waiving compliance with the right to select a judicial forum. That would directly conflict with section 14 of the same act, which declares void ''any condition, stipulation, or provision binding any person acquiring any security to waive compliance with any provision'' of the act.

With respect to cases of involuntary arbitration, therefore, the courts continue to follow the doctrine established in *Wilko* v. *Swan,* denying the forced arbitration of claims under the federal securities acts even though the investor-plaintiff has signed an agreement containing an arbitration clause. But the Supreme Court's holding that an agreement to arbitrate *future* disputes is unenforceable left undecided the enforceability of agreements to arbitrate *existing* disputes. However, the clear trend of the decided cases is that an agreement to arbitrate an existing dispute made when a party has full knowledge of all the facts and is in a position to seek legal counsel is legally enforceable. In addition, where the customer insists, he may enforce the arbitration agreement even over the objections of the broker-dealer.

To provide investors with an added measure of protection, the SEC recently adopted Rule 15c2-2, which now specifically prohibits broker-dealers from inserting provisions in customer agreements purporting to bind customers to the arbitration of future disputes arising under the federal securities laws. In addition, the new rule, which went into effect January 1, 1985, requires broker-dealers to disclose to all existing customers who have already signed arbitration clauses that they are not precluded by such clauses from bringing their claims in the federal courts.

State law generally has followed federal law with respect to the matter of arbitration. An arbitration agreement under state law will be enforced where the issues involve common law causes of action, such as negligence or breach of the fiduciary relationship. Still, the state courts follow *Wilko* v. *Swan* where the issues involve alleged violations of the federal securities laws and will not permit such claims to be arbitrated.

THE ARBITRATION PROCESS

At the present time, the rules of most exchanges and the NASD *permit* the arbitration of existing claims by investors against member brokers or their registered representatives, but generally *require* the arbitration of claims between members themselves (including claims between members and their registered representatives).

Voluntary arbitration offers both advantages and disadvantages to investors seeking redress for securities act violations. The investor who chooses to arbitrate gives up some important rights that are normally granted plaintiffs in securities litigation. These include the right to a jury trial, the surrender of discovery rights, and various other presumptions of law and allocations of burden of proof usually granted to investors in federal court litigation. An important consideration, of course, is the composition of the arbitration panel itself, which is usually securities-industry dominated and may thus be seen as inherently biased.

Still, there are some clear-cut advantages to arbitration from the plaintiff's standpoint. The proceedings are less formal than those of a courtroom and can be instituted and resolved fairly promptly. Because the plaintiff does not have to hire securities experts to explain to a jury how securities transactions are normally handled, the costs savings to the plaintiff can be enormous. Another plus is the fact that dilatory pretrial motions by attorneys that typify some of the worst aspects of civil litigation today are done away with entirely, along with other technical procedural devices that tend to delay or otherwise impede a fair hearing.

Finally, the scheduling and location of the arbitration proceeding is customarily made convenient to the parties, a major advantage for many litigants who resent having to forfeit time from their normal occupations while waiting for their cases to be called, juries to be selected, pretrial motions heard, and the like. Thus, many of the drawbacks associated with regular court proceedings simply do not occur with arbitration.

There is one area in which the choice of arbitration rather than litigation may offer a distinct advantage to a plaintiff. You will recall the earlier discussion of the trend of recent cases to deny an investor's claim for damages based upon his broker's violation of the suitability doctrine. By and large, unless the alleged violation is tantamount to fraud, and thus a direct violation of the securities acts, a claim for relief simply will not prevail. In an arbitration proceeding, however, a plaintiff may allege injury resulting from the broker's violation of the NASD's or a stock exchange's suitability rule, and the arbitration panel is not prevented from considering such violation as a basis for awarding damages.

To summarize, there may be distinct advantages for an investor to arbitrate rather than litigate an existing claim against a securities representative. Arbitration is cheaper and faster, making it particularly appropriate where the claim is small and the issues are simple. Probably its biggest drawback is the plaintiff's lack of access to the procedural weapon of discovery, which can be critically important where the plaintiff needs extensive records from the broker-defendant's files to prove his case. On the other hand, since arbitrators are not bound by the formal rules of evidence, they commonly allow the introduction of documentary evidence without formal authentication as long as it appears relevant and reliable.

Incidentally, it is common for arbitration tribunals to decide the case under consideration immediately following the open hearing. Although written decisions are required, often this consists of little more than a factual statement indicating which party prevailed. Occasionally, when the facts are complex and the issues not entirely clear, the parties may be requested to submit posthearing legal briefs that further amplify their positions.

From the planner-broker's point of view, arbitration almost always will be preferred to litigation. Emotional appeals to lay juries are eliminated, and the defendant can rely on the knowledge of arbitration panelists, some of whom will be industry experts, to weigh the facts intelligently, while not being bound by formal rules of evidence or being subjected to the tactics of trial lawyers who, to justify their fees, often place greater emphasis on legal technicalities than the circumstances of the case require.

FORMAL CIVIL LITIGATION

State Court Litigation

You will recall that, in enacting the Securities Act and the Exchange Act, Congress did not intend to preempt the field of securities regulation, and both of these statutes contain language expressly preserving "all other rights and remedies that may exist at law." Accordingly, a client who believes he has suffered loss as a result of a planner's acts or omissions, the usual grounds for a tort claim alleging negligence, may bring a lawsuit in state court to recover damages. In addition, a claim brought in state court may include allegations of fraud, breach of fiduciary relationships, breach of contract, and any other common law grounds for obtaining relief.

A state court suit may (and usually will) include violations of the state's blue-sky law, since all the state blue-sky laws make it unlawful to engage in fraud in the purchase or sale of securities, utilizing essentially the same language as in the federal laws. State court actions by private individuals may also include claims under the federal Securities Act, but plaintiffs seldom choose to do so. However, state courts do not have jurisdiction to hear claims asserting violations of Rule 10b-5 or specific provisions of the Exchange Act.

There may be special reasons for bringing suit in a state court rather than federal court. The ability to recover punitive damages is probably the strongest argument for this approach. Neither punitive damages nor attorneys' fees are allowed as a matter of course to prevailing parties in federal securities act cases, but generally are permitted by nearly all states whose blue-sky laws follow the Uniform Securities Act. Another possible reason for a plaintiff to sue in state court would be the clear-cut right to a jury trial and the possibility (at least in some states) of having the case heard sooner than if brought in a federal district court. Also, some sections of the federal acts require the plaintiff to prove "scienter" (actual knowledge on the part of the defendant), which may be difficult. And finally, in an action based on state law, the plaintiff may properly introduce in evidence specific NASD or stock exchange rules as the appropriate standard to be applied, which is not generally permissible in a federal court action.

Federal Court Litigation

The federal courts have exclusive jurisdiction over violations of the Exchange Act and concurrent jurisdiction with the state courts in actions alleging violations of the Securities Act. Where a complaint includes both federal and state law issues, the plaintiff may prefer to have the entire claim (including all state and federal issues) decided by a federal district court under the doctrine of pendent jurisdiction. This procedural doctrine provides that, when both federal and state claims arise from a common nucleus of operative facts, the federal court may decide the state claims if doing so would be in the interest of judicial economy, convenience, and fairness to the parties. Accepting such jurisdiction, however, is completely discretionary with the federal court. Where pendent jurisdiction is accepted, the federal court applies federal law in deciding the federal claims and state law in deciding the state claims, in accordance with the constitutional rule laid down in the landmark decision in *Erie Railroad* v. *Tompkins,* 304 U.S. 64 (1938).

There are a variety of legal grounds for bringing suit against a financial planner, as we have seen. Some are based on common law principles and others on alleged violations of specific sections of the securities acts. In adopting the federal securities laws, Congress recognized that private actions for damages could play an important role in bringing about compliance, and, indeed, such actions have been an important adjunct to the SEC's enforcement activities.

The following statutory provisions are the principal ones that provide remedies for aggrieved private investors:

- Section 12(1) of the Securities Act, which gives one who purchases a security sold in violation of the registration provisions a right to rescind the transaction or to recover damages if he has sold the security.

- Section 11 of the Securities Act, giving the purchaser of a security a cause of action against the issuer, the underwriters, and the distributors of offerings for false or misleading statements contained in the prospectus.

- Section 12(2) of the Securities Act, which is the general remedy for defrauded purchasers of securities against one who sold the plaintiff the security, participated in its sale, or controlled the seller of the security. The claim must allege false or misleading statements in connection with the sale of the security.

- Section 17(a) of the Securities Act, one of the general fraud provisions of the act, which makes it unlawful, in connection with the purchase or sale of securities, (1) to make an untrue statement of a material fact, (2) to make a statement that is misleading because of the omission of a material fact, (3) to employ any device, scheme, or artifice to defraud, or (4) to engage in any practice that operates as a fraud or deceit.

- Section 10(b) of the Exchange Act, which makes it unlawful in connection with the purchase or sale of any security, to use any manipulative or deceptive device or contrivance, as defined by SEC regulations. The SEC's Rule 10b-5, which implements this statutory provision, is discussed more fully later in this chapter.

- Section 14(a) of the Exchange Act, and SEC Rule 14a-9 issued thereunder, which makes it unlawful in connection with the solicitation of proxies (1) to make a false statement, (2) to make a statement that is misleading because of omission of a material fact, or (3) to fail to correct an earlier statement that has become false or misleading.

- Section 14(e) of the Exchange Act, which deals with fraudulent, deceptive, or manipulative acts or practices in connection with tender offers.

- Sections 15(c)(1) and (2) of the Exchange Act, and Rule 15c1-2 issued thereunder, relating to the activities of broker-dealers in effectuating the purchase or sale of securities. The statute and implementing rules prohibit the use of devices, contrivances, acts, and practices that are manipulative, deceptive, or otherwise fraudulent.

- Section 9 of the Exchange Act, which relates to the manipulation of listed securities.

Invoking the jurisdiction of the federal court is a simple matter of alleging and establishing the defendant's use of the mails or any other instrumentality of interstate commerce, either directly or indirectly, in connection with the securities transaction in question. In legal parlance this is often referred to as "invoking the jurisdictional means." Once the jurisdictional means has been established, the lawsuit can be brought in any federal judicial district in which the defendant is found, is an inhabitant, or transacts business. In addition, if a Securities Act violation is involved, it may be brought in the district in which the offer or sale took place; if an Exchange Act violation is involved, it may be brought in any district in which "any act or transaction constituting the violation occurred."

Bringing a claim in federal court has distinct advantages of its own. For one thing—and quite apart from any cause of action a client investor might have under express provisions of the federal securities acts—a whole body of law has grown up under section 10(b) of the Exchange Act and SEC Rule 10b-5 issued thereunder, which is generally helpful to a plaintiff. We turn now to a closer examination of this rule.

Implied private remedies under Rule 10b-5. Rule 10b-5 was

promulgated by the SEC in 1942 as a broad antifraud measure implementing section 10(b) of the Securities Exchange Act of 1934, 15 U.S.C. § 78j(b). Section 17(a) of the Securities Act of 1933, 15 U.S.C. § 77q(a), also outlaws fraudulent conduct but applies only to "the sale or offer for sale" of securities, while section 10(b) applies to "the purchase or sale" of securities, and thus is broader in scope. Taken as a whole, the various fraud provisions of the federal securities acts, even though part of a single statutory scheme, reflect considerable overlapping and duplication, mainly because they were enacted at different times.

Since its issuance in 1942, Rule 10b-5 has become the source of more disciplinary proceedings and civil litigation than any other provision of the federal securities laws. The rule reads as follows:

> It shall be unlawful for any person, directly or indirectly, by the use of any means or instrumentality of interstate commerce, or of the mails, or of any facility of any national securities exchange,
>
> (a) to employ any device, scheme, or artifice to defraud,
>
> (b) to make any untrue statement of a material fact or to omit to state a material fact necessary in order to make the statements made, in the light of the circumstances under which they were made, not misleading, or
>
> (c) to engage in any act, practice, or course of business which operates or would operate as a fraud or deceit upon any person, in connection with the purchase or sale of any security. [17 CFR Sec. 240.10b-5.]

Over the years, there never was much doubt that breaches of Rule 10b-5 could lead to SEC administrative sanctions or even criminal penalties. The law itself makes that clear. But neither section 10(b) of the Exchange Act nor Rule 10b-5 specifically authorize any private right of action by a person claiming to be injured by a violation thereof. Nevertheless, beginning with the landmark decision in *Kardon* v. *National Gypsum Co.*, 69 F.Supp. 512 (E.D. Pa. 1946), the vast majority of courts have recognized the right of a private litigant to bring an action for damages based on a violation of Rule 10b-5. *Kardon* involved a private claim for misrepresentations and omissions of the defendant in connection with the plaintiff's sale of securities to the defendant. Nearly all federal court cases decided after *Kardon* concurred in its finding of an implied private right of action under 10b-5, but it was not until 1971 that the Supreme Court formally recognized that holding in a brief footnote to *Superintendent of Insurance* v. *Bankers Life & Casualty Co.:* "It is now established that a private right of action is implied under section 10(b)" (404 U.S. 6, 13, note 9).

Various legal theories have been put forth in support of an implied private right of action under Rule 10b-5, but the most persuasive theory is based on the tort law doctrine which provides that a person injured by a violation of a statute enacted for his benefit is entitled to bring a civil suit for damages based on such violation. Few of the hundreds of cases decided since *Kardon* have even bothered to mention this legal issue. Significantly, the Supreme Court took a much more restrictive view of the implied liability concept in *Transamerica Mortgage Advisors, Inc.* v. *Lewis,* 444 U.S. 11 (1979), in which it denied the existence of a private right of action based on a violation of section 206, the antifraud provision of the Investment Advisers Act of 1940.

But 10b-5 continues to be the fraud remedy most private litigants prefer, and there is no indication it is likely to diminish in importance in the foreseeable future, notwithstanding increasing doubts about the full reach of the implied remedy doctrine brought about by the *Transamerica* decision.

Regardless of the legal basis for supporting a private right of action, the consequences are decidedly significant. For the financial planner, the most important consequence arises out of the 10b-5 prohibition against fraudulent conduct in the buying or selling of securities. Without question, registered broker-dealers and their registered representatives, as fiduciaries, are subject to rigorous 10b-5 liabilities. In addition, breaches of the rule can result in criminal penalties, court injunctions, and, of course, administrative sanctions. The liability of a securities representative to the SEC or NASD for violating Rule 10b-5 normally is established in an administrative disciplinary proceeding, as described in Chapter Five.

Broker-dealer liability. Broker-dealers, as we have seen, must conform to a wide variety of laws and regulations dealing with the purchase or sale of securities. These laws and regulations were designed to achieve a "high standard of business ethics in the securities industry," and both the SEC and the courts have tied the broker-dealer's legal responsibility to the very act of being in the securities business. The *shingle theory* was first enunciated by the SEC in a disciplinary proceeding in 1939, in which the Commission stated: "Inherent in the relationship between a [broker-]dealer and his customer is the vital representation that the customer will be dealt with fairly, and in accordance with the standards of the profession." Judicial approval of the shingle theory came in 1943, in the case of *Charles Hughes & Co.* v. *S.E.C.,* 139 F.2d 434 (2d Cir.).

By hanging out his shingle, a broker-dealer, on behalf of himself and his registered representatives, impliedly represents (among other things):

1. That he has an adequate basis for his securities recommendations.

2. That the securities he recommends are suitable for the individual client investor.

3. That he will make full disclosure of all necessary and material facts about a proposed investment.

4. That all prices charged for securities will be reasonably related to the market price.

5. That all commissions will be disclosed in advance.

6. That he will not excessively trade a client's account.

7. That he will not misappropriate the client's funds or do anything else to jeopardize the moneys under his control.

The shingle theory of responsibility has been applied by the SEC as well as the courts for many years. In addition, the more limited fiduciary theory of liability is also applicable. Early on, the SEC took the position that the relation of a securities dealer to his clients was not that of an ordinary merchant to his customers, but a position of special trust and confidence "approaching and perhaps even equaling that of a fiduciary." The courts have had little difficulty in finding a fiduciary relationship, as well. In *Hughes* v. *S.E.C.,* 174 F.2d 969 (D.C. Cir. 1949), a dealer who was also an investment adviser was accused of failing to disclose that she was not selling securities to her clients at the best price obtainable in the market. The appellate court affirmed the revocation of her broker's license on the ground that she had breached the fiduciary duty of trust and confidence. In its decision, the court held that the broker-dealer had the affirmative duty to disclose all conflicts of interest to her clients and the duty to act in their best interests at all times.

Limitations periods. Various limitations periods for bringing a lawsuit are set forth in the federal securities acts. In general, under section 13 of the Securities Act an action must be filed within one year after discovery of the facts giving rise to the claim, but in no event later than three years from the public offering or the sale in question.

Similar limitations appear in the Exchange Act in section 9(e), dealing with market manipulations, and section 18(c), dealing with false statements in required filings.

Where the lawsuit is based on an implied cause of action under SEC Rule 10b-5, there is no specific federal statute of limitations. In these cases, the courts will look to the state cause of action that most closely resembles the thrust of Rule 10b-5 and then apply the limitations provision applicable to that action. In most cases this means the state's blue-sky law limitations period or the limitations period applicable to common law fraud. These limitations periods generally are longer than the federal periods, in some cases as long as six years after the cause of action arose. While the courts are by no means in agreement on the issue, in most cases the limitations period for a Rule 10b-5 claim begins to run from the time the fraud, upon reasonable inquiry, should have been discovered. Reasonable inquiry means that the plaintiff must have exercised reasonable diligence in discovering the fraud. Clearly, where the defendant fraudulently conceals the underlying facts giving rise to a claim, the statute of limitations is tolled (i.e., the statutory period does not run during the period of concealment).

Right to a jury trial. Whether or not there is a right to a jury trial in an action against a financial planner in a federal district court will depend on the precise nature of the claim(s) asserted. The Seventh Amendment to the Constitution reads simply enough:

> In suits at common law, where the value in controversy shall exceed twenty dollars, the right of trial by jury shall be preserved, and no fact tried by a jury shall be otherwise examined in any Court of the United States than according to the rules of the common law.

Rule 38(a) of the Federal Rules of Civil Procedure provides "the right of trial by jury as declared by the Seventh Amendment to the Constitution . . . shall be preserved to the parties inviolate." Note, however, that the right to a jury trial is limited to "suits at common law," those that generally seek money damages for harms suffered. But there is no right to a jury trial in actions sounding in equity, that is, cases involving issues of fundamental fairness or moral obligation requiring special remedies other than money damages.

In the federal judicial system as it exists today, the distinction between actions at law and actions in equity have been eliminated for most purposes, *but not where the right to a jury trial is concerned.* Accordingly, there is no clear-cut right to a jury trial in a case involving the federal securities acts, since the relief sought by the plaintiff may be traceable to a traditional equitable remedy, such as restitution—the disgorgement of "ill-gotten gains," in the words of one court—rather than money damages, as in a typical negligence action.

About the most one can say with certainty is that, when both legal and equitable issues are presented (by either side) in a case, the Supreme Court has held that the basic nature of the underlying claims is determinative. Thus, if the action involves traditional common law claims such as negligence or breach of contract, the plaintiff is entitled to a jury trial, notwithstanding the equitable nature of the proceeding [*Ross* v. *Bernhard*, 396 U.S. 531 (1976)].

Measure of damages. Where the plaintiff brings an action seeking relief under one of the express remedies in the securities laws, the measure of damages is prescribed by the appropriate statutory provision. For example, in a suit seeking damages for fraud in violation of the Exchange Act, section 28(a) thereof limits the relief to "actual damages on account of the act complained of." The courts have held that "actual damages" means "compensatory damages," whether the measure of those damages be out-of-pocket loss, the benefit of the bargain, or some other appropriate standard.

A plaintiff cannot recover more than his "net economic loss," however, and sometimes making this determination is far from easy. A recently decided case in the 2nd judicial circuit raised the question whether, in an action alleging fraud in a tax shelter investment, the plaintiff's recovery must be reduced by the tax benefits he had already received. In a well-reasoned opinion, the court commented,

> Even assuming that the investor's ultimate goal is to realize a gain from an income-producing business (either through sale or income), the intervening tax benefits to the [limited] partner represents an important tangible economic advantage expected to be derived from his investment regardless whether the venture eventually operates at a profit.

The court then concluded,

> To the extent that plaintiffs invested in a tax shelter, all benefits they received from their investment, including tax benefits, would have to be deducted in calculating the recissionary damages, if any, to which

they would be entitled. [*Salcer v. Envicon Equities Corp.*, 744 F.2d 935 (2d Cir. 1984).]

When the plaintiff's claim is based on a Rule 10b-5 violation, he can either rescind the transaction or recover out-of-pocket losses based on the difference between what he paid for the security and its real value, together with interest.

A multitude of other special damages rules apply to securities cases, and it would serve no useful purpose to detail them all. It should be noted, however, that only in claims under sections 11 and 12 of the Securities Act does the court have discretion to award costs and attorneys' fees to the winning party. Such costs and fees are not allowed in 10b-5 cases.

Civil suits under RICO.

There is one other potential basis for a civil suit against a financial planner besides those already mentioned. The Racketeer Influenced and Corrupt Organizations Act of 1970 (RICO), 18 U.S.C. sections 1961–1968, was passed by Congress ostensibly to limit the ability of organized crime syndicates to enter into legitimate business enterprises. The statute as enacted, however, is considerably broader in scope and contains provisions permitting civil actions to be brought by injured parties apart from its more obvious criminal provisions. Thus, even though on the surface it does not appear to constitute a likely basis for suing a financial planner, there are circumstances under which a planner-broker theoretically could be held liable under RICO's civil provisions.

Section 1962 of the act sets forth a variety of prohibited activities, all of which are tied to some type of "enterprise" engaged in a "pattern of racketeering activity." "Racketeering activity" under RICO includes such offenses as extortion, kidnapping, arson, bribery, and gambling, not exactly the type of activities likely to involve financial planners. However, "fraud in the sale of securities" is also on the list, and if a plaintiff believes he has been "injured in his business or property by reason of a violation of" any of the operative provisions of the act (i.e., the criminal RICO provisions), he can bring a civil RICO claim. Moreover, if he can prove his case, the statute permits him to recover treble damages as well as his attorney's fees—far more than the simple compensatory damages allowable when bringing claims under the federal securities acts. For this reason, RICO has generated an explosion of civil cases in the past several years, including many in the securities fraud area, and it may in time prove to be a more important source of civil litigation than the express and implied remedies under the Securities Act and the Exchange Act.

To state a civil claim for damages under RICO, a plaintiff must allege that the defendant violated one of the "predicate offenses" under RICO's criminal provisions, "fraud in the sale of securities" being one of the listed offenses. To prevail, the plaintiff must show that the defendant has participated in an enterprise that has been engaged in a "pattern of racketeering activity. . . ." Despite the crime syndicate implications of this language, most courts have refused to restrict civil RICO claims only to defendants who have ties to organized crime, based on their interpretation of the language of the statute as well as its legislative history. Accordingly, a number of courts have held that merely proving two separate but related acts of fraud in the sale of securities within a 10-year period is sufficient to satisfy the statute. A case of major importance, *Schacht* v. *Brown,* 711 F.2d 1343 (7th Cir. 1983), went even further and ruled that civil RICO claims are applicable to the most commonplace or "garden variety" fraud.

But a later case, *Sedima* v. *Imrex Company, Inc.,* 741 F.2d 482 (2d Cir. 1984) came to the opposite conclusion, holding that the plaintiff in a civil RICO case must allege and prove *actual criminal convictions* of the underlying predicate offenses. To resolve direct conflicts on this issue between a number of lower courts, *Sedima* was accepted for review by the Supreme Court. In a major defeat for the securities industry, the court rejected the *Sedima* argument, based on its analysis of the statutory language and the legislative history of the act. [53 *Law Week* 5034, July 1, 1985]. Thus, civil RICO claims continue to represent a clear litigation threat to financial planners.

KEY POINTS TO REMEMBER

1. It is important for a financial planner to have a general idea of the procedural issues involved in litigation, since they can significantly affect the outcome of a case.

2. The securities industry has long favored arbitration of claims against brokers and broker-dealers, rather than litigation of such claims. For years, all customer contracts with brokers have had mandatory arbitration clauses.

3. In 1953, the Supreme Court ruled that a signed agreement to arbitrate future disputes is unenforceable, but later decisions have strengthened the view that voluntary agreements to arbitrate existing claims are still legally valid and enforceable.

4. SEC Rule 15c2-2 now prohibits the inclusion in customer agreements of any clause requiring the arbitration of future disputes.

5. State law has generally followed federal law on the issue of arbitration.

6. Voluntary arbitration offers advantages as well as disadvantages to persons with claims against securities personnel. The rights forfeited under arbitration include the right to a jury trial, the surrender of discovery rights, and important evidentiary rules regarding the burden of proof. The advantages include a quicker decision with less legal fuss and expense, conducted in an informal setting.

7. One big advantage of arbitration is the plaintiff's right to assert in an arbitration claim the violation of NASD or exchange rules and receive damages based thereon.

8. A claimant may choose to bring a claim against a planner-broker in state court, and in such state court action he can claim all the usual grounds for seeking relief, including negligence, breach of fiduciary duty, breach of contract, as well as violations of state blue-sky laws.

9. State courts have jurisdiction to hear federal Securities Act claims, but have no jurisdiction to hear claims under Rule 10b-5 or any provisions of the federal Exchange Act.

10. In lawsuits brought under the securities laws, punitive damages are recoverable in a state court action, but not in a federal court action.

11. Where a plaintiff has alleged both state law and federal law issues in a suit brought in federal court, the court has pendent jurisdiction, meaning it has the authority to decide the state claims as well as the federal ones in the interest of judicial fairness and economy.

12. Many sections of the federal securities acts give plaintiffs express remedies for violations by securities personnel and investment advisers. A number of these remedies overlap and duplicate one another.

13. No claim can be brought under the federal securities laws unless and until the plaintiff alleges the defendant's use of jurisdictional means, which means he has used the mails, telephone, or other instrumentality of interstate commerce to perpetuate the fraud or other violation in question.

14. SEC Rule 10b-5 is the most litigated provision of the federal securities laws. It is a general antifraud rule that, if violated and the violation causes harm to a person, entitles the latter to bring a private legal action for money damages, even though the rule contains no express language to that effect.

15. Financial planner-brokers are subject to rigorous 10b-5 liabilities and may suffer everything from disciplinary sanctions to criminal prosecution for 10b-5 violations.

16. If anything, the broker-dealer's liability under 10b-5 is even greater, because of the shingle theory of liability, which makes the broker-dealer responsible for exercising the highest degree of business ethics in all dealings with investor-clients.

17. The usual statute of limitations in a federal securities act case is one year after discovery of the facts giving rise to the claim, but in no event later than three years after discovery.

18. There is no express statute of limitations in 10b-5 cases, so the courts look to the applicable state law for guidance in that respect.

19. While the right to a jury trial as stated in the seventh amendment to the U.S. Constitution is still preserved, it is limited to suits demanding money damages. There is no absolute right to a jury trial where the claim is one seeking equitable relief, such as restitution.

20. In most federal actions under the securities laws the measure of damages is limited to actual or compensatory damages. In calculating the actual damage, courts take into consideration (and deduct) all benefits a plaintiff has already received, including all tax benefits. There is no right to recover punitive damages in the federal courts.

21. It is theoretically possible for a planner to be sued for securities fraud under the civil provisions of RICO (Racketeer Influenced and Corrupt Organizations Act) if he has been found guilty of two securities fraud violations within the past ten years. The plaintiff in such a suit is entitled to treble damages as well as attorneys' fees.

SELECTED REFERENCES

Statutes

Federal Arbitration Act, 9 U.S.C. §§ 1–14.

Limitations Periods, 15 U.S.C. §§ 77m; 78i; 78r.

General Litigation Considerations

Shearer, W. B., and Erkiletian, M. K., "Humbled Offerings," *Financial Planning*, vol. 14, no. 2, 194 (February 1985).

Robinson, R., "Litigation against Securities Brokers," *Litigation*, vol. 7, no. 4, 37 (Summer 1981).

Arbitration of Investor Claims

Malena et al. v. *Merrill, Lynch, Pierce, Fenner & Smith, Inc.*, ¶ 91,492, *CCH Federal Securities Law Reporter* (April 18, 1984).

Coenen v. *R. W. Pressprich & Co.,* 433 F.2d 367 (5th Cir. 1972).

See generally, Zepfel, R., "Arbitration of Investor-Broker Disputes," 65 *Cal. L. Rev.* 120 (1977).

Broker-Dealer Arbitration Clauses Now Prohibited

Exchange Act Release No. 20397 (Nov. 1983).

State Law Arbitration

Kavit v. *A. L. Stamm & Co.,* 491 F.2d 1176 (2d Cir. 1974).

Prima Paint Corp. v. *Flood & Conklin Mfg. Co.,* 388 U.S. 395 (1967).

Implied Remedies under Rule 10b-5

J. I. Case Co. v. *Borak,* 377 U.S. 426 (1964).

Mitchell v. *Texas Gulf Sulphur Co.,* 446 F.2d 90 (10th Cir. 1971).

See generally, Annotation, *Civil Action by Private Person under Sec. 10(b) of Securities Exchange Act,* 37 ALR 2d 649.

Jacobs, A., *Litigation and Practice under Rule 10b-5,* 2d ed. (Clark, Boardman Company, New York, 1981).

Doctrine of Pendent Jurisdiction

Prakash v. *American University,* 727 F.2d 1174 (C.A.D.C. 1984).

Financial General Bankshares, Inc. v. *Metzger,* 680 F.2d 768 (C.A.D.C. 1982).

See generally, Lowenfels, L., "Pendent Jurisdiction and the Federal Securities Acts," 67 *Colum. L. Rev.* 474 (1967).

Statutes of Limitations

Vigman v. *Community National Bank & Trust Co.,* 635 F.2d 455 (5th Cir. 1981).

Wachovia Bank & Trust Co. v. *National Student Marketing Corp.,* 650 F.2d 342 (D.C.Cir. 1980).

Vanderboom v. *Sexton,* 442 F.2d 1233 (8th Cir. 1970).

Right to a Jury Trial

In re U.S. Financial Securities Litigation, 609 F.2d 411 (9th Cir. 1979).

S.E.C. v. *Commonwealth Chemical Securities, Inc.,* 574 F.2d 90 (2d Cir. 1978).

Johns Hopkins University v. *Hutton,* 326 F.Supp. 250 (D. Md. 1971).

Damages Recoverable in Securities Cases

Petrites v. *J. C. Bradford & Co.,* 646 F.2d 1033 (5th Cir. 1981).

Young v. *Taylor,* 466 F.2d 1329 (10th Cir. 1972).

Globus v. *Law Research Services, Inc.,* 418 F.2d 1276 (2d Cir. 1969).

See generally, Note, "Rule 10b-5 Damage Computation: Application of Financial Theory to Determine Net Economic Loss," 51 *Fordham L. Rev.* 838 (Apr. 1983).

Claims under Civil RICO

Yancoski v. *E. F. Hutton & Co.,* 581 F.Supp. 88 (D.C.Pa. 1983).

Mauriber v. *Shearson/American Express,* 567 F.Supp. 1231 (D.C.N.Y. 1983).

Miller, S., and Olson, K., "The Expanding Uses of Civil RICO," *California Lawyer,* vol. 4, no. 6, 12 (June 1984).

chapter eight

Professional Liability Claims Prevention

THE NEED FOR A CLAIMS PREVENTION STRATEGY

The typical financial planner who is caught up in the throes of everyday practice is not likely to give much thought to professional liability (malpractice) claims prevention, let alone have a conscious strategy for avoiding professional liability claims. Few planners seem to be risk management oriented when it comes to their own practices, even though advising clients about the benefits of risk management is one of the planner's important functions. Whatever the reasons for this indifference, the failure to plan and implement a specific claims-avoidance strategy could prove costly from a number of vantage points.

To begin with, the planner who is unlucky enough to be the target of a malpractice suit, whether justified or not, will find that life will never be quite the same thereafter. The mere fact that someone has filed a malpractice suit is traumatic in itself, since it necessarily represents an attack on the planner's judgment, ability, and integrity. The financial planner challenged in this manner is bound to be affected psychologically, and during the entire time the case is pending will probably experience considerable mental anguish, loss of sleep, and increased nervous tension. In addition, there will be more psychological stress and loss of valuable time while giving depositions and testifying at the trial itself. Once the case is concluded, the planner may be required to pay damages to the plaintiff out of his own financial resources, unless he has adequate professional liability insurance to cover all the damages awarded. Finally, the stigma of having been sued is likely to remain long after the case has been concluded, even if the planner is totally exonerated.

Thus, there are a great many personal reasons why a financial planner should take malpractice claims prevention seriously, but there are important professional reasons, as well. Conscious efforts to minimize the likelihood of a malpractice claim necessarily involve giving the utmost attention to proper ethical conduct and meeting all legal responsibilities. This can only result in providing higher-quality service to your clients in all aspects of the planning process.

CAUSES OF MALPRACTICE LITIGATION

Essential to any structured program of malpractice claims prevention is a basic understanding of the principal factors that are likely to influence malpractice litigation against planners. Some of these are directly related to the quality of professional services rendered, while others are indirect influences of a sociological nature. The more significant of these factors are discussed next.

Indirect or Sociological Factors

A major influence on malpractice litigation is the increasing public interest in new financial products and services brought about by deregulation of the banking industry, major changes in the tax laws, and the ever-present fear of inflation. Many of these factors were outlined in Chapter One, where it was pointed out that the more informed the public becomes about financial planning and financial planners, the more likely it will resort to litigation when anticipated financial profits or gains do not materialize.

Over the last several years vast numbers of persons, attracted to the financial services field by the lure of large incomes, have presented themselves to the public as professional financial planners. Many are and have the credentials to prove it; others are little more than product hucksters seeking to maximize their incomes at the expense of uninformed investors. How is the public to know the difference? The typical investor is hardly in a position to judge the competence, let alone the ethics, of all who call themselves financial planners. Since the financial planning profession, as such, is not as yet regulated by any governmental authority, it only stands to reason that the derelictions of a certain percentage of so-called planners inevitably will stimulate malpractice claims and litigation.

From a sociological standpoint, the impetus to sue is already there. In our increasingly consumer-oriented society, a growing number of persons may be classified as *suit conscious,* meaning they are not the least bit hesitant about turning to the courts for redress of grievances of all kinds. Whether or not your client is among those who fit this description is something you will never know for sure, but you should be aware of this tendency in the populace as a whole. We have become a sue-happy nation, and providers of professional services are now considered fair game whenever their acts or omissions lead to losses that their clients believe are unwarranted and should have been prevented.

There is little doubt that the daily and financial press have contributed to the problem by publicizing egregious examples of fraudulent conduct by securities brokers and suggesting that litigation may be the most effective means of recouping the losses suffered at their hands. Nationally syndicated financial writer Dan Dorfman devoted an entire column ("Complaints about Brokers Are Beginning to Increase," *Peninsula Times Tribune,* Palo Alto, CA., C-9, December 25, 1983) based on the increasing volume of mail he had been receiving from investors decrying the "touty, questionable and at times downright unethical broker practices." Dorfman noted that growing numbers of them complained they were "tired of being ripped off and tired of playing patsy." The article cited numerous instances in which aggrieved investors filed claims to recover damages from fraudulent, unethical, or negligent securities brokers.

In a similar vein, an article by Jane Bryant Quinn in *Woman's Day* magazine in September 1984, entitled "Don't Believe Everything Your Broker Tells You," advised its readers:

> If you think you've been burned, you can take your case to arbitration at any of the major stock exchanges. . . . If you hope to recover a lot of money, take a lawyer with you; the broker will certainly have one. For large sums of money, consider a lawsuit.

Unquestionably, articles like these by such well-known financial writers tend to encourage investors to consider suing when they sustain losses at the hands of brokers or investment advisers. The increasing public awareness that financial planners and investment advisers not only make mistakes but sometimes are sued for damages has made consumers generally more sophisticated and better informed concerning malpractice litigation as a potential weapon against them. As we shall see, however, even when the client has a reasonable legal basis for a claim, malpractice litigation is not the inevitable result. Usually, there are other circumstances of a psychological nature that help tip the scales in that direction.

A final factor relating to the stimulus to sue should be mentioned. Suits involving losses sustained in securities transactions require the skills of trial lawyers who understand and specialize in securities litigation. At the moment, relatively few lawyers are experts in this area of law, but it is only reasonable to expect that more trial lawyers will acquire the knowledge and develop the skills necessary to become proficient in the handling of these cases. When this happens, there is little doubt that more malpractice cases against financial advisers will be instituted, and the publicizing of those cases will further stimulate litigation of this nature. Financial planners as a class thus far have had relatively little adverse publicity from the litigation standpoint, but all signs point to the fact that the honeymoon period is fast drawing to a close.

Direct, Professional Factors

Malpractice suits don't just happen; they are triggered by some negative financial outcome that focuses the client's thinking on ways to recoup his losses, and that invariably stirs thoughts about the possibility of bringing a malpractice claim. Chapter Six outlined the principal grounds for asserting malpractice claims against financial planners, some of which are securities oriented and others not. It was pointed out that financial planners can find themselves the targets of malpractice litigation in dozens of ways that extend beyond the liabilities of the typical stockbroker. This is because of the nature of the financial planning process itself, with its emphasis on the technical complexities associated with data gathering, data analysis, plan preparation, and plan implementation.

Suffice to say, there are many potential legal booby traps facing the financial planner in his daily professional activities, and he must be on the alert constantly to avoid making the types of errors that may later force him to defend his actions in court. In the material that follows, the major problem areas are reviewed and specific techniques for avoiding malpractice claims are suggested.

PREVENTION OF MALPRACTICE CLAIMS

Human Relations Aspects

A good planner will never underestimate the importance of the interpersonal aspects of the planner-client relationship. Not only will this result in more harmonious relations with clients, but it is likely to be a critical factor in warding off potential malpractice claims. Success or failure in the management of the planner-client relationship is dependent in large part upon the interplay between the planner's personality and the client's personality throughout the entire period of the relationship. As a general proposition, the more reasonable and mature both planner and client are, the less likely a malpractice suit will follow when the client has experienced a significant financial loss or some other unfortunate consequence. And, of course, the converse is equally true.

Ordinarily, too little attention is devoted to the human relations aspects of financial planning, with a resultant failure on the part of planners to recognize the need of many clients for psychological and emotional support in addition to the financial advice and assistance they require. It therefore behooves all planners to acquire a basic understanding of the psychological aspects of client behavior as an important risk-management tool.

Understanding the suit-prone personality. Studies have
shown that there is a type of person with specific personality characteristics who is more likely than others to bring a lawsuit when something goes wrong in the rendering of professional services. The hallmark of the suit-prone individual is his basic immaturity, a characteristic that is reflected in all aspects of his life but is greatly magnified when dealing with professionals, about whom he has decidedly ambivalent feelings. This person generally refuses to take personal responsibility for his own actions and is excessively dependent on others. He is the one most likely to say to you, "Whatever you decide is fine with me," or "You're the expert," but you will fast become his prime litigation target when disappointment is encountered, especially where his finances are concerned.

The type of person who fits the suit-prone personality exhibits emotional attitudes that provide fertile soil for the growth of resentment and dissatisfaction. Notwithstanding his professed faith in professionals, he instinctively mistrusts them, but insists that they measure up to his unrealistic goals and expectations. When these are not met, he is quick to fix blame, and this often takes the form of formal litigation. Recognizing the suit-prone individual, therefore, and making allowance for his special emotional needs can play an important part in reducing your chances of being sued by persons with these negative personality traits.

Minimizing client dissatisfaction. A malpractice suit against a professional planner usually reflects not only the client's disappointment, but his anger—for things done or said quite apart from the alleged negligent conduct. So, paying attention to the client's psychological and emotional needs can pay big dividends in more ways than one.

Intelligent management of the planner-client relationship not only requires a sensitivity to the client's expressed needs, but the ability to recognize his possible hidden motives, antagonisms, and unrealistic expectations. There is no more effective preventive measure than the establishment and maintenance of a friendly and respectful working relationship with the client. This requires viewing him as an individual, someone with highly individualized goals, aspirations, and needs. Listen carefully to what he says and how he says it. Active listening is the conscious attempt to understand both the content and the feeling another person expresses. Make an effort to become proficient in interpreting body language, facial expressions, and tone of voice as clues to what he really is thinking. If the client feels that you truly understand his situation, that you have listened to his concerns, he will develop an emotional rapport with you that will foster trust, confidence, and respect.

Several positive steps should be taken to minimize misunderstandings that might lead to later disappointment. First, *never* build up the client's expectations by making promises of future investment performance. Such promises are patently false and making them will not only get you in hot water with the client, but with the NASD as well. Second, keep the client informed, and make sure he understands. When talking to clients, many professionals have the unfortunate habit of using words and concepts that are so technical that it is difficult for the client to comprehend what is being explained. Not only does this impede true communication, it can foster great resentment on the part of the client, particularly the client who is too embarrassed to admit he does not understand what the planner is saying.

Here, again, the wise planner will be alert to his client's vocabulary and speech pattern, using them as a guide to his own language usage, tempo, and tone. You should frequently ask the client, ''Have I made that clear enough for you?'' or ''Would you like me to run over that concept again?'' Body language is also important, and as soon as the client shows tell-tale signs of confusion or nonreceptivity—a blank stare, excessive head-scratching, or other repetitive or inappropriate gestures—you know that there is a gap between what you are attempting to explain and what is being understood. Don't let it happen. Develop the necessary interpersonal skills to motivate clients to communicate freely with you. Seminars are often given on this subject.

Keeping the client informed means just that. It is your legal responsibility to keep the client abreast of significant changes in tax laws and other matters that might directly affect his financial goals and needs. Sometimes this means discussing unfavorable circumstances pertaining to an existing investment. Clients are generally aware when the stock market is down and their investments are declining in value, but they expect you to discuss these matters with them frankly and, if appropriate, to make suggestions about alternative investments. *It is precisely when investments do not perform as anticipated that the client needs you the most.* This is not the time to enshroud yourself in mystical silence.

To summarize, an effective claims prevention program requires, first and foremost, constant attention to the human relations aspects of your practice. Get to know the client as an individual and develop emotional rapport with him. Be sensitive to his special psychological needs, to the extent they are discernible. Avoid making overoptimistic projections concerning investment yields or potential profits, and *never* guarantee any yield or profit. Keep the client informed on a continuing basis, and do not hesitate to discuss unfavorable progress. A client is far less likely to turn against the planner who has dealt with him openly and honestly throughout the relationship, even if his investments do not perform as expected.

Specific Liability-avoidance Measures

Human relations matters are extremely important, but even the most vengeful client cannot bring a malpractice suit unless he can prove to a court or jury that you were negligent in some aspect of financial planning or violated a specific statute or regulation. Outlined next are the principal areas of financial planning practice that require your special attention.

Fiduciary responsibilities. Every aspect of your handling of securities transactions and giving investment advice must be carried out with scrupulous attention to all legal requirements, and one of the most important of these requirements is your fiduciary obligation to your client. This is not a requirement to be taken lightly, for alleged breach of fiduciary duty is likely to be one of the major grounds for seeking damages in suits against planners in the years ahead. Fiduciaries are held to the highest standards of ethical conduct, and their acts are evaluated with a strict eye for overall fairness.

Pared to its essentials, a fiduciary relationship is one in which complete trust and confidence is reposed by one person in the fidelity and integrity of another. As a fiduciary, you must always deal fairly and in good faith with your client, showing paramount regard for his interests, not your own. The most common circumstances in which a charge of breach of fiduciary duty is likely to prevail will occur when the planner-broker has engaged in some form of self-dealing amounting to a direct conflict of interest.

Self-dealing can take many forms, and it would not be practical to mention all of them here. Clearly, it would be a violation of your fiduciary duty to recommend an investment that is not suitable for your client simply because the commission thereon is greater than on some other (and legally suitable) investment. There may be instances in which, for example, recommending a well-managed no-load mutual fund meeting the client's overall financial needs and objectives would be more in his interests than recommending a load fund with the same general objectives.

Another example: Let us assume the client's circumstances indicate the need for fixed income and a high degree of liquidity, but you recommend instead a nonliquid, variable-income real estate limited partnership because it affords a much higher sales commission. This would be a clear-cut breach of fiduciary duty that would be indefensible in a court action or an NASD or SEC disciplinary proceeding.

The basic liability-avoidance rule is simple. Never permit your personal financial interests to outweigh the interests of your client. In making each investment recommendation, ask yourself: Am I making this recommendation on its merits, or is the existence or amount of my commission an overriding factor in the making of this recommendation? If the predominant reason is the commission, then you are violating your fiduciary obligation to your client in recommending such investment.

Closely tied to the commission issue is the matter of bonuses and gratuities offered by product sponsors as sales incentives. You cannot possibly recommend to a client a security that affords you a cash bonus or gift without laying yourself wide open to a charge of self-dealing and breach of your fiduciary responsibility. Even if the particular investment is clearly appropriate for the client, you risk being accused of having a conflict of interest. Your only proper course of action is to discuss the matter openly with your client and point out that the sales contest raises a potential conflict of interest. If the client wishes to proceed after being so informed, so much the better, but be sure to make a record of the discussion and place it in the client's file.

Disclose all material facts. You have a legal duty to disclose all relevant and material information about each investment you recommend to a client. This is both an offshoot of your common law fiduciary responsibility to act in your client's best interests as well as a statutory requirement under section 10(b) of the Exchange Act and SEC Rule 10b-5.

Never take shortcuts in disclosing the important aspects of recommended investments. The investor is entitled by law to the fullest possible disclosure. An integral aspect of "informing" a client is making sure he understands what you are saying. The amount of detail you should provide will vary with the client's age, education, and prior experience in investing. The less sophisticated he is, the more time you must spend in explaining what the investment entails. Pro forma disclosure, such as simply handing the prospectus to the client without further explanation, is not the type of disclosure contemplated by the securities laws or the NASD.

On the other hand, the importance of the prospectus should not be minimized. Always furnish one, as required by law, and obtain a prospectus receipt as evidence of having done so. Never mark up a prospectus so as to highlight an investment's favorable points; in fact, it is best not to mark it at all. Most direct participation programs include sales literature designated "For Broker-Dealer Use Only." You should never display this material or any due diligence material to the client, let alone leave it with him. To do so is a direct violation of both federal and state securities acts.

SEC Rule 10b-5 makes it unlawful, among other things, to use sales literature that is materially misleading in connection with the sale of securities. The NASD has implemented this legal prohibition in its own Rules of Fair Practice, section 35 of which deals at length with communications by broker-dealers (and their registered representatives) with the public. Among other things, section 35 provides that, in discussing securities with prospective investors, "no material fact or qualification may be omitted if the omission, in the light of the context of the material presented, would cause the advertising or sales literature to be misleading." That section defines the term *sales literature* as including any written communication to customers or the public, with specific reference to circulars, research reports, market letters, performance reports or summaries, form letters, standard forms of options worksheets, seminar texts, and reprints or excerpts of any other advertisement, sales literature, or published article.

Section 35 lays down very strict guidelines governing the conduct of broker-dealers and their representatives in providing sales literature that makes investment comparisons or otherwise promotes one investment over another. The reason for the NASD's concern is obvious. A statement made in one context may be misleading even though appropriate in another context. Comparisons of investment results are particularly troublesome, since they often omit material facts and information necessary to make the comparisons accurate and fair.

As a financial planner, your best litigation-avoidance strategy is to *refrain from providing clients with any extraneous notes or comments in writing as a matter of standard practice.* The opportunities to mislead are simply too great, and in any event all such written comments are considered sales literature in the eyes of the NASD and therefore can get you in trouble unless properly cleared. Your safest course of action is to talk about proposed investments generically and conceptually, leaving the details to the official prospectus. If you feel compelled to furnish supplementary information about an investment, make sure it gets prior approval by a registered principal of your broker-dealer (usually the person heading the office of supervisory jurisdiction, OSJ, or that person's designee). Then make sure you keep a copy of what you provided in the client's file, along with any other observations concerning your discussion of this investment with him.

Never misrepresent the facts. To misrepresent is to give a false representation about something, and when done knowingly and for the purpose of inducing the sale of a security, constitutes a violation of the securities laws as well as grounds for a common law action in deceit. Exaggeration, hyperbole, and embellishment may be par for the course in television advertising, the selling of used cars, and in virtually every aspect of the entertainment industry, but they have no place in the securities field. As the Supreme Court observed, the purpose of the securities acts was "to achieve a high standard of business ethics in the securities industry," and a vast number of SEC and NASD disciplinary actions, as well as private lawsuits, against fraudulent and unethical securities brokers has reinforced that position.

Misrepresentation has no place in the practice of any profession and should be guarded against by all who consider themselves ethical financial planners. The temptation to misrepresent is most likely to occur during the course of explaining the characteristics of a recommended investment. In expressing his enthusiasm for a particular investment, a planner may unintentionally overemphasize its expected benefits by exaggerating the anticipated yield, its tax benefits, or its overall investment potential, while minimizing (or not even mentioning) its downside risks. Even if you presently own the investment in question or plan to purchase an interest in it, resist the temptation to mention that to the client as a selling point. Being a professional requires conducting yourself like one.

By the same token, avoid using the word "guaranteed" in any presentation about a proposed investment. It should be clear by now that nothing can ever really be guaranteed in the investment world and to imply that this is possible is the worst form of misrepresentation. Incidentally, giving a guarantee is also a direct violation of Article III, Section 19(e) of the NASD Rules of Fair Practice. *Make a pact with yourself never to use the word "guaranteed" when discussing investments with clients.* In fact, it would be even better to point out that no investment yield or profit can ever be guaranteed. Make sure the client understands this clearly and then record the fact that you specifically brought this to his attention.

One of the best ways to avoid problems in discussing proposed investments with clients is to prepare a simple investment disclosure checklist and use it as a guide in covering all key points. Such a checklist should prompt discussion of the general risks of investing (e.g., the effect of bull and bear markets, interest rates, inflation), the specific risks associated with the investment being proposed (e.g., industry trends, competition, regulation), possible tax benefits, and a discussion regarding the inability to guarantee any investment yield, profit, cash distribution, or capital appreciation. An investment disclosure checklist of this nature can also be used as an aid in determining the client's suitability for the investment in question. More about this in the discussion that follows.

Recommend only suitable investments. It is your legal responsibility as a financial planner, investment adviser, and fiduciary to consider the specific financial needs and goals of each investor when making investment recommendations. This is one area in which your claim to be a true financial professional can be demonstrated most clearly.

To arrive at a conclusion about investment suitability, you must make two separate, though related, factual determinations. First, you must make a reasonable inquiry about the investor's personal financial needs and circumstances, especially the degree of risk he is able and willing to assume. As a financial planner, you will normally be in a position to make that determination based on the documentary and personal data furnished by the client during the initial interview or within a reasonable time thereafter. In those rare instances where a person refuses to divulge the information necessary to make a proper suitability determination, you have a serious problem—one that is probably best resolved by rejecting the individual as a client altogether. An individual who will not level with you—his own professional adviser—right from the outset is not worthy of your time or attention.

Second, you must at least know enough about the recommended investment itself to have a reasonable basis for recommending it. That calls for a mini due diligence inquiry that goes beyond blind reliance on self-serving statements made in the issuer's prospectus or accompanying sales literature. Incidentally, the mere fact that your broker-dealer has approved the legality of the investment and has a sales agreement with the product sponsor does not necessarily make it an appropriate investment for your client. The SEC has held that even statements made by superiors in a brokerage firm are not an adequate basis for representations made by securities representatives to clients. As a financial planner and securities representative, you are obligated to make an independent investigation to ensure that all representations about a security have a reasonable basis *in fact.*

Take a real estate limited partnership as an example. Before recommending such a partnership, it is your professional responsibility to assess all the key factors about the proposed investment. That includes evaluating the expertise and continuity of the partnership's management, assessing its track record, its fee structure, its front-end costs, the percentage of your client's investment that will be "in ground," and the partnership's liquidation fees. One way to handle this task is to do it entirely on your own; another is to join forces with other financial planners for the purpose of engaging in joint due diligence discussions on specific investment products. The latter approach makes a lot of sense, not only because there is safety in numbers, but because a group setting is ideal for keeping abreast of the thinking of your peers on specific areas of investment, as well as gaining a broader perspective on the general economy and economic trends.

Avoiding litigation based on alleged investment unsuitability calls for a combination of skills. On the fact-finding level, as just noted, you must become proficient in learning the true merits and drawbacks of each investment you intend to recommend. This includes investigating its degree of speculativeness, its ability to produce income, and its chances for capital appreciation. If the client's concern is for specific tax relief, then you must inquire into that aspect of the security as well. On the human relations level, you must do several things. Most important, you must really "get to know" your client so that you clearly understand his honest-to-goodness investment objectives. Never impose your own approach to investing on the client (e.g., don't talk about your own investment portfolio), and make appropriate allowance for the client's personal philosophy, degree of investment sophistication, and general risk threshold.

Defending a case alleging investment unsuitability is likely to boil down to the client's word versus yours. Protect yourself with careful documentation, and to assist you in this process, consider using an investor-suitability checklist along with the investment disclosure checklist mentioned earlier. The suitability checklist should prompt your consideration of the following questions:

1. Does the client meet the investment's stated financial suitability standards?

2. Are the client's overall financial objectives compatible with the investment?

3. Is the client sophisticated enough to truly comprehend the risks as well as the benefits of the investment?

4. Does the investment fall within the client's specific risk threshold?

5. Taking all the preceding into consideration, is this the right investment (i.e., is it legally "suitable") for this client?

As every financial planner knows, clients have widely varying investment goals. Some who are in their retirement years may seek safety of principal and current income; others who are still in their working years may seek only long-term capital growth; still others may need investments with tax advantages; and, of course, some clients will need various combinations of these. It is your job as a planner to help each client meet his specific goals, and it goes without saying that recommending the placement of funds in unsuitable investments will surely defeat that objective.

What would be considered an unsuitable investment for a client will depend, of course, on all the surrounding circumstances, but a few actual situations may be instructive. In a disciplinary action, the SEC held that a registered representative made unsuitable recommendations to a client where the latter indicated he was in need of "conservative" investments but the representative recommended options and securities on margin. In another case, a highly speculative security was recommended to a 79-year-old man, retired and living alone, whose physical condition had so deteriorated that it was doubtful whether he was capable of understanding or making decisions with respect to his investments or financial matters. The SEC held that no amount of disclosure to that investor could have cured the suitability violation, and further held that the broker had an affirmative obligation *not* to recommend a course of action clearly contrary to the best interests of the investor.

The following practices represent such flagrant examples of unfair dealing with clients that they are considered *per se* violations of the NASD suitability rule:

1. Recommending speculative low-priced securities to an investor without knowledge of or attempting to ascertain information about his other securities holdings, financial situation, and other necessary data. Along the same lines, the wholesale recommendation of a single security without thought to each individual investor's overall financial situation clearly violates the fairness concept embodied in the suitability rule.

2. Engaging in excessive trading in an investor's account, also referred to as "churning."

3. Trading in mutual fund shares, particularly on a short-term basis. Mutual funds are not proper trading vehicles, and excessive trading therein not only cannot lead to economic gain, but often involves substantial sales commissions and tax disadvantages.

4. Recommending the purchase of securities or the continuing purchase of securities in amounts which are inconsistent with the reasonable expectation that the investor has the financial ability to meet such a commitment.

In the decided cases, evidence put forth regarding the investor's sophistication, his degree of reliance on the recommendation, and even his personal opinion that the transaction was suitable, has not proved to be a satisfactory defense where a *per se* violation has occurred.

Diagnose with care. By holding yourself out as a financial planner, you represent to the public that you have the skills and expertise to do what is normally expected of a professional in that field. The law imposes on you the general standard of conduct of reasonable care, which means that in providing financial planning services you are expected to exercise the degree of care that would be expected of other reasonably prudent members of the financial planning profession, given the same or similar circumstances.

More specifically, as a planner you are expected to know how to analyze the factual data furnished to you by the client and, based thereon, to make considered judgments about his overall financial picture, cash flow situation, retirement needs, insurance needs, estate plan, tax situation, and investment needs. In making these judgments, you are expected to utilize the commonly accepted diagnostic tools and techniques of the profession. This includes, first and foremost, understanding and knowing how to work with accounting concepts, since they are fundamental to all financial planning decision making. Thus, a competent planner is supposed to know how to construct and interpret balance sheets, net worth, cash flow and income statements, basic business statements, and the like.

A working knowledge of the tax laws, significant IRS rulings, and IRS audit procedures is also considered fundamental, since there are important tax consequences to nearly all financial planning decisions. An important aspect of diagnosing a client's tax situation is the ability to analyze and synthesize information contained on state and federal tax returns, and the planner who is deficient in this respect will probably wind up defending his actions in court sooner or later.

Much the same can be said about the planner's knowledge of insurance principles, estate planning, pension and retirement planning, and investment planning. The best liability-avoidance strategy is to make it your business to keep up with all significant developments in the field through regular attendance at seminars, conventions, and continuing education courses. There is no better defense to a malpractice suit than becoming as expert as possible in all the key subjects and issues you must face in the normal course of your practice.

Utilize consultants whenever necessary. Earlier, we talked about the client with the suit-prone personality and noted his basic feelings of insecurity and other negative psychological traits. Financial planners sometimes exhibit many of the same characteristics, and when they do, the stage is really set for litigation! The suit-prone planner cannot admit to himself his own limitations of training and experience, so when confronted with a complex or difficult problem, he chooses to muddle his way through rather than turn to other professionals for help. This usually proves to be the wrong decision, with negative consequences for the client that he may not be willing to swallow, particularly if the planner is evasive in explaining what went wrong or, even worse, refuses to explain or discuss it at all.

The planner who takes his fiduciary responsibilities seriously should never be reluctant to consult an appropriate specialist whenever the circumstances of a case so require. No one is expected to be an expert in every phase of financial planning. In fact, one of the planner's important responsibilities as a financial professional is to recognize the need for specialized help and to act as liaison with other professionals. The use of a consultant's services can be accomplished in a completely professional manner and need raise no inference or suggestion of the planner's inadequacies or improper handling of his client's situation.

A word of caution: Choose your consultant carefully! If the individual selected by you gives advice that proves harmful to your client, you may be held legally liable for failing to exercise reasonable care in making the selection.

Supervise subordinates carefully. Financial planners can be held liable for the acts of their employees (both professional and non-professional) in many ways. This form of derivative liability arises by virtue of common law agency principles, as well as under the controlling-persons provisions in the federal securities acts. The latter applies, of course, only to planners who are their own broker-dealers, and persons in this category may wish to review the discussion on derivative liability contained in Chapter Six.

As planners expand their practices, they must cope with the increased demand for their personal services. This is not always an easy task, since it becomes increasingly difficult to accommodate the needs of both old and new clients and still provide the quality of professional services that made the planner successful in the first place. Delegating key tasks to subordinates (whether called paraplanners or something else) is the only practical solution to this dilemma. Paraplanners can assist the planner in carrying out many responsible technical tasks, such as interviewing clients, completing financial statements, performing client follow-up tasks, researching new investment products, and giving general background support to the planner. But in carrying out these activities, the paraplanner may commit an error or fail to do something that should have been done, and this will give rise to the planner's derivative liability.

The solution is obvious: you must closely supervise and control the activities of all subordinates to assure their exercise of due care. Your first task is to be sure to hire only capable persons as staff assistants, and then designate one of them as office manager with responsibility for monitoring the conduct of the others. Then you must give all employees the necessary formal and informal training to make sure that they understand fully what is and what is not expected of them. Perhaps your biggest problem will be to explain the limits of their authority and responsibility, for there may be a tendency on the part of some of your employees to undertake tasks that legally may be carried out only by you.

Close supervision means just that. Never take anything for granted. Hold staff meetings periodically to determine if all subordinate employees know their jobs and how to carry them out. If necessary, institute periodic spot-checks by asking trusted clients if they have encountered any unusual problems with office procedures or personnel. Make changes accordingly. If you are a broker-dealer, your liability is even greater, and NASD rules require that you designate a staff member as the responsible officer of supervisory jurisdiction (OSJ) to supervise the activities of all registered representatives.

Implement plans carefully. One of the surest ways to invite malpractice litigation is to assume responsibility for implementing a client's plan and then to fail to do so. It could also lead to a suit alleging breach of contract. Remember, when you enter into a formal planner-client relationship, you assume responsibility for a number of things, one of which is the responsibility to follow through on all tasks requiring your specific professional attention. Failure to do so may well lead to legal liability, especially if something significant is overlooked that could prove financially costly to the client.

Among the many follow-up tasks you are likely to have are the following:

1. Contacting and arranging to meet with lawyers, accountants, pension experts, bankers, investment analysts, and other specialists.

2. Requesting and obtaining important documents, such as wills, trust agreements, insurance policies, tax returns, company pension plans, and other such documents needed to properly analyze the client's situation.

3. Making due diligence inquiries about specific investments.

4. Executing actual purchases or sales of securities on behalf of the client.

5. Handling the normal correspondence and other paper work necessary to assure proper supervision of the client's account.

Timing is all-important in carrying out many planning functions, and your best liability-avoidance strategy in this respect is to establish and maintain efficient internal office management procedures that stress the importance of meeting all required deadlines and executing all plan implementation responsibilities with dispatch. The prudent planner will take steps to assure that matters do not get out of hand and that all necessary client-servicing needs are met within the period of time agreed upon or legally mandated. This may mean hiring paraplanners or more clerical personnel to assist in implementing some of the more routine tasks. On the other hand, it may be more prudent to limit the number of new clients you will accept, and taking this step may prove to be far less costly in the long run.

SUMMARY

By now, the reader should appreciate the fact that there are literally dozens of ways in which a disgruntled client can take you to court and make your life miserable. Why give him the chance? Do everything you can to avoid foul-ups, indiscretions, or tactical professional errors likely to cause financial loss or other harm to your clients. If properly approached, professional liability risk management can bring about better client relations as well as greater financial rewards, but it is a job that calls for constant vigilance.

In addition to the specific liability-avoidance strategies described in this chapter, and becoming aware of your legal obligations in general, as outlined in earlier chapters, give particular consideration to the following matters:

Securities Transactions

Never take shortcuts in handling securities transactions. Always observe the letter of the law; it is your only reliable legal defense. Don't forget to discuss risks as well as rewards when proposing an investment, and make sure you know enough about the client and the investment to be able to justify the recommendation as meeting all suitability requirements. Use the investment disclosure checklist and the investment suitability checklist mentioned earlier as practice aids and memory joggers.

Always provide the required prospectus and obtain a prospectus receipt from the client. Memories fade with time, and it is safest to have the receipt in your file should the client ever decide to sue. Never display "broker-dealer only" or other due diligence material to your clients, and never leave such material with them. Finally, make sure your clients understand that nothing can ever be guaranteed in the investment world, and that investments can go down as well as up. Be sure to record your discussions on this point in their files.

Office Management

Make sure to establish proper office management procedures and guidelines to assure close supervision of all subordinate personnel, both professional and nonprofessional. Your office procedures and guidelines also should assure the prompt, accurate, and efficient handling of all securities transactions. Hire competent staff and make sure they are properly trained and know the limits of their authority, particularly with respect to the giving of investment advice and the handling of securities transactions. Keep detailed records on all clients, and document all telephone discussions with them while the details are still fresh in your memory.

Client Relations

Above all, recognize the importance of the interpersonal aspects of your financial planning practice and employ the techniques necessary to make them work in your favor. Take the time to really get to know each client as an individual during the initial interview. Don't get too technical and don't bombard clients with too much information. Show them that you recognize and respect their fears, their personal concerns, and their feelings about life in general, as well as their financial problems and concerns. A warm and sincere planner-client relationship founded on mutual trust and respect will go a long way toward aborting any later thoughts of malpractice litigation, come what may.

During the initial interview, be on the lookout for psychological traits or idiosyncracies of the client that might indicate later trouble. When you spot the tell-tale signs of a suit-prone person—insecurity, reluctance to assume personal responsibility, unreasonable attitudes, refusal to provide basic factual information—decide right then and there whether you really want this person as a client. You are under no legal obligation to accept anyone as a client and you can always beg off if you want to. If you decide to proceed, make sure you never record any negative information about the client's personality traits in the file. Maintain regular contact with your clients and keep them abreast of all significant developments in tax laws, new products, and any negative developments in their own investments. Finally, make a practice of responding to their problems promptly, before they turn into complaints—or worse. Let them know you care about them personally, and the results will be worth it a hundredfold.

KEY POINTS TO REMEMBER

1. The failure of a financial planner to have a specific professional liability claims avoidance strategy could prove costly to him.

2. The trauma of being sued for malpractice can be significant. Such a suit represents an attack on the integrity of the planner, and this is bound to have many negative psychological consequences.

3. Direct professional factors and indirect sociological and psychological factors all play a role in influencing malpractice litigation.

4. An important sociological influence is the general suit-consciousness of our society, with a growing predisposition to sue for damages whenever acts or omissions lead to losses or other injuries.

5. A workable malpractice claims prevention strategy must take into consideration the human relations aspects of rendering professional services. Often, success or failure in managing the planner-client relationship is dependent on the interplay between the planner's and the client's personality. Understanding the psychological components at work can make a big difference in preventing unwanted malpractice claims.

6. Some prospective clients will have personality traits of the suit-prone person: immaturity, excessive dependency, and unwillingness to assume personal responsibility for one's own actions. Either decline to accept these persons as clients, or make up your mind you will have to deal with them very carefully.

7. Minimizing client dissatisfaction requires paying attention to each client's expressed needs, as well as his hidden motives and unrealistic expectations.

8. It is important to develop rapport with the client, and the planner must never build up his client's unrealistic expectations.

9. Always keep your client informed of changes in tax laws and other matters likely to affect his financial situation. Keeping in touch on a regular basis is one of the best ways to maintain client rapport and confidence.

10. Do not avoid discussing unfavorable events with clients. The client needs your advice and support most of all when investments turn sour. That is when it is essential to be open and frank with him.

11. Living up to your obligations as a fiduciary is one of the most effective claims prevention techniques. Shun every incentive to engage in self-dealing or other possible conflicts of interest.

12. If you find that recommending a particular investment is likely to produce a conflict of interest, mention it to the client and give him the option of refusing to make the investment. Sales incentives such as bonuses, gifts, and trips fall into this category.

13. Always disclose all relevant and material facts about investments to your client, and make sure the client understands what you are saying.

14. Where a prospectus is required, do not fail to furnish it to the client, and always obtain a receipt therefor.

15. The wisest course of action is never to provide anything in writing to your client other than the required prospectus. Instead, talk generically and conceptually about investments. All written materials, including notes, newspaper clippings,

comparisons, and so on, are considered official sales literature and must be cleared before being given to a client.

16. Avoid exaggeration in describing the purported virtues of investments, and never guarantee any investment. Doing so is a violation of NASD rules and is sure to get you in trouble with your clients.

17. Using a simple checklist will help you to cover all key points in discussing the key points about investments with clients.

18. Recommending only suitable investments is a clear-cut legal requirement. This calls for factual information about the client as well as the proposed investment.

19. Investors have different needs, goals, and financial resources; accordingly, you must tailor your recommendations to meet the specific needs and risk threshold of each client. Use of an investor suitability checklist will help you meet this legal responsibility.

20. As a professional financial planner, you must use the standard diagnostic tools of the profession, and your failure to do so will lead to liability. Keeping abreast of all important developments in the field is one of the best strategies for avoiding malpractice claims based on alleged incompetence.

21. Do not presume to have knowledge on every aspect of financial planning. It is your legal duty to call in consultants on matters that are beyond your professional competence or experience.

22. Close supervision of all professional and nonprofessional employees is an absolute must if you do not wish to be held liable for their negligent acts or omissions.

23. Proper follow-up on all financial planning implementation steps is an important aspect of claims prevention. It is essential that all securities transactions be handled carefully and on time.

SELECTED REFERENCES

Stimulus To Sue

"Bad Tip? Sue Your Broker," *Calif. Lawyer,* vol. 4, no. 2, 17 (February 1984).

Bernzweig, E. P., "Malpractice and the Financial Planner," *Best's Review,* Life/Health Ed., 26 (November 1984).

Malpractice Claims Prevention Strategies

Bernzweig, E. P., "The Ten Best Safeguards Against Malpractice Suits," *Digest of Financial Planning Ideas,* vol. 1, no. 8 (October 1984).

Human Relations Factors

> Hegarty, C., "The Key to Selling Is Listening," *Digest of Financial Planning Ideas*, 31 (September 1982).
>
> Leroy, R., "The Fine Art of Listening," *Financial Planning*, vol. 14, no. 7, 167 (July 1985).
>
> Wright, C., "Are Your Clients Comfortable?" *Digest of Financial Planning Ideas*, 78 (September 1982).
>
> Mundheim, R., "Professional Responsibilities of Broker-Dealers: The Suitability Doctrine," 1965 *Duke L. J.* 445, 476 (Summer 1965).

Fiduciary Obligations of Brokers

> *Rolf* v. *Blyth, Eastman Dillon & Co.*, 424 F.Supp. 1021 (S.D.N.Y. 1977).
>
> *Carras* v. *Burns*, 516 F.2d 251 (4th Cir. 1975).
>
> *Moscarelli* v. *Stamm*, 288 F.Supp. 453 (E.D.N.Y. 1968).

Communications with the Public

> Article III, Section 35, *NASD Manual* (Washington, D.C., 1984).

chapter nine

Miscellaneous Legal Concerns

CRIMINAL LIABILITY OF THE PLANNER

The type of person who chooses financial planning as a profession is not likely to engage knowingly in criminal conduct in providing services to clients. Nevertheless, financial planners may subject themselves to criminal liability either by doing something that the law defines as a criminal act or by omitting to do something that the law requires, the omission of which the law declares to be a crime. A person does not have to be wicked or immoral for the law to regard his conduct as criminal. For example, section 78o(a)(1) of the Securities Exchange Act of 1934 makes it mandatory for anyone meeting the definition of a broker or dealer who wishes to "effect transactions in" securities to be registered with the SEC before doing so. The willful violation of that law is made a crime. Thus, a planner who implements securities transactions on behalf of clients without first securing the appropriate license is guilty of a crime even if he has no intention of harming anyone or doing wrong in the usual sense of that word.

Certain wrongs are identified as crimes because they are regarded as harmful to the health, welfare, safety, or security of the public at large. Congress has the power to decide what wrongs constitute crimes in federal matters, and each state legislature has the power to declare what wrongs will be classified as crimes within its territorial jurisdiction. In the final analysis, it is public policy or the will of the people, as expressed in federal and state statutes, that determines what shall be classified as a criminal wrong.

Distinction between Torts and Crimes

You may recall the discussion about torts in Chapter Six, where it was pointed out that a tort is a *civil* wrong committed by one person against the person or property of another. It was also noted that a tort may result either from intentional or unintentional conduct. There are some similarities, as well as some important differences, between torts and crimes that are deserving of mention.

Both a tort and a crime may involve antisocial conduct and both may result in harm to a specific person, as opposed to the public at large. And, in fact, it is possible that the same act may be both a tort and a crime. For example, if Al and Barney get into an argument at a local bar and Barney assaults and seriously injures Al, Al could bring a tort action alleging assault and battery, while the state (through the local district attorney's office) might seek an indictment to prosecute Barney for the criminal offense of assault and battery. If Al were to prevail in his civil action, he would receive money damages; if the state were to prevail in its criminal prosecution, Barney would be fined, sent to jail, or possibly incur both penalties. The important difference is that a crime is considered an offense against the public at large, as spelled out in a particular statute or ordinance. A tort, on the other hand, is considered an invasion of the individual rights of another, for which the latter can bring a civil action to recover money damages.

Another important difference between a tort and a crime is that the concept of punishment usually does not enter into tort law, even though announced decisions in tort cases occasionally may deter others from engaging in the same type of wrongful conduct. The whole purpose of criminal law, on the other hand, is to punish and to set an example for others. The one area in which the concept of punishment does enter into tort law is when the defendant's wrongdoing has been so deliberate, intentional, and outrageous that it assumes the same characteristics as a crime. In those cases the courts in some states have permitted juries to award the injured plaintiff "punitive" or "exemplary" damages over and above the compensatory damages he is legally entitled to. As pointed out earlier, however, punitive damages are not permitted in federal securities act cases.

Federal Securities Act Criminal Liability

Under the Securities Act and the Exchange Act, the SEC is authorized to transmit to the U.S. Attorney General (more specifically, to the U.S. Department of Justice) for possible criminal prosecution such evidence as may be available regarding acts or practices that appear to the SEC to constitute violations of those acts by the person or persons in question.

The federal securities acts provide for the imposition of fairly severe criminal penalties for the willful violation of their various provisions or any rules or regulations promulgated thereunder. Under the Exchange Act, for example, conviction can bring a fine of up to $10,000, or imprisonment for not more than two years, or both. The same penalties are applicable to convictions under the Investment Advisers Act of 1940. Conviction under the Securities Act can bring a fine of up to $5,000, imprisonment for not more than five years, or both. Theft, conversion, or embezzlement of funds protected under the Securities Investor Protection Act (SIPC) can bring a fine of as much as $50,000. And it should not be forgotten that just about any act that would constitute the basis for a criminal prosecution against a planner will likewise constitute a violation of NASD and/or stock exchange rules, so the errant planner can anticipate severe NASD or stock exchange disciplinary action as well as criminal prosecution for the same conduct.

It is important to note, however, that some form of willful intent (called "scienter" by the courts) is essential to a criminal conviction for violation of the federal securities acts, whether that be an intent to defraud or merely an intent to perform the acts that constitute the violation. Generally, it is unnecessary for the government to show that the defendant knew of, or intended to violate, the *specific* prohibitory statute or rule he allegedly violated, although not all courts have decided thusly. The minority of courts that adhere to what is called the *no-knowledge* rule permit the defendant prior to sentencing to rebut the presumption that he had *actual knowledge* of the specific rule or regulation that he has been convicted of violating.

The principal violations of the Securities Act for which criminal prosecutions have been based are the securities registration provisions. For example, brokers have been convicted of violating the registration provisions of the Securities Act where they knowingly sold unregistered securities. Knowing misrepresentations made to clients about specific securities, even if there is no desire or intent that the deceived purchaser will suffer financial loss as a result of the purchase, is sufficient to convict a broker of violating the antifraud provisions of the Exchange Act. Conviction will also result if a broker (or any other person) "willfully and knowingly" makes a false statement in any application, report, or document required to be filed with the SEC.

SEC Rule 10b-5 is the general rule implementing the antifraud provisions of the Exchange Act. 10b-5 makes it unlawful, among other things, for a securities broker to employ any device, scheme, or artifice to defraud; to make any untrue statement of a material fact or to omit to state a material fact necessary to assure that the statements made are not misleading; or to engage in any act, practice, or course of business that operates as a fraud or deceit upon any person in connection with the purchase or sale of any security. The planner who is indicted on criminal charges is more than likely to find the alleged violation to be based on one of the mentioned prohibitions of Rule 10b-5.

Criminal RICO Liability

In 1970, Congress passed the Racketeer Influenced and Corrupt Organizations Act (RICO), making it unlawful to engage in certain enumerated offenses arising out of what the statute refers to as "a pattern of racketeering activity." One of the specified offenses is "securities fraud," so it is conceivable that a planner-broker who willfully engages in fraudulent conduct deemed to constitute such a pattern of racketeering activity could be criminally prosecuted therefor. The penalty for violating the criminal provisions of RICO is a fine of not more than $25,000 or imprisonment for not more than 20 years, or both.

In Chapter Seven it was pointed out that RICO also has important civil remedy provisions, under which an aggrieved claimant can obtain treble damages and attorneys' fees if he can prove he suffered loss or injury at the hands of a defendant who has engaged in a "pattern of racketeering activity" by committing securities fraud on at least two prior occasions.

State Securities Act Criminal Liability

The handling of criminal prosecutions for violations of state blue-sky laws is very similar to those under the federal securities acts, and the grounds for bringing such prosecutions are likewise similar. Penalties vary, of course, from state to state, but states that have adopted the Uniform Securities Act have made the penalty a fine of $5,000, imprisonment for not more than 3 years, or both. Note especially that violation of a state's blue-sky law may also constitute a crime under its general penal laws, and the penalties prescribed under the latter may be even more severe.

It seems to be well settled that violations of a state's blue-sky law is punishable even though the perpetrator may not be aware that his acts constitute a crime, with intent (scienter) not being an element of such a crime. Thus, unlike the distinctions between "willful" violations or violations that are "willfully and knowingly" perpetrated under the federal acts, the state criminal statutes generally do not require knowledge of the unlawfulness of the conduct in question. Obviously, this means the planner who violates a state blue-sky law has fewer legal defenses and stands a greater chance of conviction than one who violates a federal securities statute or regulation.

Among other grounds for criminal prosecution under state law, giving investment advice or selling securities without proper registration or licensing will result in conviction without regard to the defendant's alleged intent to comply with the law at some later date. Similarly, the intentional selling of unregistered securities is a crime where such registration is required prior to sale, even though registration may take place soon afterward. Note also that there is no need for the state to prove that an investor has suffered a financial loss or other detriment before an indictment can be brought and a conviction obtained against a broker who has violated the letter of the law.

There is evidence that state regulatory authorities are becoming increasingly disenchanted with the activities of persons calling themselves financial planners who are really nothing more than investment product salespersons with questionable ethical standards. Accordingly, legitimate planners can expect a definite tightening of state laws regulating their activities, either directly (as planners) or indirectly (as investment advisers and securities sellers). As this is written, legislation is under consideration in several states that would result in greater regulatory control over the activities of financial planners. California, Oregon, Minnesota, Washington, Maine, Massachusetts, Florida, and Georgia are the principal states that have been considering such legislation. In any event, strict adherence to the letter of the laws and implementing regulations with respect to the selling of securities and giving of investment advice is an absolute must if the responsible financial planner wants to avoid disciplinary action or criminal prosecution.

THE IMPORTANCE OF MALPRACTICE INSURANCE

By now the person who has chosen to become a professional financial planner must appreciate the fact that there are substantial risks in so doing. As has been pointed out, there are legal obligations owed to the state and federal governments by virtue of specific statutes and regulations, as well as legal obligations owed to the NASD and the stock exchanges. All these have significant legal consequences—disciplinary action, suspension, fines, license revocation, and possibly even imprisonment.

Of all the liabilities the planner is likely to incur, however, the only one he can insure against is his liability to his clients for professional misconduct, or malpractice. Chapter Eight outlined the major potential sources of malpractice litigation against a financial planner and pointed out that a successful plaintiff is entitled to compensatory money damages in a malpractice action. The planner who thinks "it can't happen to me" and determines not to insure against his potential malpractice liability is definitely taking a calculated risk.

Should an uninsured planner be sued, he is in for a sobering experience not likely to be soon forgotten. Chapter Eight outlined the principal negative effects of a pending lawsuit on the planner's personal and professional life, so there is no need to repeat all of them here. But just the expense involved in hiring a lawyer should be reason enough to seriously consider the purchase of professional liability (malpractice) coverage. Remember, even if the case is successfully defended, huge sums will have been incurred in legal costs. And don't forget, during the time a case is being prepared for trial a lot of the planner's time will be spent in nonremunerative matters like attendance at deposition proceedings, conferences with his lawyer, and the like. Just when the need for additional financial income is greatest, potential profits will be lost because of the inability to effectively service existing clients or attract new ones. Finally, and most important of all, if the case is lost and the plaintiff is awarded damages, the planner risks losing everything he owns.

No financial planner worthy of the name should ever consider practicing without appropriate malpractice coverage. It is unwise to assume that you are automatically covered under the malpractice policy of your broker-dealer (assuming he even has such a policy), since that is not likely to be the case. As a matter of fact, some broker-dealers specifically require their registered representatives to sign agreements (called *hold-harmless* agreements) to indemnify the broker-dealer for claims or losses paid as a result of the representative's negligence or violation of federal, state, or NASD securities rules or regulations.

In any event, a broker-dealer's liability for conduct relating to securities transactions, and his possible insurance coverage thereon, is generally more limited than the financial planner's malpractice liability for all types of conduct, including matters that extend well beyond securities transactions. So get your own policy from a carrier that offers malpractice coverage specifically tailored for financial planners. As this book goes to press, the IAFP currently offers its members this type of insurance protection through a group program. The ICFP, however, is currently looking for a new carrier for its group program following the sudden withdrawal of its original carrier in mid-1984.

When you do apply for this type of insurance, make sure you get adequate coverage in light of your client load and the scope and breadth of your professional financial planning services. The peace of mind you will be buying is well worth the price. In addition, don't take too much for granted. Read the policy's insuring clause very carefully and make sure it offers protection against any and all claims based on professional services of the type you render. Pay particular attention to the policy exclusions, for they are on a par with, and must be read in conjunction with, the insuring clause. Do not forget that what an insurer purports to cover in the insuring clause can be legally taken away in the exclusions clause, so read the proposed policy with this in mind.

Should you have any doubts about any of the exclusions in a policy offered to you by an insurer (or even some doubts about your present policy), do not hesitate to ask the carrier for an official interpretation in writing. It is better to know in advance what is and what is not covered than to have a knock-down, drag-out fight with your own insurance carrier *after* a claim has been filed against you.

One of the key benefits in any malpractice policy is the insured's right to have the company provide legal counsel to defend claims or lawsuits that are filed against him. The most beneficial policy language obligates the carrier to defend *any* claim or suit based on professional services rendered (or which should have been rendered), even if the allegations appear to be groundless, false, or fraudulent. By the same token, *make sure the policy guarantees legal counsel even if the complaint alleges that you violated a specific statute or regulation.* Most complaints against financial planners will do just that, and even if the policy won't pay for claims based on statutory violations (because that is against public policy), it is only fair that you should be entitled to legal representation on that critical issue, or else the policy is really worthless.

The "other insurance" clause in your malpractice policy is also deserving of close attention. Although this clause usually is comprised of fairly complex phraseology, don't let that deter you from trying to understand it. A reasonable "other insurance" clause will obligate the insurer to pay only its proportionate share of any loss (and its associated claim expenses) in the event you happen to have another policy that covers the same type of claim. In other words, both policies will pay their proportionate share of the total claim and claim expenses, but no more. An unreasonable ''other insurance'' clause would be one that makes the policy in question ''excess coverage.'' This means that any other policy you might own covering the same type of loss will be deemed the *primary* source of payment, while the policy in question will only pay any claims *in excess of the other policy's limits.* If you only have the one policy, there is no problem; but if you happen to have two malpractice policies, and each has an ''excess coverage'' clause, both companies are likely to deny primary responsibility in a contractual standoff. The sad fact is, even though you own two policies, you could be left holding the bag with no protection afforded by either policy. This is not theoretical; it has actually happened to policyholders in this situation. All the more reason to read all your insurance policies carefully to eliminate any confusion likely to result from clauses like the one being discussed.

Even if you seriously doubt that financial planners are going to become the targets of malpractice claims in any great numbers, why run the risk of finding out the hard way? Common sense dictates that the reasonably prudent planner should insure against the likelihood of such litigation, even if it is only a remote possibility. Having malpractice coverage won't solve all your problems, but it will go a long way toward giving you some important peace of mind.

OTHER LICENSES A PLANNER MIGHT NEED

Throughout this book the primary focus has been on the person who has taken up or plans to take up financial planning as a full-time professional activity. As noted at the outset, many entrants into this field have come directly from college with MBA degrees or other educational credits in business or finance. On the other hand, a much larger number have entered the field from other disciplines, such as law, accounting, insurance, banking, and real estate. In many cases, persons in the latter category already have acquired the specific licenses needed to practice their respective professions before acquiring the licenses necessary to practice financial planning. Indeed, many of these individuals have found that the additional knowledge required to become a professional financial planner has greatly assisted them in serving their existing clientele.

It is far less likely that a person who has first become a financial planner will thereafter pursue the rigorous educational requirements for becoming a lawyer or accountant, but he or she might well consider acquiring licenses in real estate, insurance, professional investment management, or other relevant disciplines. It goes without saying, the more knowledge and training an individual can bring to bear on the financial planning process, the better able he will be to serve his clients' needs. This book does not address the legal requirements of the various state laws with respect to those "other" licenses, but that does not mean they are not important or that they should not be given thoughtful consideration.

The planner or would-be planner wishing to obtain more information about how to become a licensed life insurance, disability insurance, or health insurance agent should contact the appropriate state insurance department. If the planner is interested in becoming directly involved in real estate matters, he should contact his state real estate board. The importance of complying with all local, state, and federal licensing laws cannot be overemphasized. The entire premise of this book is that the prudent financial planner should become familiar with these matters before they turn into intractable legal problems.

CLAIMS AGAINST EMPLOYERS AND OTHERS

There may be circumstances that will require a planner-broker to seek relief from the acts or omissions of his broker-dealer or other persons in the securities industry. Obviously, you should try to adjust such matters informally before taking more drastic measures. But if it appears that no such accommodation is possible, then you may have to take more formal action.

All NASD members, including all registered broker-dealers, all registered representatives, and all associated persons are *required* to submit all disputes, claims, or controversies between one another to arbitration in accordance with section 8 of the NASD Code of Arbitration Procedure. In such cases, the arbitration panels are comprised of no fewer than three nor more than five arbitrators, all of whom are required to be from the securities industry. A simplified arbitration process is also available for claims involving dollar amounts of less than $5,000. This process calls for submission of all pleadings and documentary evidence to the arbitration panel for review and decision, but without a hearing. A decision is required to be rendered within 30 days.

Incidentally, it may be deemed conduct inconsistent with just and equitable principles of trade for an NASD member to fail to submit a dispute with another member to arbitration—by taking the dispute to court, for example. This in itself may be grounds for imposing disciplinary sanctions on a securities representative.

SEEKING ADDITIONAL LEGAL HELP

Although reasonably comprehensive, this book does not pretend to be the final word on all the legal aspects of financial planning. And, once again, the reader is cautioned against using this book as sole authority for resolving specific legal problems. That is not its purpose. The planner with a particularly troublesome or complex problem, say, whether and how to register as an investment adviser or as a broker-dealer, should discuss the matter with an attorney who specializes in securities law. The latter point is deserving of emphasis, since the attorney who holds himself out as an all-around general practitioner is likely to find he is beyond his depth when it comes to understanding the nuances of securities law. Don't risk it. You can get the names of securities law specialists from various sources: (1) referrals from colleagues who have utilized securities lawyers in the past, (2) referrals from your local bar association, (3) referrals from accountants, bankers, or other professionals you know whose work brings them into contact with securities lawyers, and (4) listings of securities specialists in bar association directories or other comparable legal directories. With respect to the latter, most large libraries have copies of the *Martindale-Hubbell Law Directory,* which lists every attorney currently practicing in the United States. The "professional card" section of that directory includes detailed information about lawyers' specialty areas, and before a lawyer (or the firm with which he is associated) is allowed to include his professional card in *Martindale-Hubbell,* he must have been in practice at least ten years and have achieved the top professional rating ("a v") as determined by his peers.

There may be circumstances in which it would be simpler and less costly to first discuss your problem, particularly if it is of a regulatory nature, with one of the staff attorneys of the SEC in Washington, D.C., or at one of the SEC's regional offices. The SEC's staff attorneys are generally quite helpful and willing to answer these basic questions about SEC rules and the steps necessary to comply with the pertinent federal securities laws. Appendix F lists the SEC regional offices around the country and gives the names and titles of the key regional office personnel.

More complex inquiries may be directed in writing to the Chief Counsel's Office, Securities and Exchange Commission, 450 Fifth Street, N.W., Washington, D.C. 20549. State security commissions also have legal personnel who can answer general legal questions about their respective blue-sky laws and regulations. And, finally, do not overlook the legal help available from lawyers employed by the NASD, either in Washington, D.C., or in the field, on matters pertaining to NASD rules and procedural issues. Appendix C lists the NASD district offices and gives the names of their key district office personnel.

KEY POINTS TO REMEMBER

1. A financial planner may subject himself to criminal liability by engaging in conduct prohibited by statute, even though he may not intend any harm thereby.

2. Torts differ from crimes in that they are wrongs against the person or property of individuals, while crimes are considered wrongs against society as a whole.

3. The federal securities acts impose severe criminal sanctions for violation of prohibited acts, including fines up to $10,000 as well as imprisonment.

4. Any act that would be the basis for a criminal prosecution would also be grounds for disciplinary action by the SEC, NASD, or one of the stock exchanges.

5. In most instances, proving a statutory violation under the federal securities acts does not require proof of the perpetrator's specific knowledge of or intent to violate the provision in question.

6. Failure to register and commission of acts prohibited under the antifraud provisions of the securities laws, including Rule 10b-5, are the principal bases for criminal prosecutions.

7. A planner can also be criminally prosecuted for securities fraud under the criminal provisions of RICO (Racketeer Influenced and Corrupt Organizations Act of 1970).

8. State criminal prosecutions for securities act violations are very similar to the federal statutes, except that the penalties are often more severe.

9. The state criminal statutes generally do not require proof of the perpetrator's willful conduct and knowledge in order to convict. Thus, a planner who is prosecuted under state law has fewer defenses than one prosecuted under federal law.

10. Malpractice insurance is a practical necessity for any planner who understands the magnitude of his legal liability to his clients.

11. Such protection is worth it even if all it provides is the peace of mind that comes with knowing you have legal counsel to defend you in the event you are sued.

12. It will pay to learn as much as possible about the specific clauses in your malpractice policy, since some policies afford coverage that is more illusory than real.

13. There are a variety of other possible licenses a financial planner might need in order to carry out his professional duties effectively, including licenses to engage in real estate, insurance, accounting, and law.

14. When a planner-broker has a dispute with his own broker-dealer or perhaps a colleague in the securities field, he is required to arbitrate such dispute in accordance with NASD arbitration rules and procedures. His failure to arbitrate may be grounds for disciplinary proceedings against him by the NASD.

15. It is important to obtain additional legal help before attempting to resolve specific legal issues. In so doing, look for an attorney who specializes in securities law, rather than a general practitioner.

16. Excellent legal advice on procedural matters is available without charge from staff attorneys assigned to SEC and NASD regional offices, and they should be consulted on such matters for initial assistance.

SELECTED REFERENCES

Statutes

Racketeer Influenced and Corrupt Organizations Act of 1970 (RICO), 18 U.S.C., §§1961–1968.

Distinction between Torts and Crimes

Prosser, W., *Handbook of the Law of Torts,* 4th ed., Chapter 1 (West Publishing Co., St. Paul, Minnesota, 1971).

Criminal Violations of the Securities Laws

Hall v. *Security Planning Service, Inc.,* 462 F.Supp. 1058 (D.C. Ariz. 1978).
United States v. *Clark,* 353 F.Supp. 131 (S.D.N.Y. 1973).
Annotation, *Securities Law Violation—Scienter,* 20 ALR Fed 227.

Effect of Prior or Concurrent Criminal Prosecution

S.E.C. v. *Dimensional Entertainment Corp.,* 493 F.Supp. 270 (S.D.N.Y. 1980).
S.E.C. v. *Everest Management Corp.,* 466 F.Supp. 167 (S.D.N.Y. 1979).
United States v. *Sloan,* 388 F.Supp. 1062 (S.D.N.Y. 1975).

Importance of Malpractice Insurance

Darby, R., "Malpractice Insurance for Brokers," *Registered Representative,* vol. 8, no. 6, 18 (June 1984).

Bernzweig, E. P., "The Hazards of 'Going Bare'," *Financial Planning,* vol. 13, no. 8, 135 (August 1984).

Bernzweig, E. P., "Malpractice and the Financial Planner," *Best's Review,* Life/Health Ed., 26 (November 1984).

Licensing and Regulation of Insurance Agents and Brokers

Johnson, D. S., "Regulation Guideposts," *Financial Planning,* vol. 14, no. 4, 235 (April 1985).

SEC Interpretive Release No. IA-770

SECURITIES AND EXCHANGE COMMISSION
17 CFR Part 276

(Release No. IA-770)
Applicability of the Investment Advisers Act to Financial Planners, Pension Consultants, and Other Persons Who Provide Investment Advisory Services as an Integral Component of Other Financially Related Services

AGENCY.   Securities and Exchange Commission.

ACTION.   Statement of staff interpretive position.

SUMMARY.   The Commission is publishing the views of the staff of the Division of Investment Advisers Act of 1940 to financial planners, pension consultants, and other persons who, as an integral component of other financially related services, provide investment advisory services to others for compensation. The purpose of this release is to call to the attention of persons providing such services, as well as members of the general public who may utilize such services, the circumstances under which persons providing these services would be investment advisers under the Advisers Act and subject to the Act's registration, antifraud and other provisions. The guidance provided in this release should assist providers of financial advisory services in complying with the Advisers Act and reduce the number of requests for staff interpretive or no-action advice with respect to the applicability of the Advisers Act to such persons where the requests do not present any novel, factual or interpretive issues. With one exception the interpretive views set forth in the release are based on positions consistently taken by the staff in the past. In the case of the one exception, the position articulated in the release may have the effect of excepting from the definition of investment adviser certain persons the staff would not regard as being in the business of providing investment advice.

For further information contact:

Mary S. Champagne, Esq.
Investment Advisers Study Group
Division of Investment Management
Securities and Exchange Commission
500 North Capitol Street
Washington, DC 20549
(202) 272-2041

Supplementary Information

The staff of the Commission has received numerous requests for staff interpretive or no-action advice concerning the applicability of the Investment Advisers Act of 1940 (15 U.S.C. 80b-1 *et seq.*) ("Advisers Act") to persons, such as financial planners, pension consultants, sports and entertainment representatives and others, who provide investment advisory services as an integral component of, or bundled with, other financially related services. In addition, it appears that many of these persons may not be aware of the provisions of the federal securities laws which may be applicable to their activities, particularly the fiduciary standards and registration requirements of the Advisers Act. It is the view of the staff that, for the reasons set forth below, many of the persons providing such services to the public are investment advisers under the definition of investment adviser contained in Section 202(a)(11) of the Advisers Act (15 U.S.C. 80b-2(a)(11)) and are not entitled to rely on any of the exceptions from that definition provided in clauses (A) to (F) of Section 202(a)(11). An investment adviser who uses the mails or any means or instrumentality of interstate commerce in connection with his or its business as an investment adviser is subject to the registration, antifraud, and other provisions of the Advisers Act, unless the adviser is excepted from registration under Section 203(b) of the Advisers Act (15 U.S.C. 80b-3(b)). An adviser excepted from registration under the Advisers Act remains subject to its antifraud provisions.

I. BACKGROUND

Financial planning typically involves the provision of a variety of services, principally advisory in nature, to individuals or families with respect to management of financial resources based upon an analysis of individual client needs. Generally, financial planning services involve the preparation of a financial program for a client based upon information elicited from the client as to the client's financial circumstances and objectives. Such information normally would cover present and anticipated assets and liabilities, including insurance, savings, investments, and anticipated retirement or other benefits. The program developed for the client typically includes general recommendations for a course of activity, or specific actions, to be taken by the client. For example, recommendations may be made that the client obtain insurance or revise existing coverage, establish an individual retirement account, increase or decrease funds held in savings accounts, or invest funds in securities. A financial planner may develop tax or estate plans for the client or may refer the client to an accountant or attorney for these services. The provider of such financial planning services typically assists the client in implementing the recommended program by, among other things, making specific recommendations to carry out the general recommendations of the program, or by selling to the client insurance products, securities, or other investments. The financial planner may also review the client's program periodically and recommend revisions. Persons providing such financial planning services use various compensation arrangements. Some financial planners charge clients an overall fee for the development of an individual client program while others charge clients an hourly fee. In some instances financial planners are compensated, in whole or in part, through the receipt of sales commissions upon the sale to the client of insurance products, mutual fund shares, interests in real estate, or other investments.

A second common form of service relating to financial matters is that provided by "pension consultants" who typically offer, in addition to administrative services, a variety of advisory services to employee benefit plans and their fiduciaries based upon an analysis of the needs of the individual plan. Such advisory services may include advice as to the types of funding media available to provide plan benefits, general recommendations as to what portion of plan assets should be invested in various investment media, including securities, and, in some cases, recommendations regarding investment in specific securities or other investments. Pension consultants may also assist plan fiduciaries in determining plan investment objectives and policies and in designing funding media for the plan. They may also provide general or specific advice to plan fiduciaries as to the selection or retention of persons to manage the assets of the plan.[1] Persons providing such services to plans are customarily compensated for the provision of their services through the receipt of fees paid by the plan, its sponsor, or other persons; by means of sales commissions on the sale of insurance products or investments to the plan; or through a combination of fees and commissions.

---

[1] The authority to manage all or a portion of a plan's assets often is delegated to a person who qualifies as an "investment manager" under the Employee Retirement Income Security Act of 1974 (29 U.S.C. 1001 *et seq.*). Under that statute, which is applicable to private sector pension and welfare benefit plans, an "investment manager" must be a registered investment adviser under the Advisers Act, a bank as defined in the Advisers Act, or an insurance company which is qualified to perform services as an investment manager under the laws of more than one state.

Another form of financial advisory service is that provided by persons offering a variety of financially related services to entertainers or athletes based upon the needs of the individual client. Such persons, who often use the designation "sports representative" or "entertainment representative," typically offer a number of services to clients, including the negotiation of employment contracts and development of promotional opportunities for the client, as well as advisory services related to investments, tax planning, or budget and money management. Some persons providing these services to clients may assume discretion over all or a portion of a client's funds by collecting income, paying bills and making investments for the client. Sports or entertainment representatives are customarily compensated for the provision of their services primarily through fees charged for negotiation of employment contracts but may also receive compensation in the form of fixed charges or hourly fees for other services, including investment advisory services, which they provide.

There are other persons who, while not falling precisely into one of the foregoing categories, provide financial advisory services. As discussed below, financial planners, pension consultants, sports or entertainment representatives, or other persons providing financial advisory services, may be investment advisers within the meaning of the Advisers Act.

II. STATUS AS AN INVESTMENT ADVISER

A. *Definition of Investment Adviser*

Section 202 (a)(11) of the Advisers Act defines the term "investment adviser" to mean:

> . . . any person who, for compensation, engages in the business of advising others, either directly or through publications or writings, as to the value of securities or as to the advisability of investing in, purchasing, or selling securities, or who, for compensation and as part of a regular business, issues or promulgates analyses or reports concerning securities. . . .

Whether a person providing financially related services of the type discussed in this release would be an investment adviser within the meaning of the Advisers Act would depend upon all the relevant facts and circumstances. As a general matter, however, if the activities of any person providing such integrated advisory services satisfy each element of either part of the foregoing two part definition, such person would be an investment adviser within the meaning of the Advisers Act, unless entitled to rely on one of the exceptions from the definition of investment adviser in clauses (A) to (F) of Section 202(a)(11).[2] Accordingly, a determination as to whether a person providing

---

[2]See discussion of Section 202(a)(11)(A) to (F) in Section II B, *infra*.

financial planning, pension consulting, or other integrated advisory services is an investment adviser will depend upon whether such person: (1) provides advice, or issues reports or analyses, regarding securities; (2) whether he is in the business of providing such services; and (3) whether he provides such services for compensation. These three elements are discussed below.

1. *ADVICE OR ANALYSES CONCERNING SECURITIES.* It would seem apparent that a person who gives advice or makes recommendations or issues reports or analyses with respect to specific securities is an investment adviser under Section 202(a)(11), assuming the other elements of the definition of investment adviser are met, i.e., that such services are performed as part of a business and for compensation. However, it has been asked on a number of occasions whether advice, recommendations or reports that do not pertain to specific securities satisfy this element of the definition. In the view of the staff, a person who provides advice, or issues or promulgates reports or analyses, which concern securities, but which do not relate to specific securities, would generally be an investment adviser under Section 202(a)(11), assuming such services are performed as part of a business[3] and for compensation. The staff has interpreted the definition of investment adviser to include persons who advise clients either directly or through publications or writings concerning the relative advantages and disadvantages of investing in securities in general as compared to other investment media.[4] A person who, in the course of developing a financial program for a client, advises a client as to the desirability of investing in securities as opposed to, or in relation to, stamps, coins, direct ownership of commodities, or any other investment vehicle would also be "advising" others within the meaning of Section 202(a)(11).[5] Similarly, a person who advises employee benefit plans on funding plan benefits by investing in securities, as opposed to, or in addition to, insurance products, real estate or other funding media, would be "advising" others within the meaning of Section 202(a)(11). A person providing advice to a client as to the selection or retention of an investment manager or managers also would, under certain circumstances, be deemed to be "advising" others within the meaning of Section 202(a)(11).[6]

---

[3]In this regard, as discussed in detail below, it is the staff's view that a person who gives advice or prepares analyses concerning securities generally may, nevertheless, not be "in the business" of doing so and, therefore, will not be considered an "investment adviser" as that term is used in Section 202(a)(11).

[4]*See, e.g.,* Richard K. May (avail. Dec. 11, 1979); Hayes Martin (avail. Feb. 15, 1980); Pauline Wang (avail. Mar. 21, 1980).

[5]*See, e.g.,* Thomas Beard (avail. May 8, 1975); Sinclair-deMarinis Inc. (avail. May 1, 1981).

[6]*See, e.g.,* FPC Securities Corp. (avail. Dec. 1, 1974) (program to assist client in selection and retention of investment manager by, among other things, recommending investment managers to clients, monitoring and evaluating the performance of a client's investment manager, and advising client as to the retention of such manager); William Bye Co. (avail. Apr. 26, 1973) (program involving recommendations to client as to selection and retention of investment manager based upon client's investment objectives and periodic monitoring and evaluation of investment manager's performance). On occasion in the past the staff has taken no-action posi-

2. THE "BUSINESS" STANDARD. In order to come within the definition of an investment adviser, a person must engage for compensation in the business of advising others as to the value of securities or as to the advisability of investing in, purchasing, or selling securities or issue or promulgate reports or analyses concerning securities as part of a regular business. Under this definition, the giving of advice or issuing of reports or analyses concerning securities for compensation need not constitute the principal business activity or any particular portion of the business activities of a person in order for the person to be an investment adviser under Section 202(a)(11). However, a person who provides investment advice for compensation but is not *in the business* of advising others as to the value of securities or the advisability of investing in securities, or does not issue reports or analyses concerning securities as part of *a regular business*, does not come within the Advisers Act's definition of an investment adviser.

Whether or not a person's activities constitute being engaged in the business of advising others as to the value of securities or the advisability of investing in securities or issuing reports or analyses concerning securities as part of a regular business will depend on (1) whether the investment advice being provided is solely incidental to a non-investment advisory, primary business of the person providing the advice; (2) the specificity of the advice being given; and (3) whether the provider of the advice is receiving, directly or indirectly, any special compensation therefor.[7] As a general matter, the staff would take the position that a person who provides financial services including investment advice for compensation is *in the business* of providing investment advice within the meaning of Section 202(a)(11) unless the advice being provided by such person is solely incidental to a non-investment advisory business of the person, is non-specific, and is not rewarded by special compensation for such investment advice.

If a person holds himself out as an investment adviser or as one who provides investment advice, he would be considered to be in the business of providing investment advice. However, a person whose principal business is providing financial services other than investment advice would not be regarded as being *in the business* of giving investment advice if, as part of his service, he merely discusses in general terms the advisability of investing in securities in the context of, for example, a discussion of economic matters or

---

tions with respect to certain situations involving persons providing advice to clients as to the selection or retention of investment managers. *See, e.g.*, Sebastian Associates, Ltd. (avail. Aug 7, 1975) (provision of assistance to clients in obtaining and coordinating the services of various professionals such as tax attorneys and investment advisers, including referring clients to such professionals, in connection with business as agent for clients with respect to negotiation of employment and promotional contracts); Hudson Valley Planning Inc. (avail. Feb. 25, 1978) (provision of names of several investment managers to client upon request, without recommendation, in connection with business of providing administrative services to employee benefit plans).

[7]These criteria were developed as part of the staff's on-going review of prior staff interpretive letters and have not previously been articulated.

the role of investments in securities in a client's overall financial plan. The staff would, however, take the position that such a person is in the business of providing investment advice if, on anything other than rare and isolated instances, he discusses the advisability of investing in, or issues reports or analyses as to, specific securities or specific categories of securities (e.g., bonds, mutual funds, technology stocks, etc.).[8] In addition, a person who provides market timing services would be viewed as being in the business of giving investment advice. Finally, as previously indicated, a person will be regarded as being in the business of providing such advice if he receives any special compensation therefor or receives any direct or indirect remuneration in connection with a client's purchase or sale of securities. A person would generally not be considered to be receiving special compensation for the provision of advisory services if he makes no charge for the advisory portion of his services or if he charges an overall fee for financial advisory services of which the investment advice is an incidental part.

3. **COMPENSATION.**   The definition of investment adviser applies to persons who give investment advice and receive compensation therefor. This compensation element is satisfied by the receipt of any economic benefit, whether in the form of an advisory fee, some other fee relating to the total services rendered, commissions, or some combination of the foregoing. It is not necessary that a person who provides investment advisory and other services to a client charge a separate fee for the investment advisory portion of the total services. The compensation element would be satisfied if a single fee were charged for the provision of a number of different services, which services included the giving of investment advice or the issuing of reports or analyses concerning securities within the meaning of the Advisers Act.[9] As discussed above, however, the fact that no separate fee is charged for the investment advisory portion of the service could be relevant to whether the person is "in the business" of giving investment advice.

It is not necessary that an adviser's compensation should be paid directly by the person receiving investment advisory services, but only that the investment adviser receive compensation from some source for his services.[10] Accordingly, a person providing a variety of services to a client, including investment advisory services, for which the person receives any economic benefit, for example, by receipt of a single fee or commissions upon the sale to the client of insurance products or investments, would be performing such advisory services "for compensation" within the meaning of Section 202(a)(11) of the Advisers Act.[11]

---

[8]*Compare, Zinn* v. *Parrish,* 644 F.2d 360 (7th Cir. 1981), CCH Sec. L. Rep. para. 97,920.

[9]*See, e.g.,* FINESCO (avail. Dec. 11, 1979).

[10]*See, e.g.,* Warren H. Livingston (avail. Mar. 8, 1980).

[11]Section 202(a)(11)(C) of the Advisers Act excepts from the definition of investment adviser a broker or dealer who performs investment advisory services which are incidental to the conduct of its broker-dealer business and who receives no special compensation therefor. See discussion of Section 202(a)(11)(C) *infra.*

B. *Exceptions from Definition of Investment Adviser*

Clauses (A) to (E) of Section 202(a)(11) of the Advisers Act set forth limited exceptions from the definition of investment adviser available to certain persons.[12] Whether an exception from the definition of investment adviser is available to any financial planner, pension consultant, or other person, providing investment advisory services within the meaning of Section 202(a)(11), will depend upon the relevant facts and circumstances.

A person relying on an exception from the definition of investment adviser must meet all of the requirements of such exception. It is the view of the staff that the exception contained in Section 202(a)(11)(B) would not be available, for example, to a lawyer or accountant who holds himself out to the public as providing financial planning, pension consulting, or other financial advisory services. In such a case it would appear that the performance of investment advisory services by such person would be incidental to the practice of his financial planning or pension consulting profession and not incidental to his practice as a lawyer or accountant.[13] Similarly the exception for brokers or dealers contained in Section 202(a)(11)(C) would not be available to a broker or dealer, or associated person of a broker or dealer, acting within the scope of its business as broker or dealer, if such person receives any special compen-

---

[12]Section 202(a)(11) provides that the definition of investment adviser does not include:

    (A) a bank, or any bank holding company as defined in the Bank Holding Company Act fo 1956, which is not an investment company;

    (B) any lawyer, accountant, engineer, or teacher whose performance of such (advisory) services is solely incidental to the practice of his profession;

    (C) any broker or dealer whose performance of such (advisory) services is solely incidental to the conduct of his business as a broker or dealer and who receives no special compensation therefor;

    (D) the publisher of any bona fide newspaper, news magazine or business or financial publication of general and regular circulation;

    (E) any person whose advice, analyses, or reports relate to no securities other than securities which are direct obligations of or obligations guaranteed as to principal or interest by the United States, or securities issued by corporations in which the United States has a direct or indirect interest which shall be designated by the Secretary of the Treasury, pursuant to Section 3(a)(12) of the Securities Exchange Act of 1934, as exempted securities for the purposes of that Act. . . .

Section 202 (a)(11)(F) excepts from the definition of investment adviser "such other persons not within the intent of this paragraph, as the Commission may designate by rules and regulations or order."

[13]*See, e.g.,* Mortimer M. Lerner (avail. Feb. 15, 1980). The "professional" exception provided in Section 202(a)(11)(B) by its terms is only available to lawyers, accountants, engineers, and teachers. A person engaged in a profession other than one of those enumerated in Section 202(a)(11)(B) who performs investment advisory services would be an investment adviser within the meaning of Section 202(a)(11) whether or nor the performance of investment advisory services is incidental to the practice of such profession. Unless another basis for excepting such person from the definition of investment adviser is available, such person would be subject to the Advisers Act.

sation for the provision of investment advisory services.[14] Moreover, the exception from the definition of investment adviser contained in Section 202(a)(11)(C) would not be available to an associated person of a broker-dealer or "registered representative" who provides investment advisory services to clients outside of the scope of such person's employment with the broker-dealer.[15]

III. REGISTRATION AS AN INVESTMENT ADVISER

Any person who is an investment adviser within the meaning of Section 202(a)(11) of the Advisers Act, who is not excepted from the definition of investment adviser by virtue of one of the exceptions in Section 202(a)(11)(A) to (F), and who makes use of the mails or any instrumentality of interstate commerce in connection with such person's business as an investment adviser, is required by Section 203(a) of the Advisers Act to register with the Commission as an investment adviser unless specifically excepted from registration by Section 203(b) of the Advisers Act.[16] The materials necessary for registering with the Commission as an investment adviser can be obtained by writing Publications Unit, Securities and Exchange Commission, Washington, DC 20549.

IV. APPLICATION OF ANTIFRAUD PROVISIONS

The antifraud provisions of Section 206 of the Advisers Act (15 U.S.C. 80b-6), and the rules adopted by the Commission thereunder, apply to any person who is an investment adviser as defined in the Advisers Act, whether or not such person is required to be registered with the Commission as an investment adviser. Sections 206(1) and (2) make it unlawful for an investment adviser, directly or indirectly, to "employ any device, scheme, or artifice to defraud

---

[14]*See, e.g.,* FINESCO, *supra.* For a general statement of the views of the staff regarding special compensation under Section 202(a)(11)(C), see Investment Advisers Act Release No. 640 (October 5, 1978).

[15]*See, e.g.,* George E. Bates (avail. Apr. 26, 1979).

[16]Section 203 (b) excepts from registration

(1) any investment adviser all of whose clients are residents of the State within which such investment adviser maintains his or its principal office and place of business, and who does not furnish advice or issue analyses or reports with respect to securities listed or admitted to unlisted trading privileges on any national securities exchange;

(2) any investment adviser whose only clients are insurance companies; or

(3) any investment adviser who during the course of the preceding twelve months has had fewer than fifteen clients and who neither holds himself out generally to the public as an investment adviser nor acts as an investment adviser to any investment company registered under the (Investment Company Act). . . .

any client or prospective client" or to "engage in any transaction, practice, or course of business which operates as a fraud or deceit upon any client or prospective client."[17] An investment adviser is a fiduciary who owes his clients "an affirmative duty of 'utmost good faith, and full and fair' disclosure of all material facts."[18] The Supreme Court has stated that a "(f)ailure to disclose material facts must be deemed fraud or deceit within its intended meaning, for, as the experience of the 1920s and 1930s amply reveals, the darkness and ignorance of commercial secrecy are the conditions under which predatory practices best thrive."[19] Accordingly, the duty of an investment adviser to refrain from fraudulent conduct includes an obligation to disclose material facts to his clients whenever the failure to do so would defraud or operate as a fraud or deceit upon any client or prospective client. In this connection the adviser's duty to disclose material facts is particularly pertinent whenever the adviser is in a situation involving a conflict, or potential conflict, or interest with a client.

The type of disclosure required by an investment adviser who has a potential conflict of interest with a client will depend upon all the facts and circumstances. As a general matter, an adviser must disclose to clients all material facts regarding the potential conflict of interest so that the client can make an informed decision as to whether to enter into or continue an advisory relationship with the adviser or whether to take some action to protect himself against the specific conflict of interest involved. The following examples, which have been selected from cases and staff interpretive and no-action letters, illustrate the scope of the duty to disclose material information to clients in certain common situations involving conflicts of interest.

An investment adviser who is also a registered representative of a broker-dealer and provides investment advisory services outside the scope of his employment with the broker-dealer must disclose to his advisory clients that his advisory activities are independent from his employment with the broker-dealer.[20] Additional disclosures would be required, depending on the circumstances, if the investment adviser recommends that his clients execute securities transactions through the broker-dealer with which the investment adviser is associated. For example, the investment adviser would be required to disclose fully the nature and extent of any interest the investment adviser

---

[17]In addition, Section 206(3) of the Advisers Act generally makes it unlawful for an investment adviser acting as principal for his own account knowingly to sell any security to or purchase any security from a client, or, acting as broker for a person other than such client, knowingly to effect any sale or purchase of any security for the account of such client, without disclosing to such client in writing before the completion of such transaction the capacity in which he is acting and obtaining the consent of the client to such transaction. The responsibilities of an investment adviser dealing with a client as principal or as agent for another person are discussed in Advisers Act Release Nos. 40 and 470 (February 5, 1945, and August 20, 1975, respectively).

[18]*SEC* v. *Capital Gains Research Bureau*, 375 U.S. 180, 194 (1963) quoting Prosser, Law of Torts (1955), 534–535.

[19]*Id.*, at 200.

[20]David P. Aug. 1, 1977.

has in such recommendation, including any compensation the investment adviser would receive from his employer in connection with the transaction.[21] In addition, the investment adviser would be required to inform his clients of their ability to execute recommended transactions through other broker-dealers.[22] Finally, the Commission has stated that "an investment adviser must not effect transactions in which he has a personal interest in a manner that could result in preferring his own interest to that of his advisory clients."[23]

An investment adviser who structures his personal securities transactions to trade on the market impact caused by his recommendations to clients must disclose this practice to clients.[24] An investment adviser generally also must disclose if his personal securities transactions are inconsistent with the advice given to clients.[25] Finally, an investment adviser must disclose compensation received from the issuer of a security being recommended.[26]

Unlike other general antifraud provisions in the Federal securities laws which apply to conduct "in the offer or sale of any securities"[27] or "in connection with the purchase or sale of any security,"[28] the pertinent provisions of Section 206 do not refer to dealings in securities but are stated in terms of the effect or potential effect of prohibited conduct on the client. Specifically, Section 206(1) prohibits "any device, scheme, or artifice to defraud any client or prospective client," and Section 206(2) prohibits "any transaction, practice, or course of business which operates as a fraud or deceit upon any client or prospective client." In this regard, the Commission has applied Sections 206(1) and (2) in circumstances in which the fraudulent conduct arose out of the investment advisory relationship between an investment adviser and its clients, even though the conduct did not involve a securities transaction. For example, in an administrative proceeding brought by the Commission against an investment adviser, the respondent consented to a finding by the Commission that the respondent had violated Sections 206(1) and (2) by persuading its clients to guarantee its bank loans and ultimately to post their securities as collateral for its loans without disclosing the adviser's deteriorating financial condition, negative net worth, and other outstanding loans.[29] Moreover, the staff has

---

[21]*Ibid.*

[22]Don P. Matheson (avail. Sept. 1, 1976).

[23]Kidder, Peabody & Co., Inc., 43 S.E.C. 911, 916 (1968).

[24]*SEC* v. *Capital Gains Research Bureau, supra* at 197.

[25]*In the Matter of Dow Theory Letters et al.*, Advisers Act Release No. 571 (February 22, 1977).

[26]*In the Matter of Investment Controlled Research et al.*, Advisers Act Release No. 701 (September 17, 1979).

[27]Section 17(a) (15 U.S.C. 77q(a)) of the Securities Act of 1933 (15 U.S.C. 77a et seq.)

[28]Rule 10b-5 (15 CFR 240.10b-5) under the Securities Exchange Act of 1934 (15 U.S.C. 78a et seq.). *See also* Section 15(c) (15 U.S.C. 78o(c)) of the Securities Exchange Act of 1934.

[29]*In the Matter of Ronald B. Donati Inc. et al.*, Advisers Act Rel. Nos. 666 and 683 (February 8, 1979, and July 2, 1979, respectively). *See also Intersearch Technology, Inc.*, CCH Fed. Sec. L. Rep. 1974–1975 Trans. Binder para. 80, 139 (Feb. 28, 1979) at 85,189.

taken the position that an investment adviser who sells non-securities investments to clients must, under Sections 206(1) and (2), disclose to clients and
prospective clients all its interests in the sale to them of such non-securities
investments.[30]

V. NEED FOR INTERPRETIVE ADVICE

The general interpretive guidance provided in this release should facilitate
greater compliance with the Advisers Act. The staff will respond to routine
requests for no-action or interpretive advice relating to the status of persons
engaged in types of businesses described in this release by referring persons
making such requests to the release, unless the requests present novel factual
or interpretive issues such as material departures from the nature and type of
services and compensation arrangements discussed above. Requests for no-
action or interpretive advice from the staff should be submitted in accordance
with the procedures set forth in Investment Advisers Act Release No. 281 (Jan.
25, 1971). Accordingly, Part 276 of Chapter II of Title 17 of the Code of Federal
Regulations is amended by adding Investment Advisers Act Release No. IA-770,
Statement of the staff as to the applicability of the Investment Advisers Act to
financial planners, pension consultants, and other persons who provide investment advisory services as an integral component of other financially related
services; thereto.

By the Commission:

George A. Fitzsimmons
Secretary.

August 13, 1981.

[30]*See, Boston Advisory Group* (avail. Dec. 5, 1976).

State Investment Adviser Registration Requirements

State	Adopted USA*	Regis- tration Required	Initial Regis- tration Fees
Alabama	Yes	No	—
Alaska	Yes	Yes	$50
Arizona	No	No	—
Arkansas	Yes	Yes	$300 (SEC registra- tion) $500 (others)
California	No	Yes	$250
Colorado	Yes	No	—
Connecticut	Yes	Yes	$250
Delaware	Yes	Yes	$150
Florida	No	Yes	$100
Georgia	No	No	—
Hawaii	Yes	Yes	$50
Idaho	Yes	Yes	$100
Illinois	No	Yes	$200

State	Adopted USA*	Regis-tration Required	Initial Regis-tration Fees
Indiana	Yes	Yes	$100
Iowa	Yes	No	—
Kansas	Yes	Yes	$100
Kentucky	Yes	Yes	$100
Louisiana	No	Yes	$100
Maine	No	No	—
Maryland	Yes	No	—
Massachusetts	Yes	No	—
Michigan	Yes	Yes	$100
Minnesota	Yes	Yes	$100
Mississippi	Yes	Yes	$50
Missouri	Yes	Yes	$100
Montana	Yes	Yes	$200
Nebraska	Yes	Yes	$50
Nevada	Yes	Yes	$100 (waived if SEC registered)
New Hampshire	Yes	Yes	$400
New Jersey	Yes	Yes	$50
New Mexico	Yes	Yes	$50
New York	No	Yes	$100
North Carolina	Yes	No	—
North Dakota	No	Yes	$25
Ohio	No	No	—
Oklahoma	Yes	Yes	$50
Oregon	Yes	Yes	$100
Pennsylvania	Yes	Yes	$200
Rhode Island	No	Yes	$100
South Carolina	Yes	Yes	$100
South Dakota	No	Yes	$100

State	Adopted USA*	Registration Required	Initial Registration Fees
Tennessee	Yes	Yes	$100
Texas	No	Yes	$25
Utah	Yes	Yes	$10
Vermont	No	No	—
Virginia	Yes	**	$25
Washington	Yes	Yes	$150
West Virginia	Yes	Yes	$100
Wisconsin	Yes	Yes	$200
Wyoming	Yes	No	—

*Uniform Securities Act.

**Only if not registered with SEC.

NASD District Offices and Key Personnel

National Headquarters

National Association of Securities Dealers, Inc.
1735 K Street, N.W.
Washington, D.C. 20006
(202) 728-8000

NASD District Offices

District No. 1
One Union Square, Suite 1911
Seattle, Washington 98101
(206) 624-0790
Bradford M. Patterson, Director

District No. 2N
425 California Street, Room 1400
San Francisco, California 94101
(415) 781-3434
Theodore F. Schmidt, Director

District No. 2S
727 W. Seventh Street
Los Angeles, California 90017
(213) 627-2122
Kye Hellmers, Director

District No. 3
1401 17th Street, Suite 700
Denver, Colorado 80202
(303) 298-7234
Frank J. Birgfeld, Director

District No. 4
911 Main Street, Suite 2230
Kansas City, Missouri 64105
(816) 421-5700
Jack Rosenfield, Director

District No. 5
1004 Richards Building
New Orleans, Louisiana 70112
(504) 522-6527
Edward J. Newton, Director

District No. 6
1999 Bryan Street
14th Floor
Dallas, Texas 75201
(214) 969-7050
Peter M. Walker, Director

District No. 7
250 Piedmont Avenue, N.E.
Atlanta, Georgia 30308
(404) 658-9191
Bennett Whipple, Director

District No. 8
Three First National Plaza
Suite 1680
Chicago, Illinois 60602
(312) 236-7222
E. Craig Dearborn, Director

District No. 9
1940 East 6th Street
Fifth Floor
Cleveland, Ohio 44114
(216) 694-4545
George W. Mann, Jr., Director

District No. 10
1735 K Street, N.W.
Washington, D.C. 20006
(202) 728-8400
Thomas P. Forde, Director

District No. 11
1818 Market Street, 12th Floor
Philadelphia, Pennsylvania 19103
(215) 665-1180
John P. Nocella, Director

District No. 12
Two World Trade Center
South Tower, 98th Floor
New York, New York 10048
(212) 839-6200
George J. Bergen, Vice President,
Director

District No. 13
50 Milk Street
Boston, Massachusetts 02109
(617) 482-0466
William S. Clendenin, Director

International Association for Financial Planning Code of Professional Ethics *

CANON 1

Members should endeavor as professionals to place the public interest above their own.

Rules Of Professional Conduct:

R1.1 A member has a duty to understand and abide by all *Rules* of Professional Conduct which are prescribed in the Code of Professional Ethics of the Association.

R1.2 A member shall not directly or indirectly condone any act which the member is prohibited from performing by the Rules of this Code.

CANON 2

Members should seek continually to maintain and improve their professional knowledge, skills, and competence.

Rules Of Professional Conduct:

*Reprinted with permission.

R2.1 A member shall keep informed on all matters that are essential to the maintenance of the member's professional competence in the area in which he/she specializes and/or claims expertise.

CANON 3

Members should obey all laws and regulations, and should avoid any conduct or activity which would cause unjust harm to others.

Rules Of Professional Conduct:

R3.1 A member will be subject to disciplinary action for the violation of any law or regulation, to the extent that such violation suggests the likelihood of professional misconduct.

R3.2 A member shall not allow the pursuit of financial gain or other personal benefit to interfere with the exercise of sound professional judgment and skills.

R3.3 In the conduct of business or professional activities, a member shall not engage in any act or omission of a dishonest, deceitful, or fraudulent nature.

CANON 4

Members should be diligent in the performance of their occupational duties.

Rules Of Professional Conduct:

R4.1 A member shall competently and consistently discharge the member's occupational duties, to every employer, client,* purchaser or user of the member's services, so long as those duties are consistent with what is in the client's best interests.

CANON 5

Members should establish and maintain honorable relationships with other professionals, with those whom the members serve in a professional capacity, and with all those who rely upon the members' professional judgments and skills.

---

*As used throughout this Code, the term "client" refers broadly to any individual, business firm, governmental body, educational institution or other entity that engages the professional advice or services of a member, as an independent professional and not as a common law employee of the client.

Rules Of Professional Conduct:

R5.1 A member has a duty to know and abide by the legal limitations imposed upon the scope of the member's professional activities.

R5.2 In rendering or proposing to render a professional service for another individual or an organization, a member shall not knowingly misrepresent or conceal any material limitation on the member's ability to provide the quantity or quality of service that will adequately meet the financial planning needs of the individual or organization in question.

R5.3 In marketing or attempting to market a product to another individual or an organization, a member shall not knowingly misrepresent or conceal any material limitations on the product's ability to meet the financial planning needs of the individual or organization in question.

R5.4 A member shall not disclose to another person any confidential information entrusted to or obtained by the member in the course of the member's business or professional activities, unless a disclosure of such information is required by law or is made to a person who necessarily must have the information in order to discharge legitimate occupational or professional duties.

R5.5 In the making of oral or written recommendations to clients, a member shall (a) distinguish clearly between fact and opinion, (b) base the recommendations on sound professional evaluations of the client's present and future needs, (c) place the needs and best interests of the client above the interests of the member or the member's employer or business associates, (d) support the recommendations with appropriate research and adequate documentation of facts, and (e) scrupulously avoid any statements which are likely to mislead the client regarding the projected future results of any recommendation.

R5.6 Before rendering any professional service, a member has a duty to disclose, to a prospective client, any actual or potential conflict of interest that is or should be known by the member and is likely to impair the member's objectivity as an advisor or provider of professional services to the prospective client in question.

R5.7 In the rendering of a professional service to a client, a member has the duty to maintain the type and degree of professional independence that (a) is required of practitioners in the member's occupation or (b) is otherwise in the public interest, given the specific nature of the service being rendered.

CANON 6

Members should assist in improving the public understanding of financial planning.

Rules Of Professional Conduct:

R6.1 A member shall support efforts to provide laypersons with objective information concerning their financial planning needs, as well as the resources which are available to meet their needs.

R6.2 A member shall not misrepresent the benefits, costs or limitations of any financial planning service or product, whether the product or service is offered by the member or by another individual or firm.

CANON 7

Members should use the fact of membership in a manner consistent with the Association's Rules of Professional Conduct.

Rules Of Professional Conduct:

R7.1 A member shall not misrepresent the criteria for admission to Association membership, which criteria are: (1) a professional interest in financial planning; (2) sponsorship by a member of the Association, which member is in good standing and has been a member for at least one year; and (3) a written commitment to abide by the Bylaws and the Code of Professional Ethics of the Association.

R7.2 A member shall not misstate his/her authority to represent the Association. Specifically, a member shall not write, speak, or act in such a way as to lead another to believe that the member is officially representing the Association, unless the member has been duly authorized to do so by the officers, directors or Bylaws of the national Association.

R7.3 A member shall not use the fact of membership in the Association for commercial purposes but may use the fact of membership for the following non-commercial purposes: in resumes, prospectus, and in introductions if the speaker clearly states that the opinions and ideas presented are his/her own and not necessarily those of the IAFP.

R7.4 A member or prospective member applying for Association membership shall not misrepresent any credentials or affiliations with other organizations.

CANON 8

Members should assist in maintaining the integrity of the Code of Professional Ethics of the Association.

Rules Of Professional Conduct:

R8.1 A member shall not sponsor as a candidate for Association membership any person who is known by the member to engage in business or professional practices which violate the Rules of this Code.

R8.2 A member possessing unprivileged information concerning an alleged violation of this Code shall, upon request, reveal such information to the body or other authority empowered by the Association to investigate or act upon the alleged violation.

A Code of Ethics for Members of the Institute of Certified Financial Planners *

PREAMBLE. The professional practice of financial planning is (or, in the second instance, will be) bound by law; authoritative technical standards that come to be recognized by the profession; contractual requirements, explicit or implied, of employment, agency, or co-ownership; and the full requirements of moral integrity. The primary focus is upon able and dedicated *service to clients*, consistent with all reasonable expectations of organizations enjoying contractual authority over practice, or of co-owners. Responsibilities to subordinates, competitors, other professional financial planners, and other related occupational groups are also recognized.

The specific paragraphs that follow Articles 1 through 6 below are jointly *enforced* by the College for Financial Planning and the Institute of Certified Financial Planners, in accordance with the disciplinary process summarized in the appendix [to be developed by the sponsors]. These provisions are the minimum rules of professional conduct that are both vital to practice and enforceable on a fair and equitable basis. They are by no means assumed to exhaust the ethical responsibility of a Certified Financial Planner.

1. *Parameters.* In all occupational activity a Certified Financial Planner (CFP) is bound vigorously by the fundamental boundaries of defensible conduct, including the full requirements of:

   a. Law

   b. Authoritative technical standards of practice, as they become identified within the profession

---

* For simplicity of exposition the text refers throughout to "CFPs." The Code, however, equally governs the conduct of candidates for the designation. Reprinted with permission.

c. Applicable rules, regulations, or other established policies of any organization having (through an employment, agency, or co-ownership agreement) contractual authority over such activity

d. Basic human trust and fairness.

2. *Acceptance of Clients.* A client relationship should be established only on the basis of full disclosure by both parties of information relevant to the client's financial affairs. CFPs are expected to take any appropriate initiative in this regard.

    a. *Presentation of Credentials.* A CFP should neither misrepresent his or her educational or professional credentials (including the CFP designation itself) or occupational experience, nor permit them to be misunderstood.

    b. *Disclosure of Limitations.* A CFP should make clear both what he or she is, and is not, qualified and prepared to do on behalf of a prospective client. Limitations based on his or her knowledge and experience, the prevailing "state of the art," and professional ethical commitments should be fully disclosed.

    c. *Disclosure by Client.* A CFP should accept a client only after securing sufficient credible information to be satisfied that (i) such a relationship would be warranted by the individual's needs and objectives; and (ii) the CFP would have no personal reservation about providing dedicated service to the individual. Such information should be sought and protected on a confidential basis, as defined in Paragraph f of Article 3.

    d. *Conflicts of Interest.* Before entering a client relationship, a CFP should disclose any and all relationships that he or she or a related party hold with outside firms that might jeopardize service in the best interests of the prospective client. Should a conflict of interest develop subsequent to entering a client relationship, disclosure should be made to the client. Related parties would include members of the same household, a partner or co-owner, or an employer firm.

    e. *Financial Terms.* A CFP should fully explain and document the financial requirements of any financial planning agreement, or other client relationship, specifying any factors upon which fees and/or commissions may be contingent. Any estimates made should be clearly identified as such, and should be based on credible assumptions that are duly noted.

3. *Responsibilities to Clients.* A CFP should provide dedicated, capable, and responsible service to all financial planning clients.

    a. *Competence & Knowledge.* A CFP should strive consistently to maintain and enhance occupational competence, so long as he or she is engaged in the practice of financial planning. The continuing education requirements by which members of the Institute remain eligible for professional referral by that organization represent a useful objective frame of reference for pursuing this obligation. Practice on a part-time basis, or as a sideline, does not reduce the level of expectation. In areas of untested or uncertain ability, the CFP should seek the counsel of better qualified individuals (beginning with organizational colleagues), and/or refer clients to such parties.

b. *Dedication, Due Care and Suitable Advice.* A CFP will perform as ably as possible on behalf of the best interests of clients, as mutually understood. Sufficient diligence and care should be maintained, in all occupational activity addressed to those interests, to assure that recommendations will be suited to the client's circumstances.

c. *Credibility.* A CFP should not intentionally deceive or mislead clients on matters of fact, interpretation, or forecast or make representations to them for which no credible supporting evidence is available.

d. *Reasonable Fees and/or Commissions.* A CFP should limit his or her fees and/or commissions to amounts that are fair and reasonable. Potential compensation from agency relationships should be disclosed, in advance, to clients. Any prospective acceptance, from relevant financial institutions, of gratuities more than nominal in value shall also be disclosed.

e. *Objectivity and Independence.* A CFP should strive to develop judgments and recommendations without bias from personal financial considerations or other factors not relevant to client interests. So far as practicable, relationships should be avoided that might compromise the CFP's objectivity and/or independence.

f. *Confidentiality.* A CFP will only disclose client information to third parties on the basis of express contractual agreement with the client and/or due legal or regulatory process.

g. *Presentation of Recommendations.* A CFP should present and document recommendations fully and clearly to clients, along with supporting reasons and prospective benefits and risks, taking into account the client's level of financial expertise.

h. *Control.* Unless there are agreements to the contrary, after recommendations have been presented, a CFP should monitor the consequences of implementation on an ongoing basis, and keep the client apprised of any developments that might warrant review of the actions taken. If because of altered circumstances the CFP becomes unable to carry out this control function, he or she should so notify the client promptly, and provide assistance in securing competent financial counsel in this connection.

i. *Stewardship.* A CFP should keep strict account of funds or other properties of a client over which he or she has been given discretionary authority. Any commingling of funds between the CFP and his or her clients is prohibited.

j. *Disclosure of Changes.* A CFP should disclose to clients, on a timely basis, any changes in relevant credentials, qualifications, fee or commission schedules, or affiliations.

4. *Responsibilities to Employers or (in an Agency Capacity) Principals.* A CFP who is employed by a financial planning firm or an investment institution, or who serves as an agent for such an organization (the principal), ordinarily fulfills his or her responsibilities to that party and to relevant clients concurrently. Such harmony of interests is essential to professional practice by a CFP serving in either of these capacities, which are combined in the case

of a CFP who deals directly with outside parties as a representative of his or her employer firm. Standards of disclosure and of dedicated service comparable to those governing client relationships apply to both employee and agency relationships. Although focus is placed upon the business realm, a CFP engaged as an employee or agent of a nonprofit organization should observe all relevant fiduciary and other responsibilities cited below.

a. *Advance Disclosure.* A CFP should enter an employment or an agency relationship only on the basis of mutual disclosure. A CFP who represents himself or herself as a financial planner should avoid or withdraw from an institutional relationship perceived to jeopardize service to clients.

b. *Definition, and Faithful Representation, of Authority.* Before conducting business for a principal, a CFP should have his or her authority as an agent clearly defined and properly documented. Subsequently, the CFP should duly advise clients whenever he or she is doing business as an agent, and faithfully represent his or her authority in that capacity, promptly correcting any misinterpretation.

c. *Dedication and Faithful Service.* A CFP who is an employee should conduct his or her occupational tasks with dedication to the legitimate objectives of the employer, in keeping with the CFP's organizational position. Similarly, a CFP serving as an agent should faithfully follow all legitimate instructions given by his or her principal. Care and skill at a level identified with responsibility to clients are required.

d. *Loyalty to Employer.* A CFP should avoid outside affiliations that might compromise service to an employer organization; maintain the same standards of confidentiality to employers as to clients; and provide timely notice in the event of resignation.

e. *Notice to Principal.* A CFP serving as an agent should provide timely and adequate notice to his or her principal, properly documented, of any material information obtained in transacting business for the latter party.

f. *Disclosure of Suspected Wrongdoing—"Whistleblowing."* A CFP who has reason to suspect illegal conduct within his or her employer organization should make timely disclosure of the available evidence to his or her immediate superior. If that individual is suspected of involvement, he or she should either attempt to bring the matter to the attention of the next person in the management hierarchy, or contact an appropriate internal investigative staff unit.

g. *Accounting for Funds.* A CFP serving as an agent should account for all funds or other properties entrusted to his or her custody, on a full and timely basis, and not commingle them with other holdings.

h. *Employee as Agent.* A CFP who deals with outside parties as an agent of his or her employer firm is bound by the same fiduciary and other responsibilities owed by an independent agent to his or her principal.

5. *Responsibilities to Partners, or Other Co-owners.* A CFP doing business as a member of a partnership, or otherwise as a co-owner of a firm, bears to his partners or co-owners a

fiduciary responsibility of the highest order. This is based in particular upon his or her authority to act as an agent for the firm and its other members (hereafter cited in partnership terms).

a. *Advance Disclosure.* A CFP should enter a partnership from the outside only on the basis of mutual disclosure comparable to acceptance of clients or establishment of an employment or agency relationship. He or she should not enter or maintain a partnership affiliation perceived to jeopardize service to clients.

b. *Responsibilities of Agency.* A CFP who is a member of a partnership (in partnership) is bound by the basic responsibilities of agency in representing the firm and his or her partners.

c. *Good Faith.* A CFP in partnership owes to his or her partners the highest degree of good faith in all business matters. This includes (but is not limited to) full disclosure of knowledge of the firm's affairs; avoidance of any effort to secure personal gain at the expense of the firm; and adherence, both while in partnership and thereafter, to legitimate expectations of confidentiality.

d. *Transaction of Business.* In transacting partnership business, a CFP should exercise the levels of care and skill identified with service to clients, and not exceed the authority granted him or her by the underlying partnership agreement.

e. *Reasonable Record.* A CFP in partnership should keep a reasonable record of all business transacted for the firm, and make it available for timely inclusion in the partnership books.

f. *Full-time Commitment.* Unless there is a clear agreement to the contrary, a CFP in partnership should accept a full-time commitment to the firm.

g. *Withdrawal from Partnership.* A CFP in partnership who elects to withdraw from the firm should do so in compliance with the partnership agreement, and dispose of his or her interest on a fair and equitable basis.

6. *Responsibilities to Subordinates, Competitors, Other Professional Financial Planners, and Practitioners of Related Fields.* CFPs have special responsibilities to their subordinates, including promotion of ethical conduct. In keeping with service to clients, a CFP should show respect for other financial planning professionals, and related occupational groups, by engaging in fair and honorable competitive practices. Collegiality among CFPs must not be allowed to impede enforcement of Code requirements. Finally, professional responsibility extends beyond occupational conduct.

a. *Supervision.* A CFP should exercise careful and supportive supervision over the work of any immediate subordinates. He or she should take appropriate responsibility for their conduct, and not accept from them behavior contrary to his or her own professional obligations.

b. *Advertising.* A CFP should not be associated with advertising of financial planning services or products which are deceptive, misleading or focused upon nonrational persuasion (through entertainment or other means) rather than an informational function. Subject to limited qualification relative to fee schedules, comparative advertising of services should be avoided, whether involving specific individuals or general groups.

c. *Other Public Representation.* Within public representation of any kind, beyond the advertising area, a CFP should take all reasonable care to avoid misleading or deceiving the relevant audience concerning the financial planning field, his or her own professional activities, or similar matters. Personal opinions expressed should be clearly recognizable as such, and no impression should be permitted that the CFP is speaking for the Institute, the College, or any other group unless he or she has been duly authorized to do so. Public representation may occur within speeches, interviews, publications or printings, seminars and other contexts.

d. *Respect for Competitors and Related Fields.* In the course of his or her occupational activity a CFP should avoid distasteful references to the quality of service available from other financial planners, or from practitioners of fields with which financial planning overlaps.

e. *Complaint or Adverse Testimony.* A CFP having evidence of violation(s) of this Code of Ethics by another CFP should bring this information to the attention of the appropriate professional bodies, or be prepared to present it within the course of disciplinary proceedings.

f. *Extra-professional Conduct.* A CFP should observe the rule of law, and act in a socially responsible manner, outside the realm of his or her business or professional activity. He or she should avoid conduct or associations that might cast discredit upon his or her professional practice. This paragraph is not intended to limit involvement by a CFP in practices, movements, or causes based on surrounding social or political controversy or unpopularity.

SEC Regional Offices and Key Personnel

REGIONAL AND BRANCH OFFICES—ADMINISTRATORS

Region 1

26 Federal Plaza, Room 1102, New York, N.Y. 10278

Regional Administrator
Ira Lee Sorkin

Deputy Regional Administrator
(Vacant)

Associate Regional Administrators
Anne C. Flannery (Enforcement)
Charles E. Padgett (Regulation)
Edwin H. Nordlinger (Regulation)

Assistant Regional Administrators
Regina C. Mysliwiec (Enforcement)
Jason R. Gettinger (Enforcement)
Margaret McQueeney (Enforcement)
Jerome Feller (Regulation)

(212) 264-1614

Region 2

150 Causeway St., Boston, Mass. 02114

Regional Administrator
Willis H. Riccio

Massachusetts; Connecticut; Rhode Island; Vermont; New Hampshire; Maine.

Assistant Regional Administrators
Dennis R. Surprenant (Enforcement)
Peter A. Ambrosini (Regulation)

(617) 223-2721

Region 3

Suite 788, 1375 Peachtree Street, N. E., Atlanta, Georgia 30367

Suite 1114, Dupont Plaza Center, 300 Biscayne Boulevard Way, Miami, Florida 33131 (Branch Office)

Regional Administrator
Michael K. Wolensky

Assistant Regional Administrators
Joseph L. Grant (Enforcement)
James E. Long (Regulation)

Associate Administrator, Miami Office
Charles C. Harper

Tennessee; Virgin Islands; Puerto Rico; North Carolina; South Carolina; Georgia;

Alabama; Mississippi; Florida; part of
Louisiana.
(404) 892-0737

Region 4

Room 1204, Everett McKinley Dirksen Bldg.,
  219 S. Dearborn Street, Chicago, Ill. 60604
231 W. Lafayette, 438 Federal Building,
  Detroit, Michigan 48226 (Branch Office)
  Mark A. Loush—Attorney in Charge

Regional Administrator
  William D. Goldsberry

Assistant Regional Administrator
  William M. Hegan
  Minnesota; Wisconsin; Iowa; Illinois;
Missouri; Ohio; Michigan; Indiana; Kentucky.

Assistant Regional Administrators
  Phillip L. Stern (Enforcement)
  Ronald P. Kane (Enforcement)
  Joan M. Fleming (Regulation)
  Paul B. O'Kelly (Regulation)
(312) 353-7390

Region 5

411 West Seventh St., 8th floor, Fort Worth,
  Texas 76102
Suite 302, Scanlan Building, 405 Main St.,
  Houston, Texas 77002 (Branch Office)

Regional Administrator
  Wayne M. Secore

Assistant Regional Administrators
  Hugh M. Wright (Enforcement)
  T. Christopher Browne (Regulation)
  Oklahoma; Arkansas; Texas; Kansas; part of
Louisiana.

*Assistant Regional Administrator for Houston
  Branch Office*
  Edwin J. Tomko
(817) 334-3821

Region 6

Suite 700, 410 Seventeenth St., Denver,
  Colorado 80202
Post Office Courthouse Building, 350 South Main

St., Room 505, Salt Lake City, Utah 24101
(Branch Office) G. Gail Weggeland—Attorney
in Charge

Regional Administrator
  Robert H. Davenport

Assistant Regional Administrators
  John Joseph Kelly Jr. (Enforcement)
  James E. Birchby (Regulation)
  Wyoming; Utah; Colorado; New Mexico;
Nebraska; North Dakota; South Dakota.
(303) 837-2071

Region 7

5757 Wilshire Blvd., Suite 500 East, Los Angeles,
  California 90036-3648
(213) 473-3098
450 Golden Gate Avenue, Box 36042, San
  Francisco, California 94102 (Branch Office)
(415) 556-5264

Regional Administrator
  Irving M. Einhorn
  California; Nevada; Arizona; Hawaii; Guam.

Assistant Regional Administrators
  Gary Lloyd (Enforcement)
  Polly G. Bell (Regulation)

*Associate Regional Administrator for San
  Francisco Branch Office*
  Bobby C. Lawyer

Region 8

3040 Federal Bldg., 915 Second Ave.,
  Seattle, Wash. 98174

Regional Administrator
  Jack H. Bookey
(206) 442-7990

Assistant Regional Administrator
  Nobuo Kawasaki (Enforcement)
  John P. McNeall (Regulation)
  Washington; Oregon; Idaho; Montana; Alaska.

Region 9

Ballston Center Tower 3, 4015 Wilson Boulevard,
  Arlington, Va. 22203

600 Arch Street, Room 2204, Federal Bldg.,
  Philadelphia, Pa. 19106 (Branch Office)

Regional Administrator
  Paul F. Leonard

Assistant Regional Administrators
  Herbert F. Brooks, Jr. (Regulation)
  James C. Kennedy (Enforcement)

*Assistant Regional Administrator for Philadelphia
  Branch Office*
  Thomas H. Monahan
  Virginia; West Virginia; Maryland; Delaware;
District of Columbia; Pennsylvania
(703) 235-3700

State Regulatory Agencies and Key Personnel

Alabama
Alabama Securities Commission
R. Frank Ussery
100 Commerce Street
10th Floor
Montgomery, AL
36130
205-261-2984

Alaska
Division of Banking and Securities
Willis F. Kirkpatrick
Pouch D
Juneau, AK
99811
907-465-2521

Arizona
Arizona Securities Division
Matthew J. Zale
1200 West Washington Street
Phoenix, AZ
85009
602-255-4242

Arkansas
Arkansas Securities Department
Lee Thalheimer
Suite 4B 206, Capitol Mall
Little Rock, AR
72201
501-371-1011

California
Department of Corporations
Franklin Tom
600 S. Commonwealth Avenue
Los Angeles, CA
90005
213-736-2741

Colorado
Division of Securities
Royce O. Griffin
1525 Sherman Street, Room 210
Denver, CO
80203
303-866-2607

Connecticut
Securities and Investment Division
Caleb L. Nichols
165 Capitol Avenue
State Office Building
Hartford, CT
06106
203-566-5783

Delaware
Division of Securities
Donald L. Bruton
820 N. French Street
8th Floor, State Office Bldg.
Wilmington, DE
19801
302-571-2515

District of Columbia
Division of Securities
James Whitescarver
451 Indiana Avenue, N.W.
Washington, D.C.
20001
202-727-3066

Florida
Division of Securities
E. C. Anderson
1402 The Capitol
Tallahassee, FL
32301
904-488-9805

Georgia
Securities Division
H. Wayne Howell
2 Martin Luther King Drive
Suite 802, West Tower
Atlanta, GA
30334
404-656-2894

Hawaii
Corporation and Securities
Administrator
Russell Yamashita
1010 Richard Street
P.O. Box 40
Honolulu, HI
96810
808-548-6521

Idaho
Securities Bureau
Gavin Gee
700 West State Street
Statehouse Mall
Boise, ID
83720
208-334-3684

Illinois
Securities Department
Francesca Marciniak
840 South Spring Street
Suite 130
Springfield, IL
62704
217-782-2256

Indiana
Securities Division
O. Wayne Davis
One North Capital, Suite 560
Indianapolis, IN
46204
317-232-6683

Iowa
Securities Division
Craig Goettsch
Lucas State Office Building
Des Moines, IA
50319
515-281-4441

Kansas
Kansas Securities Commission
John Wurth
109 West 9th, Suite 501
Topeka, KS
66612
913-296-3307

Kentucky
Division of Securities
Ronda S. Paul
911 Leawood Drive
Frankfort, KY
40601
502-564-2180

Louisiana
Louisiana Securities Commission
Harry C. Stansbury
315 Louisiana State Office
Building
325 Loyola Avenue
New Orleans, LA
70112
504-568-5515

Maine
Maine Securities Division
Alden H. Mann
State House, Station #36
Augusta, ME
04333
207-289-2261

Maryland
Division of Securities
Susan Rittenhouse
7 North Calvert Street
Munsey Building, 2nd Floor
Baltimore, MD
21202
301-576-6360

Massachusetts
Massachusetts Securities Division
Michael Unger
John W. McCormack Building
One Ashburton Place
Boston, MA
02108
617-727-3548

Michigan
Corporation and Securities
Bureau
E. C. Mackey
P.O. Box 30222
6546 Mercantile Way
Lansing, MI
48909
517-373-0938

Minnesota
Securities and Real Estate
Division
Mike Hatch
500 Metro Square Building
St. Paul, MN
55101
612-296-6848

Mississippi
Securities Division
Peyton Prospere
401 Mississippi Street
P.O. Box 136
Jackson, MS
39205
601-359-1370

Missouri
John Perkins
Commissioner of Securities
Harry S. Truman State Office
Building
301 West High, 8th Floor

Jefferson City, MO
65102
314-751-4136

Montana
Securities Department
Rick Tucker
State Auditor's Office
Mitchell Building
Helena, MT
59601
406-444-2040

Nebraska
Department of Banking and
Finance
Patricia Herstein
301 Centennial Mall South
P.O. Box 95006
Lincoln, NE
68509
402-471-2171

Nevada
Securities Division
Abner W. Sewell
State Capitol
Carson City, NV
89710
702-885-5203

New Hampshire
Securities Division
Robert Robitaille
P.O. Box 2005
169 Manchester Street
Concord, NH
03301
603-271-2261

New Jersey
Bureau of Securities
James McLelland Smith
80 Mulberry Street, Room 308

Newark, NJ
07102
201-648-2040

New Mexico
Securities Bureau
Tommy Hughes
Lew Wallace Building
Santa Fe, NM
87503
505-827-7750

New York
Bureau of Investor Protection
and Securities
Orestes J. Mihaly
Department of Law
Two World Trade Center
New York, NY
10047
212-488-7563

North Carolina
Securities Division
F. Daniel Bell, III
300 North Salisbury Street
Room 302
Raleigh, NC
27611
919-733-3924

North Dakota
North Dakota Securities
Commission
Peter Quist
State Capitol, 9th Floor
Bismarck, ND
58505
701-224-2910

Ohio
Division of Securities
Rodger Marting
Two Nationwide Plaza

Columbus, OH
43215
614-466-7043

Oklahoma

Securities Commission
C. Raymond Patton, Jr.
2915 North Lincoln
Oklahoma City, OK
73105
405-521-2451

Oregon

Department of Commerce
Corporation Division
Jane Edwards
Corporation Commissioner
158 12th Street N.E.
Salem, OR
97310
503-378-4387

Pennsylvania

Securities Commission
Robert M. Lam
Chairman
471 Forum Building
Harrisburg, PA
17120
717-787-8061

Puerto Rico

Puerto Rico Securities Office
Fidencio Quiles Ferrer
P.O. Box S-4515
San Juan, Puerto Rico
00905
809-721-4075

Rhode Island

Department of Business
Regulation
Thomas J. Caldarone, Jr.
Director, Business Regulation

100 North Main Street
Providence, RI
02903
401-277-3048

South Carolina

Department of State
Securities Division
John T. Campbell
Secretary of State
816 Keenan Building
Columbia, SC
29201
803-758-2833

South Dakota

Division of Securities
David Haberling
Director
Capitol Building
Pierre, SD
57501
605-773-4823

Tennessee

Department of Insurance
Securities Division
John C. Neff
Commissioner of Insurance
114 State Office Building
Nashville, TN
37219
615-741-2241

Texas

State Securities Board
Richard D. Latham
Securities Commissioner
P.O. Box 13167
Capitol Station
Austin, TX
78711 3167
512-474-2233

Utah
Dept. of Business Regulation
Securities Division
Craig F. McCullough
Director
P.O. Box 5802
Salt Lake City, UT
84110
801-530-6600

Vermont
Securities Division
Harry Lantz
State Office Building
Montpelier, VT
05602
802-828-3301

Virginia
Division of Securities
Lewis W. Brothers
11 South 12th Street
Richmond, VA
23219
804-786-7751

Washington
Securities Division
Jack Beyers
P.O. Box 648
12th and Franklin
Olympia, WA
98504
206-753-6928

West Virginia
Securities Division
Jack Hall
State Capitol Building
Room W-118
Charleston, WV
25305
304-348-2257

Wisconsin
Securities Commission
Richard R. Malmgren
P.O. Box 1768
111 West Wilson Street
Madison, WI
53701
608-266-3431

Wyoming
Securities Division
Thyra Thomson
State Capitol Building
Cheyenne, WY
82002
307-777-7370

Glossary

Administrative law: That body of law that regulates the practices and procedures of agencies dealing with public health, welfare, morals, and safety.

Agent: A person hired to act on behalf of a principal and who is subject to the latter's nominal control. Generally, though not always, an agent is the principal's employee.

Allegation: A statement that a person expects to be able to prove.

Arbitration: The substitution, by consent of the parties, of another forum for resolving disputes other than customary court procedures.

Associated person: A person who is affiliated with a broker-dealer either in a selling capacity or in the supervision or training of others on behalf of a broker-dealer.

Blue-sky laws: A popular name for the securities laws enacted by the states to protect the public against securities frauds.

Bona fide: In good faith; openly, honestly, or innocently; without knowledge or intent of fraud.

Broker: Any individual, corporation, partnership, association, joint stock company, business trust, or other legal entity engaged in the business of effecting transactions in securities for the account of others, but does not include a bank.

Broker-dealer: A person or firm registered to buy and sell securities and a member of either a national securities exchange or the National Association of Securities Dealers.

Burden of proof: The duty resting on one party or another involved in litigation of producing evidence sufficient to prove a particular issue. The burden of going forward with the evidence is a procedural obligation that can shift from party to party during the course of a trial.

Capital gain, capital loss: The appreciation or loss in value from the sale of a capital asset.

Certified Financial Planner (CFP): The designation granted by the College for Financial Planning to individuals who successfully complete a rigorous six-course curriculum.

Chartered Life Underwriter (CLU): The designation granted by the American College of Life Underwriters to individuals who pass ten difficult examinations in insurance, economics, estate planning, and so forth.

Civil law: That branch of American law and jurisprudence which deals with private legal rights as distinct from criminal matters.

Clear and convincing evidence: A standard of proof required of a party to litigation that calls for establishing the facts or issues asserted by something beyond a mere preponderance of the evidence; hence, a more stringent standard.

College for Financial Planning: An organization that offers professional training curricula leading to the CFP designation.

Common law: That system of law which does not rest for its authority upon any express statutes, but derives its force and authority from universal consent and usage (precedent) over long periods.

Compensatory damages: Moneys received in a lawsuit that are intended to be sufficient in amount to cover all losses actually sustained.

Complainant: Generally, one who files a complaint against another person, and called the plaintiff in a civil suit.

Concurrent jurisdiction: Authority shared by two or more legal tribunals or administrative bodies to deal with the same subject matter.

As a rule, litigants may bring their cases before either tribunal in the first instance.

Consideration: Something of value as viewed by the law. A legal detriment to one contracting party that results in a corresponding legal benefit to the other. It is an essential ingredient of a contract. See *quid pro quo.*

Construe: To determine the sense, real meaning, or proper effect of statutory language by a consideration of the subject matter and attending circumstances in connection with the words employed.

Contract: An agreement between competent parties, upon a legal consideration, to do or refrain from doing some act or undertaking.

Controlling person: A statutory concept creating derivative or vicarious liability on the part of a broker-dealer who controls the activities of another person.

Crime: An act against society in violation of the law. Crimes are prosecuted by and in the name of the state.

Criminal law: That branch of American jurisprudence dealing with crimes and their punishment.

Damages: The amount claimed, or allowed, as compensation for injuries sustained through the wrongful act or negligence of another.

Defendant: In a civil case, the party against whom suit is brought demanding that he pay the complaining party money damages. In a criminal case, the person accused of committing a crime.

De novo: Anew; afresh. Usually refers to the right to commence a lawsuit all over again.

Discovery: Pretrial activities of attorneys to determine what evidence the opposing side will present if and when the case comes to trial. Discovery prevents attorneys from being surprised during trial and facilitates out-of-court settlement.

Discovery doctrine: Under the discovery rule or doctrine, a fraud claim does not accrue, for statutory limitations purposes, until the actual discovery by the aggrieved party of the facts constituting the fraud, or when such facts could have been discovered in the exercise of due diligence.

Discretionary account: An account in which the client gives the broker or someone else either total or limited authority and discretion to buy and sell securities on the client's behalf.

Enjoin: To command or to require someone to act or refrain from acting in a particular manner. See *injunction.*

Exchange: An organization, association, or group of persons that maintains and provides an organized marketplace or facilities for bringing together buyers and sellers of securities.

Exclusive jurisdiction: The sole authority given a court to deal with specified civil or criminal matters to the exclusion of all other courts.

Exemplary damages: See *punitive damages.*

Expert witness: A person who has special training, experience, skill, and knowledge in a particular field, and who is allowed to offer an opinion as testimony in a court case.

Fiduciary: A person having the legal duty, created by his undertaking, to act primarily for another's benefit in matters connected with such undertaking. It is a relationship having the characteristics of a trust and is founded on trust or confidence.

Finder: A person who introduces one party to another for the purpose of obtaining investment advice or buying or selling securities, but who does not participate in the negotiations between the parties.

Fraud and deceit: The gain of an advantage to another's detriment by deceitful or unfair means. It is usually based on a deliberate misrepresentation with the intention of having the other person rely on such misrepresentation. Fraud is legal grounds for a common law action against the alleged perpetrator. It may also be grounds for the state to bring a criminal prosecution.

General securities principal: A person associated with a broker-dealer member of the NASD who is actively engaged in the management of the broker-dealer's securities business. All general securities principals must pass an appropriate qualifying examination and become registered as such with the NASD.

Harm or injury: Any wrong or damage done to the person, rights, or property of another.

Independent contractor: One who undertakes work for another as a self-employed individual and not under the direction or control of another, such as an employer.

Initial Decision: The formal opinion of a hearing examiner in an SEC disciplinary proceeding that is contested, containing findings of fact, conclusions of law, and recommended sanctions against the respondent. An Initial Decision that is not reviewed by the SEC becomes the final decision of the Commission and has high precedent value.

Injunction: A prohibitive writ issued by a court forbidding a party-defendant from certain action or, in the case of a mandatory injunction, commanding such party's positive action.

Institute of Certified Financial Planners (ICFP): The professional body representing persons who are CFPs or are applying for that designation through the College for Financial Planning. It provides educational and training programs for its members and monitors their adherence to its detailed Code of Ethics.

International Association for Financial Planning (IAFP): The professional association of financial planners that provides continuing education for its members and monitors their adherence to its Code of Professional Ethics.

Introducing broker: A broker-dealer who does not directly handle securities transactions on the exchanges or in the OTC market directly, but processes all trades through a clearing member of the NASD.

Ipso facto: By the very act itself.

Judge: The person assigned to hear a case brought before a court. His duties include examining the legal processes that precede the trial and making rulings thereon. He may decide whether a jury will be permitted and conducts the proceedings in the courtroom.

Know Your Customer Rule: The New York Stock Exchange rule (Rule 405) that requires member-brokers to use due diligence to learn essential facts about every customer before making specific security recommendations. It is widely regarded as an implicit suitability rule, although not characterized as such. See *suitability rule.*

Legal consideration: See *consideration; quid pro quo.*

Liability: The legal obligation one incurs to pay another a sum of money or perform some specific act arising out of his negligence or breach of contract.

Liability insurance: An insurance contract under which the insurer, for a premium, agrees to pay for any legal liability incurred by the policy-holder. When applied to professionals, it is often called malpractice insurance.

License: A permit from the state allowing certain acts to be performed by the license holder that would otherwise be unlawful, generally involving some aspect of public health, welfare, or safety.

Limited partnership: A statutory form of partnership that consists of one or more general partners who conduct the business and are personally liable to creditors and of limited partners who do not participate in the partnership's management and whose liability is limited to the amount of their contributions. It is the most popular form of investment in tax-sheltered programs.

Litigant: Either party to a lawsuit.

Litigation: The formal court process by which the legal issues, rights, and duties between parties to a dispute are officially determined. Compare *arbitration.*

Malpractice: Professional misconduct, improper discharge of professional duties, or failure to meet the standard of care the law imposes on a professional, which results in harm or injury to another.

Malpractice insurance: See *liability insurance.*

Mandatory injunction: An order issued by a court compelling a party to perform some positive act.

Misrepresentation: A false representation or statement, usually made with intent to defraud another by inducing his reliance thereon. It is the legal basis for bringing a tort action against the person making such misrepresentation, as well as a violation of the federal and state securities laws.

NASD: The National Association of Securities Dealers. The self-regulatory organization whose members handle securities transactions for clients and themselves in the over-the-counter market. The NASD has extensive power to discipline its members, subject to SEC and court review.

Negligence: Lack of care; the failure to act as an ordinary prudent person, or action that is contrary to what a reasonable prudent person would have done. When committed by a professional person, it is called malpractice.

No-action letter: A written reply by a member of the SEC legal staff to an inquiry submitted by someone concerned about engaging in a proposed transaction or course of conduct that might be in conflict with the securities acts. A no-action letter ordinarily says no more than that if the transaction or course of conduct is carried out as proposed the staff either will (or will not) recommend that the commission take enforcement action. No-action letters are not official positions of the SEC and have little precedent value.

Off-book transaction: A private securities transaction effected for a client by a registered representative outside the scope of the representative's association with his broker-dealer.

Office of supervisory jurisdiction: Any office designated by a broker-dealer as directly responsible for reviewing and supervising the activities of registered representatives or associated persons in such office.

OTC market: A market for securities not traded on national or regional exchanges. Mainly a market made over the telephone, involving thousands of companies too small to be listed on one of the national stock exchanges.

Passive investor: An investor who does not participate in any manner in the managing of an investment, but merely invests money therein. See *limited partnership.*

Plaintiff: The complaining party in a civil suit; the party seeking money damages or other relief.

Preponderance of the evidence: A standard of proof in a civil suit in which the evidence, taken as a whole, must show that the fact or cause sought to be proved is more probable than not.

Principal: One who engages an agent to assist him or to act on his behalf. The principal controls and is legally responsible for the acts of his agent.

Private placement: A tax-sheltered investment that is offered and sold subject to the private offering exemption under the Securities Act of 1933 and comparable exemptions in various state laws. A private placement is not required to be registered with the SEC.

Private securities transactions: See *off-book transaction* and *selling away.*

Prospectus: The official document that offers a new issue of securities to the public. It is required to be furnished to each purchaser pursuant to the Securities Act of 1933.

Punitive damages: Damages allowed by a court in excess of the actual loss sustained as punishment against the wrongdoer, usually in cases of fraud or other willful behavior.

Quid pro quo: Literally, something for something; an equivalent in return; a consideration for the contract.

Real Estate Investment Trust (REIT): An equity trust that can hold income properties of all types and offers shares that are publicly traded. Operates much like a mutual fund.

Registered representative: A person who is engaged as a full-time securities broker for a broker-dealer affiliated either with a major stock exchange or with the NASD.

Regulations: Rules of conduct issued by governmental bodies to carry out the intent of specific statutes.

Regulatory agency: An official body given authority to regulate the conduct of persons in accordance with statutory guidelines. The SEC is the principal federal regulatory agency in the securities field.

Releases: Written issuances of the SEC used to propose and promulgate rules, interpret existing rules, publish investigative reports on significant issues, and announce the results of SEC disciplinary cases and important court decisions.

Respondeat superior: Let the master respond; the legal doctrine that holds an employer legally responsible for the wrongful (negligent) acts of his employees committed while acting within the scope of their employment.

Respondent: The party against whom an action or charge is filed and who must respond thereto or else be found guilty or liable.

Restitution: The act of restoring or making good for a loss sustained. A person obtains restitution when he is returned to the position he formerly occupied either by return of something he formerly had or by receipt of its money equivalent.

Scienter: The mental state that embraces a person's intent to deceive, manipulate, or defraud. Scienter is an essential element in proving a defendant's fraud in a securities case.

SEC: The Securities Exchange Commission, the chief governmental agency established by Congress to protect investors by enforcing the securities laws and assuring the maintenance of orderly securities markets.

SECO: Literally, SEC-only. Refers to the program (now terminated) under which broker-dealers not choosing to become NASD members were required to place themselves under direct SEC supervision. The SECO program was abolished in 1983.

Security: Under the securities acts, stocks, bonds, mutual funds, equipment trust certificates, oil and gas interests, and a general catchall category known as investment contracts, where one invests money in a common enterprise in which the expectation of deriving a return is dependent on the efforts of others. See, also, *limited partnership*.

Self-regulatory organization (SRO): Any national securities exchange, registered securities association, or registered clearing agency. The NASD is the SRO for the OTC market.

Selling away: The act of effecting a private securities transaction outside the scope of one's employment with a particular broker-dealer.

Shingle theory: A legal concept which states that, by the very act of hanging out his ''shingle,'' a broker-dealer assumes a number of key legal obligations to all his customers. This theory has been explicitly recognized by a number of courts.

Statute of limitations: A certain period fixed by statute within which a court action must be brought after the cause of action accrues, or else the claimant will lose his right to enforce it by law. See also, *discovery doctrine*.

Statutes; statutory law: Laws enacted by the legislative power in a country or state laying down rules of conduct in specific areas. Statutory law is legislative law, as opposed to common law, which is judge-made (decisional) law based on long-standing judicial precedents.

Stockbroker: A securities salesperson. See *broker*.

Stock exchange: An organization registered under the Securities Act of 1934 to provide and maintain physical facilities for the buying and selling of securities to the public.

Subpoena: A writ commanding one's attendance to testify in a court proceeding, either civil or criminal. A *subpoena duces tecum* is a writ compelling a person to bring with him to court specific papers or documents in his possession.

Suitability rule: The NASD rule that requires a broker-member to have reasonable grounds for believing a particular investment recommendation is suitable for the client in question on the basis of his overall financial situation, risk threshold, and investment objectives.

Tax-sheltered program: A tax-sheltered investment in which the flow-through of tax benefits is a material factor, regardless of the structure of the legal entity. Limited partnerships and joint ventures are typical tax-sheltered programs.

Tort: An injury or wrong. Wrongful conduct. Tort law is that branch of law and jurisprudence dealing with civil wrongs other than contracts.

Tortfeasor: One adjudged to be a wrongdoer in a civil suit for damages.

Vicarious liability: Liability of one person (usually a principal or employer) arising out of the wrongful conduct of another (usually an agent or employee) under the legal doctrine of respondeat superior.

Index

221